REVIVAL—Its Principles & Personalities

by Winkie Pratney

Huntington House Publishers

Huntington House Publishers
P.O. Box 53788
Lafayette, Louisiana 70505

ISBN 1-56384-058-8

All Scripture quotes taken from the King James Version, unless otherwise noted.

Preface

History. Hear that word and what do you think? Dull facts? Dead people? Useless dates? Eminently forgettable events? But the great need of the Church of the 1990s is a sense of her history and destiny. How do you "boldly go where no man has gone before" unless you first know where you really are and where you've come from?

The past is full of treasure. To slightly restate another's maxim, Christians who learn from revival history will be compelled to want to repeat it. You want history? Here are dates, people, facts and events. But if that is all you are looking for, read something else. This study is not for you. It is not, strictly speaking, intended to be a study about our past at all. It is instead a small part of the record of the awesome life and deeds of another–one who transcends our small and often shabby little human story–an infinite person who reaches time after time into lives just like yours or mine, making them memorable, giving them the greatness of a reflected glory.

Here, scenes from other times, other cultures, and other places may shock or surprise you. They might well be *your* age, *your* time, *your* generation. It is living, this Gospel of revival. It links yesterday's Bible records with tomorrow's headlines in ongoing accounts of ordinary lives moved by an extraordinary God. He who called and empowered those who changed the world before is alive forevermore; He can surely do it again.

Revivalists of the Past

Here, too, are sketches and excerpts from the lives and writings of people who saw God work. Some are perhaps well-known to you; there are those about strangers, with even stranger experiences; still others where a little-known fact about familiar figures may help you to see their lives or ministries in a whole new way.

Is this book then about people and principles you ought to know to get anything worthwhile done for Christ in our time? It is in part. We'll look at some of the important principles gleaned from past revivals. We'll meet men and women who reached out in faith.

But this study is not "our" history. This is really all about "*His-story.*" John's Gospel said it best: "This is the work of God, that you believe on Him whom He has sent." This is the Church's secret past power and present hope of survival; this, the deeds and demonstrations of the character, glory, and purity of mighty God, is the work of *revival.*

Introduction What Is Revival?

One of the problems with describing what God has done in history is that He is *still alive* and writing it. That reality has embarrassing consequences for you and me! For one thing, He is always around to contradict our interpretations of such history. For another, history isn't finished until He steps in personally to put the final "Amen" on the whole thing.

This book focuses especially on two subjects: young people and revivals. About the only thing more written on and less understood than the subject of "Youth" is the subject of "Revivals." I hope this will not add to the confusion. I am still persuaded that revival–*true* revival, heaven-born, God-authorized revival–is the critical need of the hour and the hope of this country's young. We had better understand something about this thing called revival and know how to call on God concerning it if the bright, hopeful young of the Western world in the 1990s are going to spiritually survive and triumph in the next millennium.

More Than History

This is a compilation of a pretty big sweep of history. It is a sampler, if you like, of many diverse works of God from all ages and cultures. It begins in the words and records of the Bible; it traces people and movements God used for His glory through nearly two thousand years right up to the present time. It attempts to help you meet, even for a brief moment, some of the men and women who even now affect the Christian world.

There is a great need for such an outline. Here you may find people you like, people you don't, and people you never heard of all lumped together. I have not tried to make them all agree with each other on everything, just as you or I may not agree with everything they said or did or were. I have tried to show their weaknesses as well as their strengths, their victories and failures, their trophies and their tragedies. It draws heavily on others' works, some no longer in print, but all of which I feel deserve to be heard by another generation. Others are more recent and full of value; booklists are included, and I strongly encourage you to locate the originals. If I have not included or done justice to your favorite figure, accept my apologies.

The Subject of Revival

Over the past thirty years of my travels in the Western world, I have met many hundreds of thousands of young people. I have spoken to many of them on the subject of revival, challenged them to pray and give themselves to God for revival, and even been privileged to participate from time to time in some small, but real, awakenings.

Recently the need for a general awakening in the West, particularly in Great Britain, the Pacific and North America, has become critical. Yet with so much past material available for study and so much obvious desire across the nation for revival, there is an appalling lack of understanding on the subject. For instance, if you get a chance to speak to a larger group of Christians try this little survey:

How many of you know we need a revival? (Almost everyone raises his hand here. The knowledge of this fact hardly takes scholarship or devotion.)

How many of you want a revival? (Again, a majority opinion in church groups. According to George Gallup, Jr., in the eighties, around 80 percent of the country wanted a revival. Even the lost know we need one!)

How many of you know what a revival is? (The number drops off alarmingly now. Here is something we all want and we all need, but we don't have a clue as to what it is!)

How many of you have ever experienced a real revival? (And here, very few, if any, ever respond.)

"And there arose another generation which knew not the Lord, nor yet the works which He had done for Israel" (Judg. 2:10).

And that, friend, is the reason for this book.

CHAPTER ONE

Revival—Toward a Definition

Never let a generation grow up without that knowledge of Divine things which may contain the germ of national revival in years to come.

—Rys Bevan Jones

Biblically

What is revival? The closest biblical word is *revive* or *reviving*, from *chayah* (khaw-yaw)—"a prim. root meaning ***to live*** (fig. or lit.) (14 times) or make alive, nourish up, preserve alive, quicken, recover, repair, restore, or be whole" (Strong's Concordance, 2421). It is also translated to KEEP ALIVE, PRESERVE (9 times); to SAVE, SAVE ALIVE (16 times); to RESTORE, MAKE WHOLE (5 times); to RECOVER (5 times) or to REPAIR; and to QUICKEN (12 times).

The first four times, this word is translated *revived* in the Authorized version. All deal with four increasing levels of death:

(1) Jacob: Old Man with a Lost Dream

"And they told him all the words of Joseph, which he had said unto them: and when he saw the wagons which Joseph had sent to carry him, the spirit of Jacob their father *revived*" (Gen. 45:27).

(2) Samson: Young Man with a Near-death Vision

"But God clave an hollow place that [was] in the jaw, and there came water thereout; and when he had drunk, his spirit came again, and he *revived*: wherefore he called the name thereof En-hakkore, which [is] in Lehi unto this day" (Judg. 15:19).

(3) Elijah: Restoration of a Woman's Newly-dead Child

"And the LORD heard the voice of Elijah; and the soul of the child came into him again, and he *revived*" (2 Kings 17:22).

(4) Elisha's Bones: A Group of Servants Burying a Corpse

"And it came to pass, as they were burying a man, that, behold, they spied a band [of men]; and they cast the man into the sepulchre of Elisha: and when the man was let down, and touched the bones of Elisha, he *revived*, and stood up on his feet" (2 Kings 13:21).

All these groups of people are listed as the recipients of revival in the prophecy of Joel 2:28: "Your sons and daughters (children) shall prophesy; your old men shall dream dreams; your young men shall see visions; and also on the servants and handmaids in those days will I pour out of my Spirit."

The prophet Habbakuk uses this Hebrew word in his heart-broken cry, "Oh Lord, revive thy work; in the midst of the years remember mercy!" (Hab. 3:2). Yet revival is not magic. "In contrast to the ancient near East," says the *Theological Wordbook of the Old Testament*, "where men sought to link themselves with forces of life . . . by magical recitations . . . by appropriate magical ritual, in the O.T. life is decided by a **right relationship to the righteous standards of the Word of God**" (1:280). That is why Charles Finney could succinctly define revival as "nothing more or less than a new beginning of obedience to the Word of God."

Revival is not arbitrary. It is not mystical. It is, as far as men are concerned, a heartfelt return to love and faith in the living and written Word.

Dr. Wilbur Smith notes seven "outstanding revivals" in the Old Testament in addition to the one under Jonah. They are the one in Jacob's household (Gen. 35:1-15); under Asa (2 Chron. 15:1-15); Jehoash (2 Kings 11, 12; 2 Chron. 23, 24); Hezekiah (2 Kings 18:4-7; 2 Chron. 29:31), and Josiah (2 Kings 22, 23; 2 Chron. 34, 35). There are two revivals after the Exile under Zerubbabel (Ezra 5, 6) in which Haggai and Zechariah play a prominent part, and, finally, a revival in Nehemiah's time in which Ezra was the outstanding figure (Neh. 9:9; 12:44-47).

Smith summarizes nine outstanding characteristics of these major revivals:

1. They occurred in a day of deep moral darkness and national depression.

2. They began in the heart of one consecrated servant of God who became the energizing power behind it, the agent used of God to quicken and lead the nation back to faith in and obedience to Him.

3. Each revival rested on the Word of God, and most were the result of preaching and proclaiming God's law with power.

4. All resulted in a return to the worship of Jehovah.

5. Each witnessed the destruction of idols where they existed.

6. In each revival there was a recorded separation from sin.

7. In every revival they returned to offering blood sacrifices.

8. Almost all recorded revivals show a restoration of great joy and gladness.

9. Each revival was followed by a period of great national prosperity. (Fischer, *Reviving Revivals*, pp. 63-64)

The Greek equivalent of the Old Testament word for revive is only used *five times* in the New Testament. "Why is it not more of a N.T. word? For the simple reason that New Testament Christianity IS revived Christianity" (Eric W. Hayden, *Spurgeon on Revival*, p. 11). This Greek word *anazao* (*Strong's Concordance*, p. 326) is used for the restoration of the prodigal son (Luke 15:24, 32), the resurrection of Christ (Rom. 14:9), and the physical resurrection of the dead in the last days (Rev. 20:5) but also for the deadly effect of sin (Rom. 7:9). Evil as well as righteousness can have a revival; there can be an unholy uprising as well as a holy outpouring.

Another equivalent N.T. word is used by Paul in 2 Timothy 1:6–"Wherefore I put thee in remembrance that you *stir up* the gift of God which is in thee"–*anazapureo*, (*Strong's Concordance*, 329) to "fan into flame, to revive." Some prefer the term "spiritual awakening" like the promise fulfilled in Acts 2:17. This may refer to individual quickening, but revival, as we shall use and define it, both includes and transcends this.

Lexically

Webster's 1828 dictionary defines the word *revive* as a:

1. "Return, recall or recovery to life from death or apparent death; as the revival of a drowned person." Revival brings back to life something once living that is either now dead or seemingly dead.

2. "Return or recall to *activity from a state of languor*; as the revival of spirits." Revival brings a holy shock to apathy and carelessness. Isaiah calls for God to show His power:

"Oh that you would rend the heavens, that You would come down that the mountains may flow down at Your presence . . . to make Thy name known to Your adversaries, that the nations may tremble at your Presence. When You did terrible things, which we looked not for, You came down" (Isa. 64:1-3; 63:10-15).

3. "Recall, return or recovery from a state of *neglect, oblivion*, obscurity or depression; as the revival of letters or learning." Revival restores truth and recalls to obedience that which has been forgotten. Invariably as either its cause or result, it is associated with reformation of doctrine and preaching.

4. "Renewed and more active attention to religion; an awakening of men to their spiritual concerns." Revival accomplishes what our best spiritual efforts cannot. "Revival is necessary to counteract spiritual decline and to create spiritual momentum; . . . in revival the church dormant becomes the church militant."

Other Webster meanings of the word *revive* are to "renew in the mind or memory, to recall"; 5. to recover from a state of neglect or depression 6. to comfort; to quicken; to refresh with joy or hope ("Wilt Thou not revive us again?" Ps. 85)." Revival means to reanimate, renew, awaken, re-invigorate, restore; to make the church whole and happy in God again.

Revival is more than big meetings, religious excitement, a quickening of the saints, being filled with the Holy Spirit, or great harvests of souls. One may have one or all of these without revival.

Historically

Vance Havner defined it as "a work of God's Spirit among His own people . . . what we call revival is simply New Testament Christianity, the saints getting back to normal ("*Hearts Afire*," pp. 103-104).

Some think revival only a supernatural show of unusual events, terrifying manifestations in special times and seasons; others view it as a steady, continuous work of God from a genuine, Spirit-anointed Church's functioning as it is supposed to. Both models are valid, but often the first is needed to produce a genuine example of the second.

Martyn Lloyd-Jones said, "The essence of revival is that the Holy Spirit comes down upon a number of people together; upon a whole church, a number of churches, districts or perhaps a whole country. It is a visitation or outpouring of the Holy Spirit–God has come down among them" (Revival, p.100).

In the outpouring of the Holy Spirit at Pentecost, Peter declares: "This is that . . . spoken by the prophet Joel in the last days." (He changes the phrase from "it shall come to pass afterwards"–a period of time now, not a moment like Pentecost.) True revival is marked by powerful and often widespread outpourings of the Spirit. Many times preaching has to cease because the hearers are prostrate or because the voice of the preacher is drowned by cries for mercy. "The Holy Spirit fell on all them which heard the Word" (Acts 10:44).

Jonathan Edward's son-in-law David Brainerd, who prayed in the snow until it melted around him and was stained by his blood as he coughed away his life with T.B., prevailed in prayer for revival among the American Indians. Before he died he described in his journal how it finally began in 1745:

> The power of God seemed to descend on the assembly like a rushing mighty wind and with an astonishing energy bore all down before it. I stood amazed at the influence that seized the audience almost universally

> and could compare it to nothing more aptly than the irresistible force of a mighty torrent . . . Almost all persons of all ages were bowed down with concern together and scarce one was able to withstand the shock of the astonishing operation. (Edwards, *The Life and Diary of David Brainerd,* pp. 142-143)

Brian Edward's comments: "Someone has described revival as the top blowing off and that is very true. But the top does not blow off before the bottom has fallen out" (*Revival: A People Saturated With God,* p. 130).

Arthur Wallis, in his classic study *In The Day Of Thy Power,* points out the word is determined by its usage. It had historical consistency of meaning up until recent years, where (especially in America) it began to take on a lesser, more limited sense.

Nevertheless, he says:

> "Numerous writings on the subject preserved confirm that **revival is Divine intervention in the normal course of spiritual things**. It is God revealing Himself to man in awful holiness and irresistible power. It is such a manifest working of God that human personalities are overshadowed and human programs abandoned. It is man retiring into the background because God has taken the field. It is the Lord . . . working in extraordinary power on saint and sinner." (p. 20)

J. Edwin Orr, a prolific writer and eminent authority of both scholarship and experience in the subject, defined a spiritual awakening as "a movement of the Holy Spirit bringing about a revival of New Testament Christianity in the Church of Christ and its related community" (*The Eager Feet,* p. vii). It may significantly change an individual, a group of believers, a congregation, a city, a country or even eventually the world but it accomplishes "the reviving of the Church, the awakening of the masses and the movement of uninstructed peoples towards the Christian faith; the revived church by many or few is moved to engage in evangelism, teaching and social action" (p. vii).

A. W. Tozer defined revival as that which "changes the moral climate of a community." Revival is essentially a manifestation of God; it has a stamp of deity on it that even the unregenerate and uninitiated are quick to recognize. Duncan Campbell described it as a "community saturated with God." Revival must of necessity make an impact on the community, and this is one means by which we may distinguish it from the more usual operations of the Holy Spirit" (Wallis, *Day of Power*, p. 23).

John Dawson points out, however, that the "community" of the twentieth century is different from that of previous ages; modern communities are "linked vocational villages of communication," not necessarily communities linked geographically. A revival in the eighteenth century affected your neighbor who probably did live next door; a revival that affects your neighbor in the twentieth century may touch "neighbors" who live hundreds or even thousands of miles away and are linked not by geographic location but by common vocation and communication.

Revival is what the church first experiences; evangelism is what she then engages in. Revival is periodic; evangelism is continuous. Revival cannot last; evangelism must not stop.

Do we want a revival? Do we really? James Burns, writing in *Revival, Their Laws and Leaders*, said in 1909:

> To the church, a revival means humiliation, a bitter knowledge of unworthiness and an open and humiliating confession of sin on the part of her ministers and people. It is not the easy and glorious thing many think it to be, who imagine it fills pews and reinstates the church in power and authority.
>
> It comes to scorch before it heals; it comes to condemn ministers and people for their unfaithful witness, for their selfish living, for their neglect of the cross, and to call them to daily renunciation, to an evangelical poverty and to a deep and daily consecration. That is why a revival has ever been unpopular with large numbers within the church. Because it says nothing to them of power such as they have learned to love, or of ease, or

of success; it accuses them of sin, it tells them they are dead, it calls them to awake, to renounce the world and to follow Christ.

Still interested? Then come with me. The journey begins.

Chapter Two Features of Revival

We have seen in the studies of four of the exceptional men of the first and second Great Awakenings some of the characteristics of the lives of revivalists; we have looked on these two centuries as illustrations of the New Testament model of revival. But how can we summarize the dominant features of such a New Testament pattern?

Charles Finney said it best: "The antecedents, accompaniments and results of revivals are always substantially the same as in the case of Pentecost." Albert Barnes said: "That day which shall convince the great body of professing Christians of the reality and desirableness of revivals will constitute a new era in the history of religion and will precede manifestations of power like that of Pentecost." Arthur Wallis, keying off the scriptural record of the second chapter of Acts and quoting extensively from that "Prince of Revivalists" Finney, gave an outstanding outline of a true revival's characteristics, here excerpted and partly amplified.

Allowing God to Move

Divine Sovereignty. Implicit in the phrase "When the day of Pentecost was fully come" (Acts 2:1) is the fact that every genuine revival is clearly stamped with the hallmark of God's sovereignty. Consider the timing, the significance of the day, the nations all divinely ordered there.

God times every outpouring, a *kairos* related to a thousand other plans He alone can co-ordinate. Finney, speaking of the 1859 revival, mentions this sovereignty: "When I was in Boston . . . a gentleman stated he had come from Nebraska and had found prayer meetings established throughout all the vast extent of country over which he had travelled. Think of that–a vast region of 2,000 miles, along which the hands of the people of God were lifted up to God in prayer! From North to South till you come within the slave territory, a great and mighty prayer went up to God that He would come down and take the people in hand and convert souls; and He heard and everybody stood astounded."

Likewise in the Welsh Revival: "The outpouring of the Spirit came dramatically with precision in the second week in November 1904 on the same day–both in the North and the South." Zechariah 10:1 says, "Ask ye of the LORD rain in the time of the latter rain . . ."

Spiritual Preparation. "All together in one place. . . . with one accord continued steadfast in prayer" (Acts 1:14). The two essential conditions of revival are unity and prayer. Revival has two foundation stones: "the preparedness of man and the sovereignty of God" (Wallis, *In The Day Of Thy Power*, p. 60). The Word and history teach us that an attitude of indifference and fatalism must be abandoned before revival can be expected.

If the blessing comes, then we may be sure someone has met the conditions and paid the price. "Yet . . . we cannot have revival as if God is at our beck and call. 'Thy people offer themselves willingly in the day of Thy power' (Ps. 110:3; Ezek. 36:33-37; Mark 6:5,6; Deut. 11:13,16-17)." (See *Spontaneous Working.*)

Martyn Lloyd-Jones said:

> Our essential trouble is that we are content with a very superficial and preliminary knowledge of God, His being, his cause. . . . we spend our lives in busy activism . . . instead of realizing our own failure, (that) we are not attracting anybody to Christ and that they probably see nothing in us that makes them desire to come to Him.
>
> The inevitable and constant preliminary to revival has always been a thirst for God, a thirst, a living thirst for a knowledge of the living God and a longing and a burning desire to see Him acting, manifesting himself and his power, rising and scattering his enemies. . . . The thirst for God and the longing for the exhibition of His glory are the essential preliminaries to revival. (Martyn Lloyd-Jones: *Revival*, pp. 90-91)

Expect the Unexpected

Suddenness. "And suddenly there came . . ." (Acts 2:2).

Revival is a Divine attack on society. In revival God's work may be sudden and unexpected; often even believers are caught unaware, while fear and astonishment grip unbelievers' hearts: "There was nothing, humanly speaking, to account for what happened. Quite suddenly, upon one and another came an overwhelming sense of the reality and awfulness of His Presence and of eternal things. Life, death and eternity seemed suddenly laid bare" (Joseph Kemp of Charlotte Chapel in Edinburgh 1905).

Finney said: "They would wake up all of a sudden, like a man just rubbing his eyes open and running around the room pushing things over and wondering where all this excitement came from. But though few knew it, you may be sure there had been somebody on the watchtower constant in prayer until the blessing came" (Wallis, *In The Day Of Thy Power*, p. 62).

Revival is God's springing a convicting surprise on His creation: "I have declared the former things from of old; yea they went forth out of My mouth and I shewed them; suddenly I did them and they came to pass, and new things do I declare; before they spring forth I tell you of them" (Isa. 48:3; 42:9). The effect of the sudden working of the Spirit in revival is very striking in the conviction of sinners. Often, without any preparatory concern or even thought for spiritual things, a sinner will be suddenly seized with an overwhelming conviction of sin.

Although the people in Broughshane, Ulster, of 1859 were expecting revival (that was after all, all around them) says Paisley, they were still "taken by surprise, so sudden, so powerful and extraordinary were the manifestations of the Spirit's Presence . . . about one thousand people were suddenly, sensibly and powerfully impressed and awakened."

The modern horror movie shock tactic of sudden confrontation with the unexpected is a perverted, cheap copy of a holy original–the awesome fear of the Lord. Suddenness is a divine shock tactic to remind men of their spiritual vulnerableness. "But God shall shoot at them; with an arrow suddenly they shall be wounded . . . and all men shall fear; and they shall declare the work of God and shall wisely consider His doing" (Ps. 64:7,9).

John Shearer, in *Old Time Revivals*, writes of a farmer returning from market in Ulster at Ballymena in 1859. His mind wholly intent upon the days bargain, he pauses, takes out some money and begins to count it. Suddenly, an awful presence envelopes him. In a moment his only thought is that he is a sinner standing on the brink of hell. His silver is scattered, and he falls on the dust of the highway crying out for mercy" (Wallis, *In The Day Of Thy Power*, p.63).

Wholly of God

Spontaneous Working. "There came . . . from heaven" (Acts 2:2). Revival is the result of divine, not human impulse. It cannot be worked up. Fulfilled conditions do not provide the motive force of revival. Revival, like salvation and healing, is an act of divine mercy. Like salvation, too, its grounds are Gods grace though its conditions are repentance and the prayer of faith (Acts 3:19: "seasons of refreshing . . . from the presence of the Lord").

"A movement bears this mark of spontaneity when men cannot account for what has taken place in terms of personalities, organizations, meetings, preachings, or any other consecrated activity; and when the work continues unabated without any human control" (Wallis, *Day of Power*, p. 65). As soon as a movement becomes controlled or organized, it has ceased to be spontaneous–it is no longer a revival.

The course of the 1904 revival has been outlined thus: "God began to work; then the Devil began to work in opposition; then God began to work all the harder; then man began to work and the revival came to an end" (Wallis, *In the Day of Thy Power*, p. 65).

God-Consciousness. The spirit of revival is the consciousness of God. Men were "pricked in their heart" (Acts 3:7). "Fear came on every soul" (Acts 2:43). "The effects of such manifestations of God are twofold; men are made aware both of His power and His holiness. This manifestation . . . was intensely personal" (Wallis, *In the Day of Thy Power*, p. 66). It is God's moving in power and holiness toward you; God's coming for you and calling your name!

Here is an outstanding feature of revival; it is easy to see why it results in overwhelming conviction, both among the saved and the lost whenever there is unjudged sin. At such times man is conscious that God is there; He seems to deal with him alone, until he is oblivious of all but his own soul in the agonizing grip of a holy God. If these facts are borne in mind, the extraordinary effects of past revivals will not seem incredible.

A Divine Terror

The ruthless logic of Jonathan Edward's famous discourse "Sinners in the Hands of an Angry God" could not have produced the effect it did had not God been in the midst of the congregation. "When they went into the meeting house the appearance of the assembly was thoughtless and vain; the people scarcely conducted themselves with common decency," recorded Trumbull, who goes on to describe the effects of the sermon: "The assembly appeared bowed with an awful conviction of their sin and danger. There was such a breathing of distress and weeping that the preacher was obliged to speak to the people and desire silence that he might be heard" (*Day of Power*, p. 67). Conant says, "Many of the hearers were seen unconsciously holding themselves up against the pillars and the sides of the pews as though they already felt themselves sliding into the pit" (Wallis, *In The Day Of Thy Power*, p. 67).

Finney at the village schoolhouse near Antwerp, New York, describes such conviction: "An awful solemnity seemed to settle upon the people; the congregation began to fall from their seats in every direction and cry for mercy. If I had a sword in each hand, I could not have cut them down as fast as they fell. I was obliged to stop preaching." "Did you ever witness *two hundred sinners with one accord in one place weeping*?" asked Asa Nettleton. "The scene is beyond description . . . I felt as though I was standing on the verge of the eternal world; while the floor under my feet was shaken by the trembling of anxious souls in view of a judgment to come" (Thornton, *God Sent Revival*, pp. 91-92).

A Chain Reaction

Sometimes the manifested presence of God creates a divine "radiation zone"; all coming within that expanding spiral of tangible power are brought under awesome conviction. During the 1859 revival, no town in Ulster was more deeply stirred than Coleraine. A schoolboy in class became so troubled about his soul that the schoolmaster sent him home. An older boy, a Christian, went with him and before they had gone far, led him to Christ. Returning at once to school, this new convert testified to his teacher: "Oh, I am so happy! I have the Lord Jesus in my heart." These artless words had an astonishing effect; boy after boy rose and silently left the room. Going outside the teacher found these boys all on their knees, ranged along the wall of the playground. Very soon their silent prayer became a bitter cry; it was heard by another class inside and pierced their hearts. They fell on their knees, and their cry for mercy was heard in turn by a girls' class above. In a few moments, the whole school was on their knees! Neighbors and passers-by came flocking in, and all as they crossed the threshold came under the same convicting power. Every room was filled with men, women, and children seeking God (Orr, *The Second Evangelical Awakening*, p. 44).

During the same 1859 revival in America, ships entered a

definite zone of heavenly influence as they drew near port. Ship after ship arrived with the same talk of sudden conviction and conversion. A captain and an entire crew of thirty men found Christ at sea and arrived at port rejoicing. This overwhelming sense of God bringing deep conviction of sin is perhaps the outstanding feature of true revival. Its manifestation is not always the same; to cleansed hearts it is heaven; to convicted hearts it is hell.

A Need for the Spirit

Anointed Vessels. "They were all filled with the Holy Ghost" (Acts 2:4)—there is a fresh emphasis on the person and work of the Holy Spirit. "With those stirrings of the Spirit that are the precursor of revival, there is born in many such hearts a wholesome dissatisfaction with that vague and mystic view of being filled with the Spirit that leaves one in the dark as to what it is, how it comes and whether or not one has received it" (Wallis, *In the Day of Thy Power*, p. 69). Finney again says, "Many times great numbers of persons in a community will be clothed with this power, when the very atmosphere of the whole place seems to be charged with the life of God. Strangers coming into it and passing through the place will be instantly smitten with conviction of sin and in many instances converted to Christ" (Wallis, *In the Day of Thy Power*, p. 71).

Supernatural Manifestation. "They spoke in other tongues as the Spirit gave them utterance" (Acts 2:4). The most ordinary conversion of a sinner is a supernatural work, but it is not manifestly so. Revival features conversions that are, in the eyes of men, *manifestly* supernatural and that can be accounted for in no other way. It produces in the hearts and minds of observers the reaction described here: "They were all amazed and were perplexed, saying one to another, 'What meaneth this?'" (Acts 2:12).

Revival always seems to bring a return to apostolic Christianity. Never is the church nearer to the spirit and power of the first century than in times of revival. In times of spiritual blessing, the gifts are more especially manifest. Spurgeon noted "If you read the story of the Reformation, or the later story . . . of Whitefield and Wesley, you are struck with the *singular spirit* that went with the preachers. The world said they were mad; the caricaturists drew them as being fanatical beyond all endurance; but there it was, their zeal was their power. Of course the world scoffed at that of which it was afraid. The world fears enthusiasm, the sacred enthusiasm kindled by the thought of the ruin of men and by the desire to pluck the firebrands from the flame, the enthusiasm which believes in the Holy Ghost, which believes God is still present with His church to do wonders" (Spurgeon, Sermons *On Revival,* p. 15).

"Dislike of enthusiasm," said D.M. Lloyd-Jones, "is to quench the Spirit. Those . . . familiar with the history of the Church, and in particular the history of revivals, will know this charge of enthusiasm is one always brought against people most active in a period of revival" (Lloyd-Jones, *Revival,* p. 72).

Under the Power of the Spirit

Crying out and falling down under the awesome presence of the Holy Spirit was common in the Wesley-Whitefield revivals. Lady Huntingdon wrote to Whitefield, advising him not to remove the people as it had been done, as it seemed to bring a damper on the meeting. "You are making a mistake. Don't be wiser than God. *Let them cry; it will do a great deal more good than your preaching*" (Wallis, *In the Day of Thy Power,* p. 75).

This seems a natural reaction of people in Scripture who had a divine "close encounter of the fourth kind"—the invading sense of God's convicting power. ("And when I saw Him I fell at His feet as dead." Rev. 1:17)

Wesley recorded in his journals on July, 1739:

> He (Whitefield) had opportunity of informing himself better; no sooner had he begun . . . to invite all sinners to believe in Christ than four persons sunk down close to him, almost in the same moment. One of them lay without sense or motion. A second trembled exceedingly. The third had strong convulsions all over his body, but made no noise unless by groans. The fourth, equally convulsed, called upon God with strong cries and tears. From this time, I trust, we shall allow God to carry on His own work in the way that pleases Him.

A Terrifying Blessing

Sometimes this sense of identification with the hurt of God is awesome and terrifying. An observer of the Welsh Revival, David Matthews, said of Evan Roberts,

> Mr. Roberts had an experience which I believe was never repeated. . . . Prayer was the keynote of his tireless life. No action taken or engagement entered into was done without definitely committing the matter to God in prayer. His soul appeared to be saturated through and through with the spirit of prayer. . . . He asked God to give him a *taste of Gethsemane.*
>
> . . . I am a living witness of the incident, that the prayer was answered in a terrifying way. Falling on the floor of the pulpit he moaned like one mortally wounded, while his tears flowed incessantly. His fine physical frame shook under crushing soul-anguish. No-one was allowed to touch him. . . . The majority of us were petrified with fear in the presence of such uncontrollable grief. What did it mean? . . . When Evan Roberts stood before the congregation again, his face seemed transfigured. It was patent to all he had passed through an experience that was extremely costly. No-one who witnessed that scene would vote for a repetition. One wonders whether such a hallowed scene should be chronicled. (Matthews, *I Saw The Welsh Revival.* p. 41)

The Work of the Outpoured Spirit

Divine Magnetism. "And when this sound was heard, the multitude came together" (Acts 2:6).

During the Lewis Awakening, in the village of Arnol, there was no response in the first few meetings; at the close of an evening meeting, a time of prayer was convened in a house. As one man was praying, all present became aware that the prayer was heard and that the Spirit of God was being poured out on the village. They left the house to discover the villagers also were leaving their cottages and making their way, as though drawn by some unseen force, to one point in the village. There they assembled and waited. When Duncan Campbell commenced to preach, the word took immediate effect. In a few days, that small community had been swept by the Spirit of God and many souls truly converted.

The evangelist often complains that unconverted, pleasure-loving masses will not come to hear the Gospel and that large sums are spent on publicity and advertising. But where normal means are failing to achieve the necessary end, where natural means do not succeed, we must look to the supernatural. "How long halt ye between two opinions?" Elijah said, but "the people answered him not a word" (1 Kings 18:21). But when God answered by fire, instantly the people were on their faces. What the strivings of man cannot achieve is but the work of a moment to the outpoured Spirit.

Anointed Messages

Apostolic Preaching. "Peter lifted up his voice and spoke forth to them" (Acts 2:14). Although many souls are saved in revival apart from preaching, such times are nearly always characterized by a powerful proclamation of truth. Sometimes the outpouring has come by preaching; sometimes the preaching has come by the outpouring.

> There is a rugged grandeur about the apostolic preacher which recalls the fearless prophet of O.T. days. They were clothed with the same power and impelled by the same boldness for their torches were lit from the same holy fire. . . . The primary aim is to lead souls to repentance. . . . There is so much emphasis today on believing, receiving, deciding and so on and so little on the vital step of *repenting* . . . the men dealt faithfully with the question of sin that the conscience might be aroused. (Wallis, *In The Day Of Thy Power,* p. 82)

> It was a precept of Wesley to his evangelists in unfolding their message, to speak first in general of the *love of God* to man; then with all possible energy so as to search the conscience to its depths, to preach the *law of holiness*; and then, and not till then, to uplift the glories of

> the *gospel of pardon* and of life. Intentionally or not, his directions follow the lines of the epistle to Romans. (Bishop Hadley Moule on Romans)

Finney had a fixed principle in dealing with souls: Never tell a man how to get right with God until he can no longer look him in the face. John Nelson records of Wesley at Moorfields, "His countenance struck such an awful dread upon me before I heard him speak that it made my heart beat like the pendulum of a clock; and when he did speak, I thought his whole discourse was aimed at me" (Pollock, *Wesley*, p. 154).

The realm of apostolic preaching may be divided into four categories: spontaneous preaching, anointed preaching, fearless preaching, and Christ-centered preaching. All of these are vital elements in any Spirit-led revival and have been evidenced throughout history.

Spontaneous Preaching

> For some twelve years," said Finney, "in my earliest ministry I wrote not a word; and was commonly obliged to preach without any preparation whatever, except what I got in prayer. Often I went into the pulpit without knowing upon what text I should speak or a word that I should say. I depended on the occasion and the Holy Spirit to suggest the text and to open up the whole subject to my mind; and certainly in no part of my ministry have I preached with greater success or power. If I did not preach from inspiration I didn't know how I did preach. It was a common experience with me . . . that the subject would open up to my mind in a manner that was surprising to myself. It seemed that I could see with intuitive clearness just what I ought to say, and whole platoons of thoughts, words and illustrations came to me as fast as I could deliver them. (Wallis, *In the Day of Thy Power,* p. 84)

"The very characteristic of the New Testament Church was this spontaneity, this living quality, this vivacity. But as you fall away from the Spirit and his influence, everything becomes formal" (Lloyd-Jones, *Revival* p. 76). In the Evan Mills revival, Finney recalls,

> The Spirit of God came upon me with such power that it was like opening a battery upon them. For more than an hour the Word of God came through me to them in such a manner that I could see was carrying all before it. It was a fire and a hammer breaking the rock, and as the sword that was piercing . . . I saw a general conviction was spreading over the whole audience." Far from encouraging laziness, such a manner of preaching demands incessant prayerfulness and constant meditation and feeding on the Word. (Wallis, *The Day of Power*, p. 84)

Preaching with Unction

Anointed Vessels. "The promise . . . which you do see and hear" (v. 33). Anointed preaching is "in demonstration of the Spirit and of power" so that faith does not stand "in the wisdom of men, but in the power of God" (1 Cor. 2:1-5).

One said of Savoronala, the great Italian reformer: "Nature had withheld from him almost all the gifts of the orator," yet "when we read of his intense and enrapt communion with God, his unconquerable persistence in seeking the power of the Highest till his thoughts and affections were so absorbed in God ... those who looked in his cell saw his upturned face as it had been the face of an angel." His preaching was so pathetic, melting, resistless the reporter lays down his pen with this apology written under the last line "Such sorrow and weeping came upon me that I could go no further" (Wallis, *In the Day of Thy Power*, p. 85).

Fearless Preaching

"They spoke the word of God with boldness" (Acts 4:31). Supernatural boldness in preaching is the result of God's anointing. It was noted of Gilbert Tennant, (a contemporary of Jonathan Edwards, and mightily used in the New England Revival) that:

> he seemed to have no regard to please the eyes of his hearers with agreeable gesture, nor their ears with delivery, nor their fancy with language; but to aim *directly at their hearts and consciences,* to lay open their ruinous delusions, show them their numerous secret, hypocritical shifts in religion and drive them out of every deceitful refuge wherein they had made themselves easy with the form of godliness without the power. . . . His preaching was frequently both terrible and searching (*Princes' Christian History*). Fearless preaching is calculated to produce conviction or stir up the most bitter animosity. It usually does both. (Wallis, *In the Day of Thy Power,* p. 86)

Christ-centered Preaching

"Jesus . . . by the right hand of God exalted" (Acts 2:32-33).

In the thirty years following the outpouring of the Spirit on the Moravian congregation at Herrnhut (1727), their evangelists, with a motto of "To win for the Lamb that was slain the reward of His suffering," had carried the gospel not only to nearly every country in Europe but also to many pagan races in North and South America, Asia, and Africa.

Dr. Warnek, a German historian of Protestant missions, wrote, "This small church in twenty years called into being more missions than the whole evangelical church has done in two centuries" (Wallis, *In the Day of Thy Power,* p. 88). More than a hundred missionaries went forth from this village community in twenty-five years.

Superabundant Blessing

"And there were added unto them in that day about three thousand souls" (Acts 2:41). "Many that heard the word believed; and the number of men came to be about 5,000" (Acts 4:4). "And believers were the more added to the Lord, multitudes of both men and women" (Acts 5:14). "And the number of the disciples multiplied . . . exceedingly; and a great company of priests were obedient to the faith" (Acts 6:7).

If these records were not part of inspired Scripture, we might think them exaggerated; yet down through the years there have been seasons of revival numerically comparable to Pentecost. An estimated 30,000 souls were converted through Whitefield's revivals in America. In the Second Great Awakening, Dr. Henry Ward Beecher remarked to Charles Finney, "This is the greatest revival of religion that has been since the world began." One hundred thousand were converted that year in the United States. At the peak of the great 1857 revival, conversions numbered fifty thousand a week, and over the whole U.S. there could not have been less than five hundred thousand conversions, according to Finney's conservative estimate in 1859, when the revival was still spreading. "A similar movement began in the United Kingdom affecting every county in Ulster, Scotland, Wales, and England, adding a million accessions to the evangelical churches" (Wallis, *In the Day of Thy Power*, p. 90). The 1904 revival touched almost five million people in two years. The closing years of this century have witnessed even more massive ingatherings.

Whole Communities Come to the Lord

Far more significant is the proportion of a community affected. Of the New England revival (18th century), Conant commented ". . . at least 50,000 souls were added to the churches of New England out of a population of about 250,000. A fact sufficient to revolutionize, as indeed it did, the religious and moral character and to determine the destiny of the country" (Wallis, *In the Day of Thy Power*, p. 90). Of the Northhampton, Massachusetts, (1735) revival, Edwards wrote, "There was *scarcely a single person in the town, either old or young that was left unconcerned about the great things of the eternal world* . . . souls did, as it were, come by flocks to Jesus Christ" (Edwards, *Works*, p. 91). Finney wrote of the revival in Rome, New York. "As the work proceeded it gathered in *nearly the whole population*." Of the 1858 revival in Stockholm, Sweden, "At least two hundred thousand persons have been awakened out of a population not exceeding three million" (Edwards, *Works*, p. 91).

Divine Simplicity

"And continued steadfastly in the apostles doctrine, and fellowship and in breaking of bread, and prayers . . ." (Acts 2:41). Wallis said:

> As faith and spirituality decline, the power of the Spirit is gradually withdrawn. Soon it becomes necessary to substitute human arrangements worked without the Spirit's power for the divine arrangements dependent on that power. . . . How simple were the channels along which the rivers of that first outpouring flowed! When the Spirit of God is poured out again it will be seen that nothing more is needed. (Wallis, *In the Day of Thy Power*, pp. 94-95)

In a return to the simple methods of the first century, many are surprised to discover they not only still work, but they still work the best.

CHAPTER THREE

Features and Impacts

Revivals are dangerous. They are fatal to the kingdom of darkness, but few realize the cost such a divine visitation exacts from humanity also. They are like a temporary transfer of humanity to heaven, a transient glimpse of what it is like living in the manifest glory of God. But a mortal body was never designed for continual revival; Enoch, Elijah, and Moses, who all spent inordinate amounts of time with Him, were all taken home by Him. By definition revival cannot be other than occasional: "And the people served the Lord all the days of Joshua and all the days of the elders that outlived Joshua who had seen all the great work of the Lord that He had wrought for Israel . . . and there arose another generation after them which knew not the Lord, nor yet the work which He did for Israel" (Judg. 2:7,10,11).

Besides, God the Father will never spoil His children, and to live on such special visitations would be spiritually unhealthy. "Nevertheless–there is nothing more calculated to stay the rot, wean the heart from earth and attract it to heaven, and produce spiritual steadfastness than to experience such a mighty work of God. One recalls D.M. Panton's pithy definition of revival as 'the inrush of the Spirit into a body that threatens to become a corpse!' . . . It is, after all, a sound military principle that the best method of defence is attack" (Wallis, *Day of Power*).

Static and Sliding Friction

One of the observations of physics is the marked difference between static and sliding friction. An object at rest resists a change of location more than the same object in motion. Put simply, it is always harder to get something moving than to keep it moving once it has started.

We have a parallel personal responsibility to be sensitive to the Holy Spirit when He is dealing with mankind; the initial stage of a real awakening is critical. Consider people pushing a stalled car. Initially, only one man in front pushing against them in the wrong direction can stop it cold; but once it begins to move, heaven help anyone who gets in the way! Revival is like this. Anyone privileged to participate in the initial dealings of God must be wise enough in His ways to not grieve Him and to allow the work to continue through to the moving; but once underway it will move anything out of its path.

The Steel Punch

Revival is a divine attack on society. Have you ever seen a karate champion break a stack of bricks with his hand, or a straw driven into a piece of hardwood by the violence of a tornado? Immense power concentrated in one small spot creates breakthroughs previously thought impossible.

Israel's recapture of the Golan Heights from an entrenched Syria is a modern classic of military victory. The Syrian army was dug into three consecutive trenches in the top of the hill; they had planted over a million landmines between their position and Israel's position. Russian advisors had assured Syria their position was unassailable. While Israel's Air Force strafed the enemy trenches to minimize Syrian troop groundfire, Israeli farmers drove tractors in a straight line up the side of the hill. Driving directly behind each exploded tractor, another took its place, ploughing the ruins out of the way. Followed by Israeli troops, they cut a straight single line up the side of the hill. They called it "The Steel Punch"; Israel took the Golan Heights.

Wallis notes the well-known military principle known as concentration of force: "a commander husbands his reserves, concentrates them at a strategic point for a vital blow at the crucial moment. A powerful thrust like this may accomplish what routine patrolling, skirmishing or harassing tactics could never effect" (*Day of Power*, pp. 45-50). He likens this to an ancient reservoir fed by a mountain stream supplying a village community with water. One day the wall collapses. The waters root up large trees, carry boulders like playthings, and destroy houses and bridges and all that lies in their path.

> What had before been ignored or taken for granted now becomes an object of awe, wonder and fear. People from far and near who never went near, now hurry to see this great sight. In picture language this is revival; in fact it is the sort of picture language that Scripture uses to convey the irresistible power of God. Often in the period just preceding the movement, the stream of power and blessing has been unusually low. The people of God and work of God have been "in great affliction and reproach," despised or ignored by those around them. In response to the burdened prayer of a remnant, God has been quietly "heaping the flood." "So shall they fear the name of the Lord from the west and His glory from the rising of the sun; for He shall come as a rushing stream, which the breath of the Lord driveth." ([Isa. 59:19] Wallis, *In the Day of Thy Power,* p. 4)

The Purpose of Revival

Arthur Wallis was mightily used of the Lord to further the work of the Holy Spirit towards revival, especially in New Zealand. His classic study on revival, *In the Day of Thy Power,* often quoted and excerpted from in sections of this study, was condensed and re-issued as *Rain from Heaven* (Bethany Press,

1981). In the section called "This Is the Purpose," Wallis further analyzes why God works in history by means of revivals.

God is our Creator; so we will not forget His reality or drift easily into deism, He still periodically alters human history by sudden, mighty moves of His spirit. P. V. Jenness said:

> The world of mankind has not advanced by evolution but revolution, by violent upheavals in society. Eden, the Flood, Exodus, [and the] Captivity era are O.T. examples, Pentecost the conspicuous [N]ew [Testament Example]. The Renaissance and Protestant Reformation in the fifteenth century changed the whole thought and life of Europe. Modern history dates from them. (Wallis, *In the Day of Thy Power,* p. 45)

The great missionary advance of the 19th century took momentum from the widespread revivals that blessed America and Britain during those years; much of the evangelistic explosion in many Third World countries today can be directly traced to revivals. "Revival is Divine military strategy; first to *counteract spiritual decline*, and then to *create spiritual momentum*" (Wallis, *In the Day of Thy Power*, p. 45).

Who Is Affected?

The Saints. "The quickening of saints is the root; the saving of sinners is the fruit. To see the primary effect of revival look to the church. Revival marks the awakening of the Church; when asleep one is out of touch with the world of reality. The Church asleep is out of touch with the world of spiritual reality and needs to be awakened" (Wallis, *In the Day of Thy Power,* p. 49). Scripture says: "Knowing the season, it is high time for you to awaken out of sleep; for now is salvation nearer to us than when we first believed . . ." (Rom. 13:1).

Here is the primary effect of revival–the Church awakes, casts off the works of darkness, and puts on the armor of light. She puts on strength ("awake, awake, put on Thy strength, oh Zion") and holiness ("Awake, awake, put on thy beautiful garments O Jerusalem the holy city" [Isa. 52:1].) The church asleep is not only denuded of power but also holiness. Holiness is not optional but obligatory. If there is no revival of righteousness, there is no revival at all. It is characteristic of revivals that sins long hindering blessing are exposed, confessed, and forgiven; relationships wrecked by pride, envy, and evil speaking are wonderfully restored.

Jonathan Edwards wrote: "Abundance has been lately done making up differences, confessing faults one to another and making restitution; probably more within these two years than in the thirty years before" (Wallis, *In the Day of Thy Power,* p. 50).

The Sinners. "Whenever there comes this awful sense of God's presence stealing over the hearts of men, the fountains of the great deep are broken up. Gone is the voice of the sinner who inwardly debates whether or not he will patronize the Son of God" (Wallis, *In the Day of Thy Power,* p. 51).

The Godhead. "It is the usual thing that men of the world should treat their Creator with indifference or contempt. . . . As for the Comforter . . . how seldom is that gracious unseen Presence truly recognized, relied upon or given His rightful place in the Church which He established. How often is He grieved and hindered because the people of God prefer human organization and the methods of the world to that which costs more than money to secure–His own gracious presence and power. . . . Revival has its repercussions even in the realms of the Triune God. It is a time when the rights of humanity give way to the rights of Deity" (Wallis, *In the Day of Thy Power,* p. 52, 55).

CHAPTER FOUR

O.T. Pattern of Change–Reformers

As it has been said, history repeats itself. But are there any patterns to revival? Perhaps if there are, we can learn from them. Richard Lovelace, in his contribution to the historical and experiential theology of revivals, points out that both history and Scripture show two patterns of divine intervention:

1. The New Testament pattern is one of revitalization of the Church, such as that treated by many historians of revival, such as J. Edwin Orr, and dealt with in some detail by men like Arthur Wallis.

2. The Old Testament model of reform is one of structure and doctrine that moves the Church toward "certain norms of life and health" and calls out the blessings of God upon a nation (Lovelace, *The Dynamics of the Spiritual Life,* p. 52).

Every new generation experiences what the sixties called the "Generation Gap," often phrased as "God has no grandchildren." The Bible puts it like this: "All that generation were gathered unto their fathers: and there arose another generation after them, which knew not the Lord" (Judg. 2:10). We face it today, as did our spiritual fathers before us: the cycle of change and decay, of reformation and apostasy, the existence of a nation with a godly heritage that follows the pattern of Israel's four-fold collapse:

Israel forgot God;
Israel forgot God's laws;
Israel made up new gods;
Israel made up new laws.

The Law of Moral Entropy

Why do nations leave the ways of God? There is, of course, an active Devil; he never sleeps, knowing what can happen if people get carried away with being godly. People forget their roots, and spiritual history is no exception. But there is another factor at work, one illustrated by the best-authenticated physical law in the universe, the Second Law of Thermodynamics. Put simply, things tend to run down, not up; to move from order to chaos, from cohesive complexity to random simplicity. The Second Law means you can't get out of a system all the energy there is in it. The measure of this disorder is called entropy. The Bible reveals there has been a moral entropy introduced in our race by the Fall of man; without a constant investment of higher power and ordering wisdom, man left to himself will decay and die. All these add up; an active Devil, a godly generation's death, and a law of internal decay. For this reason revival is mandatory; we need continuous reform and re-awakening.

In Israel's time, under God's judgment, people awakened to a realization of better days and linked this back to their previous relationship with Him. Prayer went up in agony for deliverance, and God raised up another leader and another restoration. You can see it in the cyclical story of Biblical history, in the Gideons, Jepthas and Jehosaphats, the Hezekiahs and the Josiahs, where one man had to plead with God for the many, where one godly man had to stand up for the nation instead of a godly nation's standing up as one man. It is the record of the book of Judges, where those like Samson stood in the gap for an apostatizing nation as other heroes before him had.

The Moral Majority

Here perhaps is a valid contribution of a "moral majority." It takes no scholarship to realize that many of such a majority need not be Christian at all; just "nice" people who want to preserve a previous life-style from a threatened destruction. Essential evangelical experience is not required to feel outrage at a collapsing society that may seriously threaten your freedom, security, and peace. But as Francis Schaeffer pointed out in *A Christian Manifesto*:

> . . . We must realize that regardless of whether we think the Moral Majority has always said the right things . . . they certainly have done one thing right; they have used the freedom we still have in the political arena . . . they have carried the fact that *law is king, law is above the lawmakers, and God is above the law* into this area of life where it always should have been. The Moral Majority has drawn a line between the one total view of reality and the other total view of reality and the results this brings forth in government and law. And if you personally do not like some of the details of what they have done, do it better. But you must understand that all Christians have got to do the same kind of thing, or you are simply not showing the Lordship of Christ in the totality of life. (Schaeffer, *A Christian Manifesto*, pp. 61-62)

Such conservative groups represent attempts to bring society back towards these "norms of life and health." Like Josiah of old, who tore down idols and cleaned out Israel without knowing why his nation was so deeply fallen, not all have "the Book of the Law." But God has worked through imperfect men before; God has raised up men with a little light where there has been no light at all in order to bring greater light. One such critical time we remember today as the Reformation.

The Great Reformation

There were outbreaks of true revival long before the Reformation. Let's not take much time to detail here the incredible influence of some of the true Catholic saints who preceded the Reformers.

Early Reformers

Some names, of course, stand out. In the dark days of the twelfth century, there was Francis of Assisi, in his brown woolen robe with a rope belt. An ex-soldier and playboy, he had a vision of Christ "with eyes fixed on him in tender love" that utterly freed him from his pleasure-mad ways and made of him a radiant apostle of love. "His words were like fire, piercing the heart" (Harold A. Fischer, *Reviving Revivals*, p. 78).

Having nothing, Francis possessed all things. With his happy band of twelve, he was granted permission from Pope Innocent to found an order that stirred all Italy and touched Egypt and Spain. Whole audiences responded to his challenge to forsake all and follow Jesus. The brothers eventually numbered in the thousands.

As early as the fourteenth century, following the Dark Ages, there were pious priests like Savonarola, who soaked themselves in the Scriptures and got a prophetic word of judgment for their corrupted generation. A fasting, praying, fifteenth century John the Baptist of his time, Savonarola spoke prophetic messages that were fire, light, and searing conviction; listeners paled, and trembled. Their "eyes glazed with terror. . . tears gushed from their eyes; they beat their breasts and cried to God for mercy" (Harold A. Fischer, *Reviving Revivals*, pp. 85-86).

One famous scholar, Pico della Mirandola, said "the mere sound of Savonarola's voice was as a clap of doom; a cold shiver ran through the marrow of his bones; the hairs of his head stood on end as he listened." Another tells how his sermons caused "such terror and alarm, such sobbing and tears that people passed through the streets without speaking, more dead than alive" as he prophesied coming judgment on the church and the country (Harold A. Fischer, *Reviving Revivals,* pp. 84-86).

Judgment came, and Savonarola became a civic leader. He continued to preach fearlessly for righteousness until a fierce reaction and opposition resulted in his ultimate arrest, torture, and hanging.

Wycliffe and Hus, on the other hand, were Protestants who heard from heaven. Here were men who dared attack the religious leadership of their day and stack up all going on in God's Name against the sacred standard of Scripture. But it took a century more before God put His hand on the hearts of some rough-cut saints-in-the-making and used them to jolt the world out of its lip-service into a beginning of true obedience.

Reformation Leaders

God has such unlikely heroes. His man in Switzerland had a weak voice and short sight, and, to put it kindly, "lacked the gifts of a popular orator"; yet his preaching set Switzerland afire (one hearer felt as if he had been "lifted up by the hair and suspended in space!"), put contracts on his life, and finally ended with his being cut into four pieces and tossed into a fire.

The second, an earthy German, wouldn't even shake hands with his brother Swiss reformer because he didn't like what he thought about the nature of bread and wine. Blunt, crude, rough, and often shockingly harsh in condemning people he didn't agree with, he nevertheless launched what has been called "the most gigantic revolution in the history of the Christian church," and his profound experience of forgiveness in Christ gave him the bravery to stand almost alone against the entire weight of established and entrenched religious deception and blow it to the winds.

The third leader had no hand in initiating the Reformation. He thought of himself as a "quiet scholar" (his opponents thought otherwise). He was an aristocrat, "practically destitute of humor or imagination." Yet by the age of twenty-six, he had finished the first draft of his most famous work, *Institutes of the Christian Religion.*

Here, in a little more detail, are the stories and contributions of these early pioneers out of darkness.

Huldrych Zwingli 1484-1531

Zwingli, "the most rational and unsuccessful of the reformers," was born January 1, 1484, in a little, gabled house in the mountain village of Wildhaus, Switzerland. He was the third child of a family of eight sons and two daughters. His father was a shepherd and chief magistrate of the city, his uncle the village priest. It was a time of great discovery: when Zwingli was eight, Columbus set sail and reached the Bahamas; when he was ten, Leonardo Da Vinci drew a flying machine; and by the time he was seventeen, music was printed for the first time in moveable type. His Bern humanist education in Latin, dialectics, and music (he played six instruments) did not bring a deep spiritual experience like Luther's. Early in his life, faith to him was little more than an intellectual encounter, and he was not averse to amorous encounters with village women, like his barber's daughter.

Freedom of Conscience

In 1519, at thirty-five, he moved to Zurich, assuming a new position as the people's priest. Then, in 1522, following a close call with plague and "hovering for weeks between life and death," he became "overwhelmed with a sense of God's mercy and majesty." Now much more Christ-dependent, he admitted that "religion took its rise when God called a runaway man back to himself; otherwise that man would have been a desert forever." His first famous sermon, "On the Choice and Free Use of Foods," made the eating of meat at Lent a matter of conscience, underscoring this further great Reformation contribution of what Robert Dale called "the right of every man to listen for himself to the voice of God" (Fry and Arnold, "Reclaiming Reformation Day," *Christianity Today*, 22 October 1982, p. 36).

Zwingli was certainly not a gifted speaker; he couldn't see too well, and he had a soft voice; yet Gordon Rupp says of him ". . . his preaching is the secret of his dominance of the great city, and not all his actions in the councils could match it. It is something with few parallels (Calvin, Knox, Latimer)—*continuous Biblical exposition adjusted to the practical needs of each changing day in a community small enough for everybody to be known and where all the effective city leadership sat under the Word;* . . . scriptural preaching went on here, first of all the cities of Switzerland" (*Twenty Centuries of Great Preaching.* Vol. 2. pp. 77-

91). It was marked by "ample scholarship, simplicity, conviction and fervor." His short sight and weak voice could not have distracted too much the hearer; who felt during one message as if he had been "lifted up by the hair and suspended in space!"

Sixty-seven Theses

Zwingli did not stop with freedom of conscience on foods. In 1953 he published his *Sixty-seven Theses,* a summary of his doctrines, presenting his case for reform before the council, people, and town leaders of Zurich.

In subsequent meetings he opposed many other common church practices, including transubstantiation, papal authority, saint worship, pilgrimages, purgatory, statues, fasts, and the Mass itself. As in Luther's case, this did not help him to win friars and influence governments. Attempts were made on his life; rumors spread about him.

As with Luther some opposition to him was certainly just. Zwingli, like Luther, felt that complete religious freedom would lead to anarchy and approved restrictive measures which he earlier would have considered tyrannous.

Opposition

While they accomplished an amazing amount of good in God's kingdom, neither of the two Reformers got on with each other. "To Zwingli the will of God rather than Luther's way of salvation was the central fact of theology. To Luther the Christian life was one of freedom in forgiven sonship, to Zwingli the Christian life was conformity to the will of God as set forth in the Bible (Walker, *A History of the Christian Church,* p. 363). In a meeting with Luther over the nature of the communion table elements, the two reformers reached no agreement; Luther refused to clasp hands with him as a brother in Christ. Disappointed, Zwingli returned to Zurich.

Increasingly isolated and drawn into war, Zwingli, along with thirty other pastors, finally lost his life; his enemies cut his body into four pieces and tossed them into a fire. Luther's sad comment was, "Live by the sword, die by the sword." But none among the German-speaking Swiss ever attained his powerful influence.

What can we learn from Zwingli of benefit to our time? People need to hear the Word of God practically applied to life in all its aspects; Christian faith is no mere pietism but something powerful and effective in all levels of society. Put simply, preaching can change a nation. If a Zwingli, hampered as he was by inaccurate theology, inadequate gifts, hindering legalism and a past of shaky character could affect the world, so can anyone. So, in the providence of God, can you and I.

Martin Luther 1483-1546

Europe, religiously and economically, reached a critical mass by the beginning of the sixteenth century. Her church was a military power, mostly hated or feared. Huge numbers of her religious leaders were blatantly hypocritical and essentially lost. The Italian clergy all supposedly took vows of lifelong poverty and chastity, but many merely paid a token church fine as regular clients in the "best little whorehouses" in Rome. Even Leo X, the Pope (one of the notorious Medicis), an outwardly decent sports fan and literary man, squandered one-seventh of the entire papal reserve (one hundred thousand ducats) on his coronation party alone. In just seven years of rule, he blew some five million ducats and left a debt of over a million; his coffin had to be lit by half-burned candles borrowed from another's funeral (*Christian History,* Issue 34, p. 38). Cunningham Geikie says, "It was the fashion to call in question the very principles of Christianity" (Geikie, *The English Reformation,* p. 114). Men were cynical, frivolous, and unbelievably flippant towards God.

Indulgences

To pay for his parties and finish the luxurious St. Peter's Church begun by his predecessor, Julian II, Leo spent much of his time asking for money. Almost any source was acceptable. He chose the sale of indulgences, a popular, though not strictly authorized, fund-raising technique for the Roman Catholic church dating from the eleventh Century. "Didn't Christ's infinite merits and the saints' excess good works not needed for their own salvation form an inexhaustible treasury from which the Church might draw benefits on special occasions?" some asked. (For instance, to release yourself or others out of "purgatory" pains after death.)

To qualify originally, you had to go on a "recover-the-Holy-Lands Crusade"; later, by hiring a knight for you instead; finally, anyone benefited who gave money for any purpose a Pope specified. By the time of Julius II, anyone giving (for themselves or dead relatives) to help Leo's St. Peter's project would surely escape church censure here and purgatory after. Leo extended it to the rest of the world's parishes for a percentage of the profits. The Archbishop of Magdenburg, Germany, was one of many who bought in for a large sum and then sent his own fund-raising hucksters, like Johann Tetzel, throughout Germany, equipped with tricky jingles and slogans.

Life in Germany

Germany was then the drunkest nation in Europe. Her monasteries too, were affluent, with large holdings criticized both by the nobles who wanted them and the peasants who worked on them. The poor in general were restless, chafing at the money demanded by the local clergy, who had "acquired a vast collection of relics . . . a branch from the Burning Bush; three thousand particles from the holy innocents, a portrait of Christ, a twelve-foot beam on which Judas supposedly hung himself, and one of the coins paid for betraying Christ." Its value had notably increased notes Gordon Lindsay, tongue-in-cheek, "and was now able to confer an indulgence of fourteen hundred years" (Gordon Lindsay, *Men Who Changed the World*, p. 63).

Yet it was dangerous to disagree. In the fifty years before the English Reformation began in 1517, the Spanish Inquisition alone had burned alive thirteen thousand men, women and children, and had racked, tortured and thrown into fearful dungeons a hundred and seventy thousand more (Geikie, *The English Reformation*, p. 120).

A Creative Time in History

It was an age of excitement, of discovery, of danger; the

age of Machiavelli, Michelangelo, Raphael, Copernicus and Columbus, though they were hardly known in Germany. Humanism was the current intellectual fad, unified under Reuchlin, a leader accused of heresy by the Moral Majority of his time. Humanist advocates looked on this charge as an ignorant and unwarranted attack on scholarship, and rallied to his support. Add to this intellectual ferment the stirrings of a popular religious awakening; people had a deepening sense of terror and concern for salvation. Such an age filled with hurt and spiritual hunger needed a bold, determined leader to speak up and speak out against sin.

In Need of Leadership

That leader and that protest came. "Made in no unusual or spectacular fashion by a monastic professor in a recently founded and relatively inconspicuous German university on Oct. 31, 1517," It found immediate response; it launched what has been called "the most gigantic revolution in the history of the Christian church" (Walker, *A History Of The Christian Church*, p. 336).

The Protestant was Martin Luther, one of the few whose work profoundly altered world history. Not a great scholar, organizer, or politician, Luther moved men by "the power of a profound religious experience, resulting in unshakable trust in God, in direct, immediate, and personal relationship to Him, which brought a confident salvation and left no room for the elaborate hierarchical and sacramental structures of the Middle Ages" (*History of Church*, p. 336). While profoundly one with his age in aspirations and sympathies, his vivid, compelling faith and heroic physical and spiritual courage transcended his time.

Luther's Background

Born 10 November 1483, in Eisleben, Luther's dad was a peasant miner; his family had a simple, though stern faith in God. Mr. Luther Sr. wanted his son to be a lawyer and entered him in a university in 1501, where Martin was known as an earnest, companionable, and music-loving student. But still he strongly felt a deep sense of sinfulness, the ground-note of the religious revival of the age in Germany.

After graduating with a M.A. in 1505, he was profoundly moved both by the sudden death of a friend and a narrow escape from lightning. ("Help me Saint Anna!" he prayed. "If I survive this storm, I will become a monk!") He broke off his career, and in deep anxiety for salvation, entered a monastery for Augustinian hermits in Erfurt in July 1505. The monastery enjoyed deserved local respect under the supervision of the kindly Johann von Staupitz (1469-1524), one of the best of the mediaeval monastics and vicar-general of Germany's Augustinian friars.

Luther's Education

Staupitz's school made much of preaching and included some pious mystics sympathetic to Augustine and Bernard. Luther even read one of John Huss's tracts that deeply touched him: "I wondered why a man who could write so Christianly and powerfully had been burned . . . I shut the book and turned away with a wounded heart" (Beard, *Martin Luther And The Reformation*, p. 165). Martin did well; he "performed the lowliest duties with a proud humility; recited prayers, froze in an unheated cubicle, fasted and scourged himself hoping to exorcize demons from his body" (Durant, *The Reformation*, p. 343).

"If ever a monk got into heaven by monkery, I should have gotten there . . . if it had lasted longer I should have tortured myself to death . . ." Luther recalled later. He survived. Sent to Wittenberg next year by his superiors for a future professorship, he got a Bachelor of Theology in 1509. Luther was picked to go to Rome in 1510 on a mission, where he did every pilgrim devotion possible, even climbing the Santa Scala stone steps on his bare knees. He earned so many "indulgences" he almost wished his parents dead so he could deliver them from purgatory–all without any peace of heart. "Who knows if it is true?" he said, in disappointment at the top of the steps of Santa Scala.

Rome's immorality and corruption horrified him. ("If there is a Hell, Rome is built on it.") He later described it as "an abomination" where the papal court was "served at supper by six naked girls" (Durant, *The Reformation*, p. 344). He returned, still searching, to Wittenberg. Made a Doctor of Theology in 1512, he began to study and lecture on the Bible. Though eventually made District Vicar over eleven monasteries, he still had no peace; his sense of sinfulness overwhelmed him.

Staupitz helped by pointing out that true penitence began not with a fear of a punishing God, but with love to God; "Man, God is not angry with you," he said to Luther. "You are angry with God. Don't you know God commands you to hope?" Tauler's works also helped. Best of all, the other monks cared enough about this intense young friar to give him what was then a rare personal possession–a Latin Bible.

The Beginning of Reform

Lindsay notes: "His search of the Scriptures opened up altogether new truths to him. He saw that the whole nature of man needed to be changed." Luther gradually saw that many of the doctrines he had been taught had no Biblical basis. By the time he lectured on the Psalms (1513-1515), he was convinced that salvation was a new relation to God based not on any work of merit on man's part, but on absolute trust in the Divine promises.

Some scholars note this important re-emphasis of Paul's teaching was not reformed enough; that to Paul, a Christian man is primarily a renewed son; to Luther understandably enough, he is first of all, a forgiven sinner. To some, it seemed that Tetzel's Roman Catholic indulgence money was to be replaced by a cheaper Protestant version. Luther, anxious to avoid works-righteousness, certainly did not help by cheerfully writing: "Christianity is nothing but a continual exercise in feeling you have no sin, although you sin . . . sin cannot detach us from Him were we to commit a thousand fornications a day, or as many murders" (Luther, *Werke*, XL 436, XXV, 330, 142, 130).

Salvation by Faith

Still, like Paul, Luther set off a spiritual H-bomb in an age of religious legality; he proved salvation was in essence a right relationship to God. Sometime between 1515 and 1518, while studying and speaking on the latter part of Romans, his confidence turned to the conviction that Godly faith gave personal assurance. From then on, the sum of the Gospel for him was forgiveness of sins. It was "good news," filling his soul with peace, joy, and absolute trust in God. It was absolute dependence on the divine promises, on God's Word.

John Tetzel

Sympathetic ears in Wittenberg listened to this new concept of salvation. Then, John Tetzel (1470-1519), a polished Dominican monk with the best indulgence spiel yet came near Luther's town. Intent on fund raising, he painted the benefits of indulgences in the crassest terms, best seen in the proverb "*As soon as the coin in the coffer springs, the soul from purgatory's fire springs.*"

If Tetzel had only stayed away from Luther's turf, history would no doubt have been radically different. To Luther, now convinced that only a right personal relationship with God brought salvation, such nonsense was a declaration of war.

From his Wittenburg university door, the reckless friar mailed his "95 Theses" to his superiors and other German scholars. He challenged to public debate all he found false and abusive in this and other church practices. Tetzel felt compelled to answer with his own "One Hundred and Six Anti-Theses" (December 1517). This proved the spark that kindled the fire.

Luther's Compatriot

Luther was later joined by the brilliant young intellectual Philipp Melanchthon (1497-1560), a twenty-one-year old Greek professor at Wittenberg. Melanchthon (whose real name was Schwarzerd) was small, homely, frail, shy, and retiring but without equal in scholarship. When five or six hundred students daily jammed into his lectures, Luther himself sat humbly among them.

Years later, Luther was able to powerfully intercede for his life-long friend. Often sick, he now apparently lay dying; eyes set, still, and scarcely breathing. Deeply concerned Luther, (quoting promises of Scripture) went to prayer. God gave him a word. Taking his friend by the hand he said: "Be of good courage Philipp, you shall not die. Trust in the Lord who is able to kill and make alive." While he was speaking, Philipp began to move. His breath came back, and he eventually fully recovered, to say, "I should have been a dead man had I not been recalled from death itself by the coming of Luther" (Lindsay, *Men Who Changed the World*, pp. 77-78).

Luther declared spiritual war with powerful tracts that set his times on fire. Contrasting his style with that of the "gardener" Melanchthon, he wrote: "I have been born to war and fight with factions and devils . . . I must root out stumps and stocks, cut away thorns and hedges, fill up the ditches ...break a path and make things ready" (Ledderhose, *Life of Philipp Melanchthon*, p. 38).

Serving God in Ordinary Life

One of Luther's most important contributions to Protestant thought (as well as one of the most significant departures from ancient and mediaeval Christian conceptions), was to declare natural human life the best field of service for God rather than the unnatural limits of a monk's asceticism: "*Next to faith this is the highest art; to be content in the calling in which God has placed you. I have not learned it yet.*"

His later decision at forty-two to marry Katharina von Bora, a runaway nun, scandalized many. For Luther, the shock was "waking up in the morning with pigtails on the pillow next to me" (*Christian History*, Issue 34, p. 17). They had three sons, Hans, Martin and Paul, and three daughters, Elizabeth, Magdela, and Margaret.

Luther's Books

"No other German author," said Will Durant, "has equalled him in clarity or force of style, in directness and pungency of phrase, in happy–sometimes hilarious–similes, in a vocabulary rooted in the speech of the people and congenial to the national mind" (Durant, *The Reformation*, p. 368). Luther wrote some 400 works; between 1517 and 1520, thirty of his works ran through a total of 370 editions; at a thousand copies an edition, almost four hundred thousand of his tracts alone flooded Germany during the crucial years (*Christian History*, Issue 34, p. 34).

His German translation of the Bible is still the greatest prose work in the national literature; his style and even the ordering of its sixty-six books profoundly influenced William Tyndale. He said of his translation method: "I try to speak as men do in the market-place. In rendering Moses I make him so German no-one would suspect he was a Jew." His title to leadership was confirmed in 1520, with three epoch-making works. The first was *To The Christian Nobility of the German Nation,* written with burning conviction by a master of the German tongue, ran the length and breadth of the nation. Here, Luther argued, it was no use pretending the priests were superior beings since all believers are priests.

This universal priesthood meant the Pope had no exclusive right to interpret Scriptures; others than the Pope could call for a reform council; and a true free council for the reform of the church should be summoned by temporal authorities. He spelled out programs for practical reform, including cutting Papal taxes, reducing bulky government, closing brothels, and theological reform in university education. He urged rulers to take church reform in their own hands.

Two months later (in scholar's Latin) his *Babylonish Captivity of the Church* attacked sacramentalist teachings of the Roman church, reducing their seven sacraments first to three (Baptism, Lord's Supper, and Penance) and finally, just two. Later, in *On Christian Liberty,* he wrote on the paradox of Christian experience: "A Christian man is the most free lord of all, and subject to none; a Christian man is the most dutiful servant of all, and subject to every one." Free, because of Christ; a servant, because he is bound by love to conform to God's will and be helpful to his neighbor. Yet Luther's revolt was far more against Roman organization and ritual than Roman doctrine; others later would take up where he left off.

The Results

Luther had deeply rocked the boat of the church world. The full imposing might of a papal council was called against him; they summoned him before them to Worms, demanding he recant. Terrified, some of his best friends left him. Yet Luther set his face like a flint. He bravely set out for the trial saying: "If there be as many devils at Worms as tiles on the roof-tops, I will enter!" (Beard, *Martin Luther And The Reformation*, p. 432).

There, on that awesome day, they pointed to a row of his books; he was asked whether or not he would retract them. Faced with the combined might of his intellectual and theological peers, his courage almost failed him. He requested time to think it over. They gave him a day. Friends came to encourage him, and on the next afternoon he was once more before the assembly. He acknowledged that in the heat of controversy he had expressed himself too strongly against persons. But the substance of what he had written he could not retract, unless convinced of its wrongfulness by Scripture or adequate argument.

The Emperor could hardly believe someone would dare deny the infallibility of a general council and cut the discussion short. Eck, a chief Church official, told him (in Latin): "Martin, your plea to be heard from Scripture is the one always made by heretics. You do nothing but renew the errors of Wycliffe and Huss . . . would you put your judgment above that of so many famous men and claim you know more than any of them? . . . I ask you, Martin–answer candidly and without distinctions–do you or do you not repudiate your books and the errors they contain?"

In German Luther replied: ". . . Unless I am convicted by the testimony of Sacred Scripture or by evident reason . . . my conscience is captive to the Word of God. I cannot and I will not recant anything, for to go against my conscience is neither right nor safe." Then, fully prepared to die for what he believed, Luther supposedly cried out the words engraved on his memorial at Worms: "*Here I stand; I can do no other. God help me. Amen*" (Durant, *The Reformation*, p. 361).

Proof of the highest courage, he had borne a great historic witness to the truth of his convictions before the highest tribunal of his nation. The packed audience applauded triumphantly, drowning out the authorities hissing hatred. Shortly after, though condemned to death by the state, Luther was abducted on the way to his sentence by the friendly King Fredrick the Wise, who hid him in his castle in Wartburg. Here, in forced exile, disguised as a bearded nobleman ("Knight George"), he was able to finish much more writing, including Scripture translation.

Luther's Legacy

What is Luther's legacy to us today? By 1517 he gave us the basic framework of Protestant theology; he had been convinced of at least three points:

1. A man is justified by faith alone and not by works. (In our day how much is made of status, power, and success, even in the Christian world)

2. Each believer has access to God directly apart from any human intermediaries. (And today, do we not feel compelled to go to our own Christian superstars for guidance, instead of learning to seek God?)

3. The Bible is the supreme source of authority for both faith and life (a foundation not to be lightly discarded without dire spiritual consequences).

By modern standards Luther was certainly no saint; he was impetuous, rough, sometimes even crude. When he was angry, he issued shockingly harsh statements. He encouraged people to "smite, slay and stab openly or secretly" the peasants who were dangerously anarchistic in their attempts by revolt to right just grievances (Luther, *Open Letter Concerning the Hard Book Against the Peasants*, July 1525, Works IV, p. 261). He recommended the execution of the Anabaptists for their excesses, advocated that all Jews be deported to Palestine, their synagogues and books burned. His attacks on the Pope were utterly unrestrained, many of them vulgar and tasteless. Yet despite these glaring faults, many springing out of an as-yet-uncorrected theology and a not-reformed-enough Reformation, it is still all but impossible not to like Luther. Full of faults, large in his mistakes, he loves, fights, laughs, sings, plays, and writes as a man utterly real; despite his flaws, in Christ he lives. His preaching, like his life, was blunt, vigorous, creative. "The truth" he said "is mightier than eloquence; the Spirit greater than genius, faith more than education." And again: "If the learned men are not well pleased with what they hear, well, the door is open" (*Christian History*, Issue 34 p. 27).

With songs like "A Mighty Fortress Is Our God" his songwriting talents did much to put the truth into the hearts of the common people. "The Devil should not be allowed," he said, "to keep all the best tunes for himself." Spurgeon notes: "in Luther's day his translation of the Psalms and his chorales did more to make the Reformation popular than even his preaching; for the ploughman in the field and the housewife at the cradle would sing one of Luther's Psalms; in Wycliffe's day fresh psalms and hymns were scattered all over the land" (Spurgeon, *The Metropolitan Tabernacle Pulpit*, #3514, p. 261).

Here is a man of prodigious courage, earthy and crude, stubbornly dogmatic in debate, but a genuinely warm human being. He considers the great subject of preaching "the glory of God in Jesus Christ"; in almost every sermon he deals with man's moral duty to act, good works growing out of inner faith. Always a common man's man, in one of his churches he preached for the "young people, children and servants of which there are more than two thousand" not the "doctors nor magistrates" of which there were "about forty."

Luther Goes Home

Luther, whose life first split a world church over truth, oddly enough died attempting personal unity for others. In 1546 he became sick from overexposure after a cold January journey, in an attempt to reconcile two friends who had quarreled. By February 18th it was plain he was on his deathbed. Friends gathering around him heard him quote John 3:16 and say, "Father into Thy hands I commend my spirit; Thou hast redeemed me, thou true God." "Do you still stand by Christ and the doctrine you preached?" they asked.

"Yes," he said. Then, with a sigh and a nod, "Who hath believed my word shall never see death."

With that, at sixty-three, he fell asleep in Christ. His body is laid in the Castle Church in Wittenburg, but his works go marching on.

John Calvin 1509-1564

He had no hand in initiating the Reformation. When he was born in 1509, Luther had already spent four agonized years of searching. While Calvin was learning how to read, Luther was already giving evangelical lectures at Wittenberg on Romans. John was still a schoolboy when Luther publicly questioned indulgences. Yet by 1580—only sixteen years after his death—the world had been more deeply influenced by his thought than any other Reformer. His influence in "religion, theology, politics, sociology and economics goes far beyond that of any other reformer" (*TCOGP* , Vol. II, p. 134).

Some time in 1534, Calvin experienced a "significant religious conversion"; from then on to 1536, he traveled through France, studying theology. By 1534 he had completed the first draft of *Institutes of Christian Religion*, a lawyer's exercise in logic that he published the next year. He was only twenty-six when he finished the last chapter of his most famous book of the Reformation, a book that has been called "the single most influential book on theology in church history."

The Importance of Calvin

What significance does this Reformer have to our century? He participated in no revivals in his time. He was no world-shaking preacher—definitely not an evangelist. He was not particularly known for his prayer life. His definition of a Christian even lacks the standard stress on being "born again." His importance is this: Calvin gave the world a picture of Gods' awesome power and reverence; he was the first Reformer to stress the transcendental nature of conversion.

Calvinism can be summed up in one phrase, "*the sovereignty of God in grace,*" says B. B. Warfield in *Calvin as a Theologian*. He was "pre-eminently the theologian of the Holy Spirit . . . who first related the whole experience of salvation specifically to the working of the Holy Spirit" (Warfield, *Calvin as a Theologian*, pp. 8-9).

Calvin emphasized the supernatural in salvation, the Holy Spirit as prime witness to Truth. "The authority of Scripture cannot be asserted by arguments and disputations. . . . (but) established rather by the testimony of the Holy Spirit. For as God alone is a sufficient witness of Himself in His own Word, so the Scriptures will never gain credit in the hearts of men till they be confirmed by the internal testimony of the Spirit" (Calvin, *Institutes*, p. 30, Condensed version; Timothy Tow, Ed).

How this has been forgotten today by the evangelical church!

> I Look at the many books that have been written in this present century and try to find me a paragraph or a section or a chapter on revival. . . . They do not even mention it. . . . There is no thought in their minds of the Spirit suddenly coming on people in the way He always does in revival and doing His wonderful works. . . . And surely this is to quench the Holy Spirit because (He) not only has His ordinary work; He has his extraordinary work and that is revival. Of course we must evangelize, of course we must preach about being filled with the Spirit, yes; but over and above that we must cry unto God to pour His Spirit out upon the whole church. And that is revival, the descent, the outpouring of the Spirit over and above his usual, ordinary work; this amazing, unusual extraordinary thing which God in His sovereignty and infinite grace has done to the church from time to time during the long centuries of her history. (Martyn Lloyd-Jones, *Revival*, p. 53-54)

Calvinism

For this fact alone, John Calvin's stress needs to be restored to our time, when we are so bound by religious rationalism, cold-hearted apologetics, and man-centered evangelism. "The central fact of Calvinism is the vision of God. Its determining principle is a zeal for divine honor" (Doumergue, *TCOGP*, p. 143).

Another of Calvin's great contributions to the church was the authority and majesty of the Christian ministry, the awesome power represented in serving an absolutely omnipotent God who holds total sway over the future of all mankind. Our age has been stripped once again of any overarching cosmic direction; the ministry has been cynically mocked and belittled. Millions have turned to science fiction and fantasy in a hollow attempt to recapture this missing feeling of significance. This sense of destiny, of God's intervention, of history revolving not around our own little actions and doings but around God's great purposes is a badly needed emphasis in our evangelically humanistic, twentieth-century church.

Calvin on Preachers

Calvin said of preachers:

> Let them argue with the mountains, let them rise up against the hills; in other words, do not be dazzled by men but let them show that the word they carry, that is committed to them is like the royal Scepter of God under which all creatures bow their heads and bend their knees . . .
>
> Let them boldly dare all things and constrain all the glory, highness and power of this world to obey and to yield to the Divine Majesties; let them by this same Word have command over everyone; let them edify the house of Christ, overthrow the reign of Satan; let them lead the flock to pasture, and kill the wolves; let them bind and let loose thunder and lightning if that is their calling; but all in God's name." (TCOGP, Vol. 2 pp. 144-145)

Challenging a City

We cannot really call Calvin a "revivalist." His influence belongs squarely in the Old Testament mold of reform, often through legal or merely moral means. In 1536 he met Farel, who tried to persuade him to go to Geneva, a city of thirteen thousand people and full of immorality and drunkenness. By 1555 Calvin had made two trips there; on his second visit he gained the upper hand. With more experience in policing than words of knowledge he set up a system of spies to search out moral breachments of the law.

It was ultimately effective; Geneva became a model of reform, and a God-fearing if not an entirely God-loving one. But his influence extended far beyond Geneva. He molded the thought and inspired the ideals of French, Dutch, and Scottish Protestants, as well as the English Puritans. His ideas penetrated Poland and Hungary; before his death Calvinism was taking root in southwestern Germany itself.

> Men thought his thoughts after him. His was the only system the Reformation produced that could organize itself powerfully in the face of government hostility as

> in France and England. It trained strong men, confident in their election to be fellow workers with God in the accomplishment of His will, courageous to do battle, insistent on character and confident that God has given in Scripture the guide of all right human conduct and proper worship. (Walker, *A History of the Christian Church*, p. 400)

Calvin founded the Geneva Academy, now the University of Geneva, which became the greatest center of theological instruction in the Reformed communions. By 1564 he was seriously ill, and he died on May 27.

Behind the Man

He was a disciplined, hard worker (twelve to eighteen hours a day); his letters alone fill eleven volumes. For twenty-five years he preached an average of five times a week. He had an amazing memory: though he frequently preached without preparation, Beza said of his preaching, "every word weighed a pound." Taking nothing but Scripture with him to the pulpit, yet he supposedly preached in one year alone 286 sermons and gave 186 lectures on theology. He slept little, ate sparingly, fasted frequently, and amazed his friends that one man could carry so heavy and varied a burden.

Yet it is so often true in history that our greatest strengths are also our great weaknesses. Roland Bainton said, "If Calvin wrote anything in favor of religious liberty it was a typographical error!"

Such essential concepts as destiny (election and predestination) Divine sovereignty (giving a sense of security and purpose in history) and the Lordship of Christ (Divine authority) can become dead orthodoxy or worse: smug self-satisfaction, religious fatalism and legal bibliolatry. Later studies show how sometimes faulty premises adopted by the Reformers led them to interpret these doctrines in ways that later only hurt and embarrassed the Church. (See chapter one of Verduin, *The Reformers and Their Stepchildren*, Paternoster London, 1968, and Forster and Marsden, *God's Strategy in Human History*, 1973, Tyndale/Send the Light Press, forward by F.F. Bruce.) Nevertheless, its heritage remains centrally significant. And even those who doctrinally disagree with the extremes of early Reform thought acknowledge how much we need the essentials.

Applying What We Learn

What is the place of doctrine in revival? As A. W. Tozer said, "No revival without reformation." In a true work of God, there is always something to do and something to know. The two conditions of true unity are common understanding and common unselfishness. Wisdom and love–if we want revival, we need them both.

And how do we deal with areas of doctrinal disagreement? Some truths are without question fundamental; others are not as central to awakening as we might believe. God reserves the right to use people you do not agree with. Revival has come even when Christians disagree. We are to love God and each other until we "come to the unity of the faith." Jesus said, "If any man will do His will–he shall know the doctrine . . . " (John 7:17). Obedience must precede understanding; we can love even when we cannot fully see. Revival begins with our crying out for a genuine love for Christ and a servant's heart, to "seek first the Kingdom of God and His righteousness." Get our hearts right with God first and He will help us get right with our brother. Pianos tuned to the same tuning fork will also be tuned to one another. From such a true commitment to His Lordship, differences can be accommodated and distinctions maintained without hurtful division. Brothers in the same family may not always agree, but they must not forget they are still brothers. Those true to Him will not hate each other. And that commonality of affection and convictions sets the stage for His entry.

Chapter Five The Reformers' Message

Zwingli, Luther, Calvin. From these three men and their co-workers we can derive three great truths that are absolutely foundational to understanding the stream of true revival. Spurgeon wrote:

> That great religious excitement has occurred apart from Gospel truth we admit; but anything which we as believers in Christ would call a r*evival of religion has always been attended with clear evangelical instruction upon cardinal points of truth*. What was the sinew and backbone of the Reformation? Was it not clear enunciation of Gospel truths which the priesthood had withheld from the people? Justification by faith, starting like a giant from its sleep called to its slumbering fellows; and together these great doctrines wrought marvels.
>
> The Reformation was due not so much to the fact that Luther was earnest, Calvin learned, Zwingli brave and Knox indefatigable, as to this–old truth was brought to

> the front and to the poor the Gospel was preached. Had it not been for the doctrines which they taught, their zeal for holiness and their self-sacrifice, their ecclesiastical improvements would have been of no avail. The power lay not in Luther's hammer and nails, but in the truth of those theses which he fastened up in the sight of all men. (C. H. Spurgeon, *The Sword and the Trowel,* p. 216)

> The concealing and the neglect of certain truths and certain aspects of Christian truth has always been the chief characteristic of every period of declension in the long history of the Christian church. . . . No revival has ever been known in the history of churches which deny or ignore certain essential truths. . . . And without a single exception it is the rediscovery of these cardinal doctrines that has led to revival (Martyn Lloyd-Jones: *"Revival,"* pp. 33, 35).

Justification, Lordship, Sovereignty

George Fry and Duane Arnold in their *Christianity Today* article "Reclaiming Reformation Day" summarize some of the Reformers major contributions; the recovery of Scriptures, the centrality of faith, liberty of conscience, and the priesthood of all believers. In our day these have implications in the areas of personal Bible study, one's personal relationship to Christ, every Christian's right and privilege to hear God's voice for himself and true community in believers' fellowship (*Christianity Today*, 22 October 1982, pp. 35-37). To crystallize what we have already explored in their lives, we can also say they gave to us three great contributions:

Justification by Faith–Freedom

Behold, his soul [which] is lifted up is not upright in him: but the just shall live by his faith (Hab. 2:4).

For therein is the righteousness of God revealed from faith to faith: as it is written, The just shall live by faith (Rom. 1:17).

But that no man is justified by the law in the sight of God, [it is] evident: for, The just shall live by faith (Gal. 3:11; also Heb. 10:38).

Blessed [is] the nation whose God [is] the LORD; [and] the people [whom] he hath chosen for his own inheritance (Ps. 33:12).

Ye [are] my witnesses, saith the LORD, and my servant whom I have chosen: that ye may know and believe me, and understand that I [am] he: before me there was no God formed, neither shall there be after me (Isa. 43:10).

Who hath saved us, and called [us] with an holy calling, not according to our works, but according to his own purpose and grace, which was given us in Christ Jesus before the world began (2 Tim 1:9).

For the gifts and calling of God [are] without repentance (Rom. 11:29).

Ye have not chosen me, but I have chosen you, and ordained you, that ye should go and bring forth fruit, and [that] your fruit should remain: that whatsoever ye shall ask of the Father in my name, he may give it you (John 15:16).

Wherefore the rather, brethren, give diligence to make your calling and election sure: for if ye do these things, ye shall never fall (2 Pet. 1:10).

> For ye see your calling, brethren, how that not many wise men after the flesh, not many mighty, not many noble, [are called]: But God hath chosen the foolish things of the world to confound the wise; and God hath chosen the weak things of the world to confound the things which are mighty; And base things of the world, and things which are despised, hath God chosen, [yea], and things which are not, to bring to naught things that are. (1 Cor. 1:26-28)

According as he hath chosen us in him before the foundation of the world, that we should be holy and without blame before him in love (Eph. 1:4).

But we are bound to give thanks always to God for you, brethren beloved of the Lord, because God hath from the beginning chosen you to salvation through sanctification of the Spirit and belief of the truth (2 Thess. 2:13).

These shall make war with the Lamb, and the Lamb shall overcome them: for he is Lord of lords, and King of kings: and they that are with him [are] called, and chosen, and faithful (Rev. 17:14).

God has chosen the ignoble things of the world to confound the privileged that no flesh should glory in His presence; the simple to confound the wise; the weak to confound the strong. He calls out of darkness into His marvellous light, from the power of Satan to the power of God, from mists of the endless darkness to the realm of eternal light. And because He was lifted up in your place, *you can go free*. Bankrupt hearts need have nothing to pay. You don't have to earn a place in this holy kingdom! Gone is all striving for merit—you can rest in Jesus and His righteousness alone. And whoever you are, whatever your vocation or position, Christ in you can make a holy calling of it.

The Lordship of Christ—Authority

Let the heavens be glad, and let the earth rejoice: and let [men] say among the nations, The LORD reigneth (1 Chron. 16:31).

The LORD reigneth, he is clothed with majesty; the LORD is clothed with strength, [wherewith] he hath girded himself: the world also is established, that it cannot be moved (Ps. 93:1).

Say among the heathen [that] the LORD reigneth: the world also shall be established that it shall not be moved: he shall judge the people righteously (Ps. 96:10).

The LORD reigneth; let the earth rejoice; let the multitude of isles be glad [thereof] (Ps. 97:1 cf. Ps. 99:1).

The heart of a return to the authority and inspiration of Scripture is confidence in the absolute power and rulership of the one who gave it. Every Christian has the right to hear God speak for himself, because every Christian can know God as his own Father. Liberty of conscience does not degenerate into immorality if we are truly ruled by the Lord Jesus Christ. It is time for a renewal of zeal for God's honor! If Jesus rules the earth and He is my King, then His rulership gives me a derived authority on earth as his servant and representative.

A soldier, apparently hunting for Luther in order to arrest him, knocked on his door and asked, "Who lives here?" Luther answered, "Christ lives here!" Could you wake, as Luther supposedly did one night, to see the Devil at the foot of your bed, say "Oh–it's only you!" and go back to sleep?

The Sovereignty of God–Destiny

The LORD has prepared his throne in the heavens; and his kingdom ruleth over all (Ps. 103:19).

And said, O LORD God of our fathers, [are] You not God in heaven? and do You (not) rule over all the kingdoms of the heathen? and in Your hand [is there not] power and might, so that none is able to withstand You? (2 Chron. 20:6)

And I heard as it were the voice of a great multitude, and as the voice of many waters, and as the voice of mighty thunderings, saying, Alleluia: for the Lord God omnipotent reigns (Rev. 19:6).

But ye [are] a chosen generation, a royal priesthood, an holy nation, a peculiar people; that ye should shew forth the praises of him who hath called you out of darkness into his marvellous light (1 Pet. 2:9).

"Who knows if you are come into the Kingdom for such a time as this?"

The power of Christian community lies in this; we are not only members one of another because we are blood brothers and sisters; we are members also of all peoples He has redeemed for Himself down through history.

This holy thing, the Church, is not an invention of the West, nor an innovation of recent history. We are linked indissolubly to a chain reaching back all the way to what God had in His heart before the beginning of earthly time. We are part of the essence of history, and thus have opportunity above all others on earth to carry a high and holy sense of destiny. We are a chosen generation, a royal priesthood, a holy nation. And all power is given to Him in heaven and on earth. God can do anything He wants to. The final future is not in the hands of men; the outcome of history is not limited to what we can do and what we can concoct. God is the King of the whole earth; and He is Lord of the Church.

Beyond the Reformation

But when the Pilgrim fathers first came to the United States, seeking to put these principles into practice in a nation, their pastor, John Robinson, reminded them: "We have come to a period in religion (when) the Lutherans cannot be drawn beyond what Luther saw. And the Calvinists stick where Calvin left them. Luther and Calvin were precious shining lights in their times, yet God did not reveal His whole will to them. I am very confident that the Lord hath yet more truth and light to break forth out of His Holy Word" (Fry and Arnold, *Reclaiming Reformation Day,* p. 36).

Leaving the Reformers' contributions to their champions, their critics, and the sure mercies of God, we launch into the next great visitation of God in history–the First Great Awakening.

John Wesley's Enemies

"The hand of our God [is] upon all them for good that seek him; but his power and his wrath [is] against all them that forsake him" (Ezra 8:22b).

We hear of the blessings of revival; what was it like to stand before the enemies of such a revival and preach? Again from Quiller-Couch's biography comes this moving account:

"All the world has heard how John Wesley rode, eight years later into Epworth; and how, his father's pulpit having been denied to him, he stood outside on his father's tomb and preached evening after evening in the warm June weather the Gospel of justification by faith to the listening crowd.

Eight evenings he preached from it, and on the third evening chose for his text "Unto him that worketh not but believeth on Him that justifieth the ungodly, his faith is counted to him for righteousness" (Rom. 4:5).

John Whitelamb

Under the sycamore, by the churchyard wall a little distance from the crowd, a man stood and listened. He was a clergyman with a worn black gown, a man not old in years but with a face prematurely old and shoulders already stooped under the burden of life–John Whitelamb. He watched, lingering between fear and hope of being recognized. When the preacher mounted the slab, stroked his hair, and turned his face toward the sycamore, he fixed his eyes (as it seemed) upon the figure. Whitelamb felt sure he had been recognized; a moment later he doubted whether that gaze had passed over him in forgetfulness or contempt.

They had been too hard for him, these Wesleys. They had all departed from Epworth years before and left him who had been their brother alone with his miserable doubts. No letters, no message of remembered affection or present good will ever came from them. He had been unfaithful to his religion; they had cast him off. For seven years he had walked and labored among the men and women here gathered in the midsummer dusk; but the faces to which he had turned for comfort were faces of the past—some dead, others far away.

So the preacher's voice came as one rending the tomb: "*Son of man, can these bones live?*"

The bones of Christ's warrior beneath the slab laid to rest in utter weariness were stirring, putting forth strength and a voice that pierced his living marrow. He listened, letting the tears run. Only once did he withdraw his eyes, and then for a moment they fell on John Romely, loitering too on the outskirts of the crowd and plainly in two minds about interfering.

A Denied Pulpit

Romely was, at this time, the Curate of Epworth; the delegate of an absentee sporting rector, and had in truth set this ball rolling by denying John Wesley his pulpit. He had miscalculated his flock, this stubborn English breed, so loyal in enmity, loving the memory of a foe who had proven himself a man. Romely watched with a loose-lipped sneer, too weak to conquer his own curiosity, far too weak to assert his authority and attempt to clear the churchyard of that "enthusiasm" which he had denounced in his most florid style the past Sunday within his church.

Whitelamb heard men and women—notorious evil-livers, some of them crying aloud. Ah, the great simplicity of it was beyond him! And yet not perhaps beyond him. Could he believe the truth, in bygone years never questioned by him, that Jesus Christ was very God? He waited for the last word and strode back to his lonely home with a mind unconvinced, yet wondering at the power he had witnessed, a heart bursting with love.

He sat down to write at once but tore up many letters. With Christ to believe was to be forgiven. If Christ could not be tender to doubt, how much less would John Wesley be tender? It was not until Friday that he found courage to despatch the following:

> Dear Brother:
>
> I saw you at Epworth on Tuesday evening. Fain would I have spoken to you, but that I am quite at a loss to know how to address or behave to you. Your way of thinking is so extraordinary that *your presence creates an awe, as if you were an inhabitant of another world.*
>
> God grant you and your followers may always have entire liberty of conscience. Will you not allow others the same? Indeed I cannot think as you do, any more than I can help honoring and loving you. Dear sir, will you credit me? I retain the highest veneration and affection for you. The sight of you moves me strangely. My heart overflows with gratitude. I feel in a higher degree all that tenderness and yearning with which I am affected towards every branch of the Wesley family. I cannot refrain from tears when I reflect this is the man who at Oxford was more than a father to me; this is he whom I have heard expound, or dispute publicly or preach with such applause–and oh that I should ever add–whom I have heard lately preach at Epworth on his father's tombstone?
>
> I am quite forgot. None of the family ever honor me with a line. Have I been ungrateful? I have been passionate, fickle, a fool; but I hope I shall never be ungrateful. Dear sir, is it in my power to serve or oblige you in any way? Glad I should be you would make use of me. God open all our eyes and lead us into truth wherever it be!

The answer was delivered to him that same evening. It read: "Dear brother–I take you at your word, if indeed it covers permission to preach in your church at Wroote on Sunday morning next. I design to take for text–and God grant it may be profitable to you and to others! 'Ask and it shall be given you'" (All information taken from Quiller-Couch, *Hetty Wesley*).

CHAPTER SIX

The First "Great Awakening" (1732-1791)

The second great pattern of revival (the New Testament model), can be clearly seen in many of the events that surrounded the next major eruption in divine destiny. Scholars have chosen to call this period "The Great Awakening" or the "Evangelical Revival" of the 1700s, surfacing decades later in the "Second Great Awakening."

Here the heroes were British and American, with a radical German thrown in for good measure. The Church had grown in grace; this breed had less warts and more power. The Puritans and the Pietists had contributed doctrine. Now the world waited for fire.

The Rise of Deism

Our glance goes back to 1660. Dallimore describes this previous century as follows:

> In the violent rejection of Puritanism that accompanied the Restoration of the English monarchy, much of the nation threw off restraint and plunged into godlessness, drunkenness, immorality, and gambling. Puritans be-

came a thorn in the side of the state church and faced increasing legal hassle. Finally, in 1662 nearly two thousand ministers—all who would not submit to an Act of Uniformity—were ejected from their churches. Forbidden to preach under severe penalties, many, like John Bunyan, were imprisoned. Hundreds suffered and some died.

Then deism rose in the nation from 1660 to 1670; a vicious thought-war against supernatural Christianity, seeking to rationalize the Bible, the Virgin Birth, and miracles. Of course, the Church responded but with coldly correct apologetics that lacked soul and fire. Large numbers, both high and low class, dropped out of the church, believing Christianity to be false. Religion became ritual; the people above all feared "enthusiasm"—anyone whose practice of Christianity showed any true fervor. Empty formality was the order of the day. (*Whitefield*, Vol. 1, pp. 19-21)

Continued Unrest

Dallimore further notes the horror of the times:

The Gin Craze began with Prohibition in 1689; and within a generation every sixth house became a gin shop. The poor were unspeakably wretched—over 160 crimes had the death penalty! Gin made the people what they never were before—cruel and inhuman. Hanging was a daily gala event, those jerking on the ropes, watched and applauded by men, women, and children who crowded the gallows for the best view. Prisons were unimaginable nightmares; young and old, hard crook and first offender were thrown together to fight for survival.

Women were treated even worse than the men; hundreds of hardened hookers and murderesses where locked into battle over scant and rotten rations, with mothers caught when forced to steal to keep their children from starving. Open sewer trenches for toilets ran

> through the cells; hundreds were jammed together in cells made to hold a score of prisoners; there were rats and insects everywhere. One man took a dog into prison with him to help protect him against the vermin; the vermin killed the dog!" (Dallimore, *George Whitefield*, pp. 19-27)

Thus, in the decade between 1730 and 1740, life in England was morally corrupt and deeply crippled by spiritual decay. Yet among these conditions, remarkably similar to those worldwide today, God rose in a mighty exercise of His power, which became the eighteenth-century revival.

A World Record Prayer Meeting

The German who started it all was Nikolas Count Ludwig Von Zinzendorf, a Moravian of unlikely name, who established a community called *Herrnhut* ("The Lord's Watch") in 1727. It almost wasn't. Division and argument nearly destroyed the work until repentance, forgiveness, and a prayer-meeting were established to hold it together. This went on for an even more unlikely duration—100 years, 24 hours a day! Even children wept and prayed with power before God. In 1732 these Moravians sent out their first missionaries. Two kinds of teams left—to win the lost and to win the church. By 1792 they had mobilized over three hundred such radicals. Their motto was "To win for the Lamb that was slain the reward of His suffering." One such team bumped into an unsaved Anglican missionary. Born on the 17th of June, 1703, and now thirty-two he was on board a ship to America. In contrast to the English, the Moravians never complained when struck or pushed and showed a "great seriousness."

On Sunday evening, January 18, 1736, in a deck service during a storm, a wave broke over the deck of the *Simmonds*, split the main sail in pieces, and covered the decks. "A terrible screaming began among the English. The Germans calmly sang on." The would-be missionary asked one of them afterwards, "Were you not afraid?" He answered, "I thank God no." "But were not your women and children afraid?" "Our women and children are not afraid to die" (*Journals*; Vol. 1, Bicentenary Edition, London, 1938, p. 143).

After landing in America, the wondering Anglican asked

one of the Moravian pastors (a Mr. August Spangenberg) for advice with regard to his own conduct. In reply he received the most embarrassing question any minister can be asked. He recalled in his journal: "He (Spangenberg) said "*Do you know Jesus Christ?*" I paused, and said "I know He is the Savior of the world." "True," he replied, "but do you know He has saved *you*?" I answered "I hope He has died to save me." He only added–"Do you know yourself?" I said "I do." "*But I fear they were vain words*" (*Journals*, p. 151).

The Conversion of a Missionary

January 24th, 1738, on the *Samuels'* homeward voyage, after an utter failure in Georgia as a missionary, the crestfallen English minister recorded in his diary: "*I went to America to convert the Indians; but oh, who shall convert me?* . . . I have a fair summer religion; I can talk well . . . and believe myself, while no danger is near. But let death stare me in the face and my spirit is troubled, nor can I say 'to die is gain'." On February 1, the day he landed, he wrote, "It is now two years and four months since I left my native country in order to teach the Georgian Indians the nature of Christianity; but what have I learned of myself in the meantime? Why, what I least suspected; that I who went to America to convert others, was never myself converted to God! I am not mad, though I thus speak; but I speak the words of truth and soberness" (*Journals*, p. 148). A prominent Bishop said of him, "If he was not a good Christian when he went to Georgia then God help the majority of those who call themselves Christians!"

Thus began his pilgrimage out of self-seeking righteousness, involving conferences with other Moravians like Peter Bohler, much prayer, and study of the Scripture. It finally ended, three months later, in a little Aldersgate prayer meeting, listening to Luther's *Preface to Romans* on Wednesday, 24 May 1738. He records: "About a quarter to nine, while he was describing the change which God works in the heart through faith in Christ, *I felt my heart strangely warmed.* I felt I did trust Christ, Christ alone for salvation; and an assurance was given me that He had taken away my sins, even mine, and saved me from the law of sin and death" (*Journals*, pp. 475-476).

A Ministry Begins

He woke next morning with "Jesus, Master" in his heart and on his lips. That spring, the man who would change England's history began a spiritual society at the Fetter Lane Moravian Chapel, the pattern of all his later societies. That winter, he visited the Moravians in Germany; on his return, he began aggressive measures on home heathenism, following his friend Whitefield's example. Thus began the ministry of a man who rose daily at 4:00 A.M. and was preaching at 5:00 A.M. so working men could attend services; who during the next fifty-two years, from 1739 to 1791, travelled 250,000 miles, mostly on horseback, and preached over 40,000 sermons. "Never," says Ryle, "did any man have so many irons in the fire at one time and yet succeed in keeping so many hot" (J. C. Ryle, *Christian Leaders Of The 18th Century*, p. 78).

To unite his people in one body, to give everyone something to do, to make each consider his neighbor and seek his edification; call out latent talent and utilize it—in his words to keep "all at it and always at it"—were his aims and objects. In those years, travelling some twenty-five miles a day (over ten circuits of the globe on horseback) he wrote 233 books on all sorts of subjects, including home health remedies (*Primitive Medicine*, in use for almost two hundred years) and one of the earliest texts on electricity! A contemporary remarked that those who knew his travels wondered he had time to write and those who know his writings wondered he had time to travel. "Leisure and I have taken leave of one another. I propose to be busy as long as I live, if my health is so long indulged me," he said. "Lord let me not live to be useless," he prayed, after seeing a once-active and useful man now old, enfeebled, and slow of speech (Ryle, *Christian Leaders Of The 18th Century*, p. 84).

His rule for Christian living was "Do all the **good** you can, by all the **means** you can, in all the **ways** you can, in all **places** you can, at all the **times** you can, to all the **people** you can **as long as ever** you can!" Things the most opposite and unlike, petty and trifling, the thoroughly spiritual and secular, all alike are mastered by an omnivorous mind, finding time for all and giving directions about all. One day he is condensing old divinity, publishing fifty volumes of theology called the *Chris-*

tian Library and writing a complete commentary on the whole Bible. Another day we find him calmly reviewing the current literature of the day and criticizing all the new books with cool and shrewd remarks as if he had nothing else to do.

He composes (with his brother) over eight volumes of hymns that live to this day; or he is "drawing up minute directions to his preachers, forbidding them to shout, scream and preach too long, insisting on their reading regularly, lest their sermons become threadbare, requiring them not to drink spirits and charging them to get up early in the morning." Like Napoleon nothing seems too small or great for his mind to attend to; like Calvin he writes as if he had nothing to do but write (over 5,000 tracts and pamphlets), preaches as if he had nothing to do but preach and administers as if he had nothing to do but administer" (Ryle, *Christian Leaders of the 18th Century*, p. 85).

He preached for sixty-five years, dying finally at the age of eighty-eight. His last words were "The best of all, God is with us" and the first words of the hymn "I'll praise My maker while I've breath; And when my voice is lost in death; Praise shall employ my noblest powers." At about 10:00 in the morning, he said "Farewell"; then, without a groan, he fell asleep in Christ. He left behind him 750 preachers in England and 350 in America; 76,968 Methodists in England and 57,621 in America; by 1957, forty million worldwide. He was the ninth child of at least thirteen. With his brother Charles, a songwriter of some nine thousand hymns and poems, including "And Can It Be" and "Oh For a Thousand Tongues to Sing," and with other evangelist friends and followers he moved all England and eventually touched the world. He was, of course, John Wesley.

John Wesley's Contribution

Howard Snyder's research on Wesley (*The Problem of Wineskins, Community of the King, The Radical Wesley*) are important studies of Wesley's methods, organizational skills, discipline and community principles, and his reliance on spiritual power to accomplish God's work. Others point to Wesley's teachings on **Christian Perfection** (experienced as a second blessing distinct from justification) as the major introduction of this thought into Protestant Christianity. Some Reformers, like B. B. Warfield, reared on Calvin and Luther, understandably view with horror what they perceive as extreme and what they therefore choose to label as "perfectionism." Right or wrong they chose to opt for a more positional view of purity or a gradual, progressive sanctification, with proper stress on man remaining fallen, though Christian. ("We sin every day in thought, word and deed.")

Wesley's Teaching

Criticism, in reaction to what is correctly seen as a departure from Reform tradition, has been levelled at his teaching on perfection, from those who trace all second-blessing, holiness—Keswick, Pentecostal and Charismatic movements—to Wesley's teachings. Still, it is true (as we shall later see), that Finney, Mahan, Caughy and Dr. Walter and Phoebe Palmer, who preached a modified Weslyan doctrine of Christian perfection, almost dominated American revivalism for thirty years, and their teaching was especially important to the revival of 1857-58. Wesley's work, carried on by others, significantly affected the theology of American churches. It moved them away from their earlier roots, often for the better. These Holiness evangelists spread this "layman's revival" to Europe in the beginnings of the "Second Evangelical Awakening"; we shall consider their message later.

Wesley was attacked in his day, both physically and in print. When he was still in college in 1732, *Fogs Weekly Journal* had the dubious distinction of being first to publicly criticize him. William Law defended him in a way that turned out to be prophetic:

> It looks as if the strict rule of primitive Christianity is removed a great way out of sight, that we are not able to behold the attempt to revise it without wonder and offence. If it shall please God to give these gentlemen the grace to persevere and the Blessing of so long a Life, they may be the means of reforming a vicious world; and may rejoice at the good they have done perhaps half a century after most of their social oppo-

nents, the gay scoffers of the present generation are laid low and forgotten as if they had never been. (Garth Lean, *Strangely Warmed,* pp. 28-30)

George Whitefield (1714-1770)

"Of all the spiritual heroes of a hundred years ago, none saw so soon as Whitefield what the times demanded and none were so forward in the great work of spiritual aggression" (J. C. Ryle, *Christian Leaders Of The Eighteenth Century* [1885] Banner of Truth).

Into the spiritual barrenness of the day came another friend of John Wesley who became quite the opposite of him in theology, mannerisms, and style. As a boy, a self-confessed liar, thief, and a gambler, addicted to filthy talk, cursing, foolishness, and fantasy (like many of the boys his age), he had a love for novels, plays—and a talent for mimicking ministers! His parents ran a hotel tavern called the Bell Inn, where he lived for the first sixteen years of his life among highway robbers that picked their victims and planned attacks around the tables, and pimps who plied their trade among the customers. Here, he developed a vivid imagination and a voice that became so powerful and expressive that it was later apocryphally rumored that on a clear day you could hear him for five miles. (David Garrick, the top celebrated Shakespearian actor of his day, said he would give "one hundred guineas to be able to say the word 'Oh!' like George Whitefield.")

A Different Upbringing

Unlike Wesley, Whitefield did not grow up a church kid. From eight to fifteen, he lived in a home that was poor, with a stepfather and his mother, who had been disillusioned, hurt, and who had finally surrendered to a broken marriage. Sent off on his own at seventeen to Oxford for a chance to make it in life, he began to re-evaluate his ways and think about his future.

Convicted and lonely under the dealings of the Holy Spirit, he became deadly serious about spiritual things, and in 1733 Charles Wesley invited him to join the Oxford "Holy Club." This gathering for spiritual discipline, Bible study, and prayer, though an object of deist and rationalist derision on campus, was not evangelical, famous, or even significant to the revival to come. It was only a legal attempt by the Wesleys and others to be better people. It did not really meet any of their deep inner needs. Here, young George read Henry Scougal's tract, "The Life of God in the Soul of a Man." It so directly contradicted all he believed that it alarmed him. In response to what he'd read, he said:

> *God showed me I must be born again or be damned!* I learned a man may go to church, say his prayers, receive the sacrament and yet not be a Christian. . . . Shall I burn this book? Shall I throw it down? Or shall I search it? I *did* search it; and holding the book in my hand thus addressed the God of heaven and earth: "Lord if I am not a Christian, or if I am not a real one, for Jesus Christ's sake show me what Christianity is, that I may not be damned at last!" . . . from that moment . . . did I know that I must become a new creature." (Whitefield, *Journals*, p. 52)

Legality Grips Whitefield

Then followed not faith but a fearfully increased asceticism, with Whitefield wearing patched gown, dirty shoes, eating the worst food, and "whole days and weeks . . . spent lying prostrate on the ground . . . bidding Satan depart from me in the name of Jesus . . . begging for freedom from those proud hellish thoughts that used to crowd in upon and distract my soul" (Whitefield, *Journals*, p. 52).

For a year, the fearful pressure ruined his studies, almost drove him mad, and finally cost him his friendship in the Holy Club. He felt that perhaps his love for the other members was the final idolatry holding him back. Two years earlier another Club member, William Morgan, had lost his mind and his life; now Whitefield, grimly resolved to "die or conquer," seemed about to do the same. Finally, at the end of all human resources, God revealed Himself to the overjoyed young zealot. A Gospel faith gave him the peace he had struggled so long to attain, and he wrote: "Oh what joy—joy unspeakable—joy full and big with glory was my soul filled when the weight of sin came off, and an abiding sense of the pardoning love of God and a full assurance of faith broke in on my . . . soul!"

An Astonishing Introduction

Sunday, June 27, in the church of St. Mary de Crypt, he preached his first sermon. His mother, relatives, Robert Raikes—the founder of the Sunday-School—and some three hundred other people crowded impatiently together to hear him. It was a startling introduction. Fifteen people were, said the presiding Bishop, "driven mad!" Whitefield was twenty-one years old. Thus began the "preaching that startled the nation." Ryle says,

> No preacher has ever been so universally popular in every country he visited, in England, Scotland and America. No preacher has ever retained his hold on his hearers so entirely as he did for thirty-four years. His popularity never waned. It was as great at the end of his day as it was at the beginning . . .
>
> "Weekdays or Sundays, wherever he preached the churches were crowded and an immense sensation produced. The plain truth is that a really eloquent extempore preacher preaching the pure gospel with most uncommon gifts of voice and manner was at that time an entire novelty in London. Congregations were taken by surprise and carried by storm." (Ryle, *Christian Leaders of the 18th Century*, p. 49)

Overwhelming Influence

He attracted high and low, rich and poor alike. Eminent critics and literary men like Lord Bolingbroke and Lord Chesterfield were frequently his delighted hearers. Bolingbroke said, "He is the most extraordinary man in our times. He has the most commanding eloquence I ever heard in any person." Ben Franklin, the calculating Quaker by profession, spoke in no measured terms of his preaching powers; Hume, the historian, said it was worth riding twenty miles to hear him" (Ryle, *Christian Leaders of the 18th Century*, p. 35-36).

None of the seventy-five recorded sermons under his name

do him justice; shorthand recorded without correction, they are terribly disjointed and dismembered. He was exceptionally simple, lucid, bold, direct, and full of the Gospel. "He met men face to face, like one who had a message from God to them; 'I have come here to speak to you about your soul' (Ryle, *Christian Leaders Of The 18th Century*, p. 52). He dramatized so vividly that his sermons seemed to move and walk before your eyes, drawing such vivid pictures his hearers sometimes actually believed they saw and heard them. Lord Chesterfield was so entranced by Whitefield's description of the sinner as a blind beggar that when Whitefield moved him to the edge of a cliff, about to take the final fatal step, he actually "made a rush forwards to save him, exclaiming aloud 'He is gone! He is gone!'" (Dallimore, *George Whitefield*, Vol II, p. 388).

Whitefield was tremendously earnest; one poor uneducated man said:

> He preached like a lion. His sermons were life and fire; you must listen whether you liked to or not. There was a holy violence about him which firmly took your attention by storm. "I have not come in my own name. No! I have come in the Name of the Lord of hosts (and he brought down his hand and foot with a force that made the room ring) and *I must and will be heard!*" (Ryle, *Christian Leaders of the 18th Century*, p. 54)

Sincere Concern for People

His sermons were filled with *immense* feeling and pathos. He commonly wept profusely in the pulpit; Cornelius Winter, who later travelled often with him, said he had not seen him get through a sermon without a tear. This was no affectation; he felt deeply for the souls before him; it awakened affections and touched secret springs that no amount of reasoning and demonstration could have moved. It smoothed prejudices; people could not hate a man who wept so much over their souls. "I came to hear you with a pocket full of stones to break your head," said one convert, "but your sermon got the better of me, and broke my heart." His actions, voice, and fluency of language were of the highest order, his manner in the pulpit so curiously graceful and fascinating it was said none could hear him for five minutes without forgetting he squinted.

Persecuted but Not Broken

Under Wesley's request Whitefield went to Georgia for about a year to help with the Savannah Orphan House set up for children of the colonists. On his return the bulk of the Anglican clergy were no longer favorable to him; scandalized by his preaching regeneration, or the "new birth," as a thing that many baptized persons greatly needed, many began to denounce him openly and deny him pulpits. Ryle says: "The plain truth is that the Church of England of that day was not ready for a man like Whitefield. . . . [it was] too much asleep to understand him and vexed at a man who would not keep still and leave the devil alone" (Ryle, *Christian Leaders of the 18th Century*, p. 39).

The door to Church of England ministry began to close, and Whitefield, seeing thousands out of church, resolved in a "spirit of holy aggression" to "go out into the highways and byways and compel them to come in." His first attempt was among the Kingswood colliers near Bristol in February 1739. He began on a hill to speak to about one or two hundred of these coal miners on Matthew 5:1-3. He said of them:

> Having no righteousness of their own to renounce they were glad to hear of Jesus who was a friend to publicans and came not to call the righteous but sinners to repentance. The first discovery of their being affected was the sight of the white gutters made by their tears which fell plentifully down their black cheeks as they came out of the coal-pits. . . .
>
> Sometimes when twenty thousand people were before me I had not in my own apprehension a word to say either to God or them. But I was never totally deserted. . . . The open heavens above me, the prospect of the adjacent fields with the sight of thousands some in coaches, some on horseback, and some in the trees and at all times affected and in tears was almost too much for me, and quite overcame me. (Whitefield, *Journals*, p. 225)

Astonishing Crowds

The word spread. The next audience was two thousand, the third four to five thousand, and then audiences multiplied and expanded—ten thousand, fourteen thousand, twenty thousand! Shortly, he would be preaching to up to thirty thousand people at one time. Thousands came to hear him preach at 6:00 A.M in the snow; whole cities turned out to hear the young man with the golden voice and a supernatural authority from heaven. From 1739 till his death in 1770, thirty-one years of immense effect, his life was one uniform outreach, his vision one thing: to preach Christ and entreat men to repent and be saved.

In a deist nation, God often supernaturally moved to confirm His reality and power in Whitefield's meetings. In Yorkshire with Lady Huntingdon, when Whitefield was about to preach from a gallows scaffold on the text "It is appointed unto man once to die," a wild, terrifying shriek came from the audience; Grimshaw, one of his workers, pressed through the crowd and cried, "Brother Whitefield, you stand amongst the dead and the dying. An immortal soul has been called into eternity. The destroying angel is passing over the congregation. Cry aloud and spare not!" After a moments silence, he began again, only to hear a second shriek and a second man fall dead near where Lady Huntingdon and Lady Margaret Ingham were standing. After that the entire mass of the people seemed, predictably enough, "overwhelmed" by his appeal.

Sometimes, like his friend Wesley, he faced intense opposition both from churches and the unrepentant: at the fields of Mary Le Bon in London, some of his rough opponents tried to push over his pulpit, and one tried to stab him with a sword. Others pelted the preacher with filth. Some tried to drown out his voice. One even climbed a tree and exposed himself (Edwards, p. 220). Yet here God had found another man He could trust. Whitefield was a light-sabre in His hand for the nations. In one single week after preaching at Moorfields he received one thousand letters from people under spiritual concern, and admitted 350 to communion.

Dauntless Zeal

He worked tirelessly, like his friend Wesley, embarrassing in his zeal. He usually rose at 4:00 A.M. and often spent whole nights in reading and devotion, sometimes getting up after going to bed at his usual hour of 10:00 P.M. to do so. He preached morning, afternoon, and night on Sundays, at 6:00 every morning and evening, Monday to Thursday, and Saturday night–thirteen messages a week, sometimes forty to sixty hours of speaking each week, at the same time carrying on massive correspondence with people in almost every part of the world.

In the thirty-four years of his ministry, he visited almost every town in England, Scotland, and Wales. He crossed the Atlantic seven times and, with Americans like Gilbert Tennant (1703-1764), captured souls in Boston, New York, and Philadelphia. He publicly preached an estimated eighteen thousand messages. Yet this was no grim-lipped determination like his Oxford legal days; he was so singularly happy that one New York woman, speaking of the influences of the Holy Spirit that had won her, said, "Mr. Whitefield was so cheerful it tempted me to become a Christian."

He had a deep humility and broad catholicity and charity towards others, loving all others who loved Jesus in sincerity. If other Christians misrepresented him, he forgave them; if they refused to work with him, he still loved them. Whitefield, influenced deeply by Jonathan Edwards and the Huntingdon Connection, was a Calvinist; Wesley, the scholar, moved towards a more Arminian view of the Gospel. One censorious professor of religion, knowing the sharp theological differences between them, asked George if he thought he would see John Wesley in heaven. "I fear not," he said. "He will be so near the throne and we at such a distance that we shall hardly get a sight of him."

In Tribute of Whitefield

For most of his adult life, George Whitefield was as "famous as any man in the English-speaking world. From the age of twenty-two till his death, he was the foremost figure of the immense religious movement holding the multitudes' attention on both sides of the Atlantic" (Ryle, *Christian Leaders of the*

18th Century, p. 31). Arnold Dallimore says in the preface to his massive and definitive two-volume study of Whitefield:

> This book was written with the desire–perhaps in a measure of inner certainty–that we shall see the great Head of the Church once more bring into being His special instruments of revival, that He will again raise up unto himself certain young men whom He may use in this glorious employ. And what manner of men will they be? Men mighty in the Scriptures, their lives dominated by a sense of the greatness, the majesty and holiness of God, and their minds and hearts aglow with the great truths of the doctrines of grace.
>
> They will be men who have learned what it is to die to self, to human aims and personal ambitions; men who are willing to be 'fools for Christs sake', who will bear reproach and falsehood, who will labor and suffer and whose supreme desire will be, not to gain Earth's accolades, but to win the Master's approbation when they appear before His awesome judgement seat.
>
> They will be men who will preach with broken hearts and tear-filled eyes, and upon whose ministries God will grant an extraordinary effusion of the Holy Spirit and who will witness "signs and wonders following" in the transformation of multitudes of human lives. Indeed this book goes forth with the earnest prayer that amidst the rampant iniquity and glaring apostasy of the twentieth century God will use it toward the raising up of such men and toward the granting of a mighty revival such as was witnessed two hundred years ago." (Dallimore, *George Whitefield*, p. 16)

Whitefield's Gift

Whitefield died as suddenly as he had lived, almost literally "in harness" during one of his U.S. tours at Newbury Port, Sunday, 29 September 1770, of a single spasmodic fit of asthma (almost before his friends knew he was ill) at the comparatively early age of fifty-six. Though ill and tired, he preached his last open-air sermon the day before on 2 Corinthians 13:5 to a huge crowd. He prayed, "Lord Jesus, I am weary in Thy work but not of Thy work. If I have not yet finished my course let me go and speak for Thee once more in the fields, seal Thy truth and come home and die" (J. R. Andrews, *Life of George Whitefield*, p. 385). He ate with a friend, rode on to Newbury Port though terribly tired, and went to turn in early.

Tradition says as he was headed for bed with a lighted candle in his hand he could not resist the opportunity to turn at the head of the stairs to speak to friends who had come to meet him; the candle burned down to the socket before he quit. "Sudden death," he had often said, "is sudden glory. Whether right or not I cannot help wishing I may go off in the same manner. To me it would be worse than death to live to be nursed and to see friends weeping about me" (Ryle, *Christian Leaders of the 18th Century*, p. 42).

From Whitefield we learn this: God can use anyone who loves enough to care and who gives without sparing a gift of utter devotion to Him.

Jonathan Edwards (1703-1764)

At the same time God had raised up Whitefield and Wesley, He was doing something unusual in the United States among the young people of Northampton, Massachusetts. His instrument was Jonathan Edwards, recognized today as one of the most original and creative native U.S. minds of all time, later a president of Princeton. Here was a man who often studied thirteen hours a day, whose writing and eyesight was so bad he had to screw his face down close to a sermon manuscript to read it (in a monotone), and who inherited his Grandfather's church so dead he described it succinctly as "Dry Bones."

A Different Point of View

Edwards was a convinced Calvinist, though he called for repentance, confession of sin and decision, and his modified view of sin as selfishness and virtue defined as "disinterested benevolence" or "love to intelligent being in proportion to the amount of being each possesses" gave him a commendable evangelical and social concern (Richard Lovelace, *Dynamics of*

Spiritual Life, p. 364). His son taught that Christ died for all, not the elect only, and preached Christ's death as a sacrifice to "general justice," a governmental theory of the cross that dominated New England thinking till the middle of the nineteenth century, producing a great missionary impulse.

Edwards most famous (and much maligned) sermon, "Sinners in the Hands of an Angry God," in which he said things like "The God Who dreadfully abhors you . . . Who dangles you over the precipice much as one would dangle a spider over a flame" was not at all typical of his preaching. Edwards' astonishing results on that day are probably much more due to the manifested power of God in answer to prayer than the convicting content of his message.

Nevertheless the effect was awesome; people screamed aloud, clutched the backs of pews and the stone pillars of the church, lest the ground open and swallow them alive into hell. The congregations of his day were full of lost people who attended for the social or political influence membership conferred; the pulpits likewise. Political oppression from England, philosophical skepticism from France, and personal degradation from selfishness combined to create an atmosphere of carelessness towards God in the Colonies.

"It seemed," he wrote, "to be a time of extraordinary dullness in religion; licentiousness prevailed among the youth of the town" (Edwards, *Thoughts on the Revival in New England*).

Conversion of Young People

These lost church kids were Puritan children or grandchildren with a spiritual inheritance of discipline and the Puritan vision of divine destiny, but they carelessly assumed their salvation as secure no matter how they lived. They ignored their parents (who were likewise mired by land acquisition and affluence), walked the streets, and partied all night. They hit the bars and lived lewdly. If they had lived in our day, they would no doubt have been "users, cruisers, and boozers."

Yet as Harold A. Fischer notes, "Edwards' town was mild as far as being an example of . . . the prevalent sins of New England . . . the state of society and morals were becoming more and more corrupt. For a time it appeared as if God had forsaken New England" (Fischer, *Reviving Revivals*, pp. 152-153).

Then two young people died unexpectedly, and some of Edwards sermons began to get through.

By December 1734, half-a-dozen of the congregation got saved. After one girl "who had been a bold flirt" was converted, others became concerned. God was on the loose in New England. The young rebels of the town began to turn to Christ, and as Lovelace put it, this awakening became the "Jesus movement" of its generation as the "hearts of the fathers were turned to their children and the children to their fathers" (Lovelace, *Dynamics of Spiritual Life*, p. 38).

A "great and earnest concern" about eternity and spiritual things gripped all social classes and ages. It accelerated rapidly until souls came, as it were, "by flocks to Jesus," about three hundred in six months. Edwards noted:

> In the spring and summer following 1735, the town seemed to be full of the presence of God as it never was so full of love, nor so full of joy, and yet so full of distress as it was then . . . Our public assemblies were then beautiful; the congregation was alive in God's service, every one earnestly intent on the public worship, every hearer eager to drink in the words of the minister . . . the assembly . . . from time to time in tears while the Word was preached; some weeping with joy and distress, others with joy and love–still others in pity and concern for the souls of their neighbors. (Fischer, *Reviving Revivals*, p. 158)

The Roots of the Great Awakening

It was the beginning of the "most far-reaching and transforming event of the eighteenth-century religious life of America"; the revival that became known as the Great Awakening. The analogue of German Pietism and British Methodism, it "emphasized conversion as the normal entrance into the Kingdom of God; gave general diffusion to the Congregational view of the church as a company of experiential Christians" (Walker, *A History of the Christian Church*, p. 571).

The wave kept spreading through other communities and

towns—Connecticut, New York, New Jersey—ultimately affecting over a hundred towns. Edwards' record and analysis of the revival, "*A Narrative of Surprising Conversions,*" crossed the Atlantic to Wesley, who saw it as "surely . . . the Lords doing and . . . marvellous in our eyes." It prepared the way for the young spiritual ignitionist George Whitefield, who would range the nation, "digging trenches" between the filling pools of spiritual power.

Revival Spreads

On Whitefield's second visit to Philadelphia, Benjamin Franklin said:

> The multitudes of all sects and denominations that attended his sermons were enormous . . . it was wonderful to see the change so soon made in the manners of the inhabitants. From being thoughtless and indifferent about religion, it seemed as if all the world was growing religious; one could not walk through town in an evening without hearing psalms sung in different families in every street." (Fischer, *Reviving Revivals,* p. 155)

Joining Edwards were men like Gilbert Tennant. Though "less polished" than Edwards, his sermons had such power that the Rev. Jonathan Parsons reported of his ministry in Lyme, Connecticut,

> Many had their countenances changed; their thoughts seemed to trouble them, so that their loins were loosed and their knees smote one against the other. Great numbers cried aloud in the anguish of their souls. Several stout men fell as though a cannon had been discharged and a ball made its way through their hearts. Some young women were greatly disturbed." (Fischer, *Reviving Revivals*, p. 156)

Under Tennant and other preachers, like Blair, Finley, Dickenson and Davies, the work spread through the Middle Colonies and, by 1743, the South. Through the prayer and missionary effort of Edwards' son-in-law, David Brainerd, it even reached the Indians. In twenty years, between twenty-five thousand and fifty thousand were added to the churches—over a one hundred percent increase in both churches and preachers during this massive revival. It culminated in a moral consensus that could no longer tolerate the oppression of George II in England and fueled America's bid for ultimate freedom. Thus, it justly deserves the title "The First Great Awakening."

Edwards on Revival

Jonathan Edwards wrote in great detail, describing and later defending this First Great Awakening. What did he think of the nature of a true work of God? In his account of the work, he writes:

> The highest transports I have been acquainted with, where the affections of admiration, love and joy, so far as another could judge, have been raised to the highest pitch, the following things have been united:
>
> A very frequent dwelling for some considerable time together in view of the *glories of the Divine perfections and Christ's excellencies* . . . the soul has been, as it were, perfectly overwhelmed and swallowed up with light and love, a sweet solace, and a rest and joy of soul altogether unspeakable. The person has more than once continued for five or six hours together without interruption in a clear and lively sense of the infinite beauty and amiableness of Christ's Person and the heavenly sweetness of His transcendent love. . . . The heart was swallowed up in a kind of glow of Christ's love coming down as a constant stream of sweet light, at the same time the soul all flowing out in love to Him; so that there seemed to be a constant flowing and reflowing from heart to heart. *The soul dwelt on high, was lost in God and seemed almost to lose the body. . . .*
>
> Extraordinary views of Divine things and the religious affections were frequently attended with very great effects on the body. . . . The person was deprived of all ability to speak. Sometimes the hands were clenched and the flesh cold but the senses remaining. Animal nature was often in a great emotion and agitation, and the soul so overcome with admiration and a kind of

> omnipotent joy, as to cause the person unavoidably to leap with all their might with joy and mighty exaltation.
>
> Nearly three years ago they greatly increased upon an extraordinary self-dedication, renunciation of the world and resignation of all to God; which were made in a great view of God's excellency in high exercise of love to Him and rest and joy in Him. . . . All that is pleasant and glorious and all that is terrible in this world seemed perfectly to vanish into nothing and nothing to be left but God, in whom the soul was perfectly swallowed up as in an infinite ocean of blessedness.
>
> This great rejoicing has been with *trembling, i.e. attended with a deep and lively sense of the greatness and majesty of God and the persons own exceeding littleness and vileness.* Spiritual joys . . . were never attended with the least appearance of laughter or lightness either of the countenance or the manner of speaking; but with a peculiar abhorrence of such appearances in spiritual rejoicing. These high transports, when past have had abiding effects in the increase of sweetness, rest and humility which they have left upon the soul; and a new engagedness of heart to live to God's honor and watch and fight against sin." (Edwards, *Works of Jonathan Edwards,* p. 301)

The Charge of "Enthusiasm"

A charge critics often made when the work of revival seriously threatened established values and traditions was "enthusiasm," or what we would call fanaticism. Edwards, in common with others in the First Great Awakening, gave little credence to any spiritual gifts or manifestations that smacked of fleshly demonstrations. He makes two important comments on the spirit of a true revival:

> These transporting views and rapturous affections are not attended with any enthusiastic dispositions to follow impulses, or any supposed prophetical revelations; nor have they been observed to be attended with any appearance of spiritual pride but very much of a con-

trary disposition—an increase of *humility and meekness* and a disposition *in honor to prefer others. . .*

These two things were felt in a remarkable manner:

(1) A peculiar *AVERSION TO JUDGING* other professing Christians of good standing in the visible church with respect to their conversion or degrees of grace; or at all . . . so much as to determine against and condemn others in the thoughts of the heart. Such want of candor appeared hateful, as not agreeing with that lamblike humility, meekness, gentleness and charity which the soul then above other times saw to be beautiful.

(2) Secondly . . . was a very great sense of the importance of *MORAL SOCIAL DUTIES* and how great a part of religion lay in them. There was such a new sense and conviction of this beyond what had been before that it seemed to be as it were a clear discovery was made to the soul.

Characteristics of Revival

Edwards also noted the following characteristics of revival:

(a) An extraordinary sense of the awful majesty, greatness and *HOLINESS OF GOD* so as sometimes to overwhelm soul and body; a sense of the piercing, all-seeing eye of God so as to sometimes take away the bodily strength; and an extraordinary view of the infinite terribleness of the WRATH OF GOD, together with a sense of the ineffable misery of sinners exposed to this wrath.

(b) Especially longing after these two things; to be *MORE PERFECT in HUMILITY and ADORATION.* The flesh and the heart seem often to cry out, lying low before God and adoring Him with greater love and humility. . . . The person felt a great delight in singing praises to God and Jesus Christ, and longing that this present life may be as it were one continued song of praise to God. There was a longing, as one person expressed it, "to sit

> and sing this life away"; and an overcoming pleasure in the thoughts of spending an eternity in that exercise. Together with living by faith to a great degree, there was a constant and extraordinary distrust of our own strength and wisdom; a great dependence on God for His help in order to the performance of any thing to God's acceptance and being restrained from the most horrid sins.

Further Revival

Thus, the convicting Spirit of God was the impetus to lead on to further revival and deeper awakening. The new American frontiers also desperately needed a divine visitation, and their needs were met in the Second Great Awakening.

Charles Finney (1792-1875)

"When he opened his mouth, he was aiming a gun. When he spoke the bombardment began. The effects of his speaking were almost unparalleled in modern history. Over half a million people were converted through his ministry . . . in an age when there were no amplifiers or mass communications. He spearheaded a revival which literally altered the course of history" (Miller, *Charles Finney,* cover).

Finney was born the year after Wesley died. Thus, the revival events of his life became the link from the Great Awakening of one century to the Second Great Awakening of the next. The Harvard professor Perry Miller wrote, "Charles Grandison Finney led America out of the eighteenth century" (Finney, *The Heart of Truth*, cover).

His Early Life

A tall (6' 2"), impressively blue-eyed young frontiersman from a totally non-Christian farming family, Charles was the seventh child of Sylvester and Rebecca Finney. He was a musical, gently mocking pagan. Most available sketches and pictures (taken near the end of his life) do not do him justice. Surviving portraits rarely catch his irrepressible sense of humor, his zest for life, or his rugged and athletic build. He was apparently deeply attractive and personable. Why else would his new wife not mind waiting for months when revivals repeatedly broke out on his way to take her home after the wedding? Their deeply moving love for each other is recorded in his private letters. Yet following her death Finney was able to marry again, and even again!

An expert marksman, sailor, and athlete, "when he was twenty he excelled every man and boy he met in every species of toil or sport. No man could throw him, no man could knock his hat off, no man could run faster, jump further, leap higher or throw a ball with greater force and precision" (Edman, *Finney Lives On*, pp. 25-26).

Though he regularly attended the gentle Dr. George Gale's Presbyterian church, he scorned prayer meetings because he "never saw any of their prayers answered." Nevertheless he played cello, directed the choir, and was in love with Lydia Root Andrews, one of the pretty young Christian girls who visited there (later his first and deeply loved wife).

Charles was then studying to be a lawyer. Reading *Blackstone's Law Commentaries* (then the ultimate authority on the subject), he was struck by this Christian's constant reference to the Bible as the basis for all civic and moral law. He obtained a copy and began to study it seriously. Perhaps of all the great evangelists and revivalists, Finney's originality and distinction owes much to the fresh approach he took, confronted for the first time by the truth of Scripture which he believed to be God's Word.

Finney's Conversion

He later noted:

> I often said to myself, "If these things are really taught in the Bible, I must be an infidel." But the more I read my Bible the more clearly I saw that these things were not found there upon any fair principles of interpretation such as would be admitted in a court of justice. . . . But the Spirit of God conducted me through the darkness and delivered me from the labyrinth and fog of a false philosophy, and set my feet upon the rock of truth—as I trust." (Finney, from the Preface, *Systematic Theology*, p. x)

His conversion reads like something from the book of Acts. Under deep conviction from the Scripture and dealt the Holy Spirit, he vowed one October Sunday evening in the Fall of 1821 to "settle the question of my soul's salvation at once, that if it were possible I would make my peace with God" (Finney, *Autobiography*, p. 12).

For the next two days, his conviction increased, but he could not pray or weep. He felt if he could be alone and cry out aloud to God something might happen. Tuesday evening, he became so nervous he felt if he did not cry out he would sink into hell, but he survived until morning. Setting out for work, he was suddenly confronted by an "inward voice" that riveted him to the spot in front of his office: "What are you waiting for? Did you not promise to give your heart to God? What are you trying to do—work out a righteousness of your own?"

The whole essence of conversion opened to him there in what he called "a marvellous manner": the finished work of Christ, the need to give up his sins and submit to His righteousness. The voice continued, "Will you accept it, now, today?" Finney vowed, "Yes; I will accept it today or I will die in the attempt" (Finney, *Autobiography*, p. 15).

Conviction of Sin

Sneaking away over the hill to a small forest where he liked to take walks, avoiding anyone who might ask him what he was doing, the young lawyer fought a battle with his pride. Several times he tried to pray, but rustling leaves stopped him cold; he thought someone was coming and would see him trying to talk to God. Finally, near despair, thinking he had rashly vowed and that his hardheartedness had grieved away the Holy Spirit, he had a sudden revelation of his pride:

> An overwhelming sense of my wickedness in being ashamed to have a human being see me on my knees before God took such powerful possession of me that I cried at the top of my voice . . . I would not leave that place if all men on earth and all the devils in hell surrounded me. . . . The sin appeared awful, infinite. It broke me down before the Lord. (Finney, *Autobiography*, p. 17)

Just then a Scripture verse seemed to "drop into his mind with a flood of light": "Then shall you go and pray to Me and I will hearken to you. Then shall you seek Me and find Me when you search for me with all your heart" (Jer. 29:13). It came to Finney with a flood of revelation, though he did not recall ever having read it. It shifted faith for him from the intellect to the choice. He knew that a God who could not lie had spoken to him and that his vow would be heard. Quietly, walking back towards the village, he was filled with such a sense of peace that it "seemed all nature listened." He realized it was noon. Many hours had passed without any conscious sense of the passage of time.

A Manifestation of Jesus

Back at his office, his boss, Judge Wright, had gone to lunch. He took down his bass viol and began to play and sing some hymns: "But as soon as I began to sing these sacred words, I began to weep. It seemed as if my heart were all liquid; my feelings were in such a state that I could not hear my own voice in singing without causing my sensibility to overflow . . . I tried to suppress my tears, but could not" (Finney, *Autobiography*, p. 20).

All that afternoon, filled with a profound sense of tenderness, sweetness, and peace, he helped Judge Wright relocate their office. The work finished, he bade his employer goodnight. "I had accompanied him to the door; and as I closed the door and turned around my heart seemed to be liquid within me. All my feelings seemed to rise and flow out and the utterance of my heart was: 'I want to pour out my whole soul to God'" (Finney, *Autobiography*, p. 21). He rushed into a back room of the office to pray. Then it happened:

> There was no fire, no light in the room; nevertheless it appeared to me as if it were perfectly light. **As I went in and shut the door after me, it seemed as if I met the Lord Jesus Christ face to face**. It did not occur to me then, nor did it for some time afterward, that it was a wholly mental state. On the contrary, it seemed to me that I saw Him as I would see any other man. He said nothing, but looked at me in such a manner as to break

> me down right at His feet . . . it seemed to me a reality that He stood before me and I fell down at His feet and poured out my soul to Him. I wept aloud like a child, and made such confessions as I could with a choked utterance. It seemed to me that I bathed His feet with my tears, and yet I had no distinct impression that I touched Him. (Finney, *Autobiography*, p. 21)

Baptized in the Holy Spirit

For a long time, Finney continued in this state. Eventually he broke off the interview and returned to the front office, where the fire had nearly burned out. As he was about to take a seat by the fire, he received, in his own words,

> **a mighty baptism of the Holy Ghost.** Without any expectation of it, without ever having the thought in my mind that there was any such thing for me, without any recollection that I had ever heard the thing mentioned by any person in the world, the Holy Spirit descended on me in a manner that seemed to go through me, body and soul. *I could feel the impression, like a wave of electricity, going through and through me. Indeed, I could not express it any other way. It seemed like the very breath of God. I can recall distinctly that it seemed to fan me like immense wings.*
>
> No words can express the wonderful love that was shed abroad in my heart. I wept aloud with joy and love; and I do not know but I should say, *I literally bellowed out the unutterable gushings of my heart.* These waves came over me and over me and over me, one after the other until I recollect I cried out "I shall die if these waves continue to pass over me." I said, "Lord I cannot bear any more; yet I had no fear of death" (Finney, *Autobiography*, p. 22).

Later, a church choir member knocked on his door. He found him loudly weeping and asked if he was sick or in pain. Eventually able to speak, Finney said, "No, but so happy that I cannot live."

The Beginning of a Powerful Ministry

The following morning, with the sunrise, his baptism of power and love returned, and with it a call to the ministry. From that day on, Finney realized it was goodbye to his legal profession. He launched out on a life of fire and power such as few have paralleled in Christian history.

Like all other men of God, he had his faults. He was sometimes extravagant and emotive in language. So careful to bring glory to God, he attacked anything that seemed in any way to him to harbor an attitude of resistance to God's Spirit.

Later, analyzing the strengths and weaknesses of his own earlier ministry, he felt he had been too apt to teach and inform before bringing people up to their known obligation to submit to Christ. This he found did not encourage faith but could lead to a cynical, fault-finding, rationalistic spirit in converts. In later years he put more stress on the power of the Holy Spirit and the simplicity of trust in Christ as the key to all victory and perseverance in ministry. Some estimate that over 80 percent of his converts during the revivals stayed true to Christ without ever backsliding, an awesome testimony to the power of a pure life and an urgent message of holiness. . . . Even his enemies and detractors admitted the awesome way God used him. They attributed it to his prayer life, the sovereignty of God, or the mood of the times while decrying the obvious implications of a theology and experience that helped break the back of a religious fatalism that had dominated the land.

Finney's Uniqueness

Three things stand out in Finney's astonishing life; his willingness to change, his deep and loving devotional life and prayer, and his radical message of practical and immediate holiness. "Denounced by clergy and secularist alike for his innovations in evangelism, he was intolerably ahead of his time. One preacher (Lyman Beecher) threatened to oppose him with cannon if he dared venture into his parish" (Finney, *The Heart Of Truth,* cover). (Beecher later relented and extended an invitation to Finney.)

"Swinging above your heads are two distorted figures suspended on ropes. At the touch of the torch they leap into flames and the crowd screams in sheer delight. Sound like a scene from a lynching . . . a race riot? Not at all. *It is a religious gathering.* The charred creatures smouldering in the air represent the public's expression of opposition to the preaching and praying of America's greatest evangelistic team. Charles Grandison Finney and his partner-in-prayer, Father (Daniel) Nash, have just been burned in effigy. Preachers and pew-warmers alike joined forces against the two men who did more to spearhead revival than any other pair in American history. . . . Finney became so **incredibly alive** that everywhere he went life leaped from him to others like flames in a fire-storm. It is impossible to read about this man without being shaken. (Basil Miller; *Charles Finney—A Biography*, cover)

Charles Finney (among the twenty-three million Americans and forty thousand ministers of his time) was unquestionably the most impressive religious revolutionary that America has ever produced. When he first gave a public account of his own conversion, the tumult began. A fellow lawyer left the meeting with the comment, "He is in earnest . . . but he is deranged . . ." When he stood up to preach his first revival messages in the backwoods regions of New York, startling chaos ensued. One man came to the meeting with a pistol, intent on killing the speaker of the evening. Instead he fell to the floor and was soundly saved. Everywhere he went for some forty years the tumult spread. (Finney, *Finney On Revival*, cover)

His Works Go Marching On

It would be true to say that his life and writings influenced more people towards revival and social reform than any other preacher of the last century. "His convictions were born in the fires of revival and shaped by a keen lawyer's mind committed to the full authority of the Bible. So effective were his theological writings that they have been the impetus for revivals around the world since his death" (S.E. Shalhemer, ed., *Finnney on Revival*, cover).

Many of his materials go into reprint generation after generation, sourcing new desires for holy awakening in each one. There is his biography, a deeply moving account of his ministry; *Reflections on Revivals*, a succinct analysis of his early mistakes and dangers in revival ministry; *Lectures to Professing Christians* and *Sermons on Gospel Themes* (re-arranged and re-issued under various titles) are powerful attacks on compromise and counterfeit conversion. Many sermons from the *Oberlin Evangelist*, a "Jesus Paper" he edited during revival, have been republished with titles like "The Promise of the Spirit" and "Principles of Victory."

V. Raymond Edman, a past president of Wheaton College, said, "In all my reading on revival I have found nothing to be the equal of Finney's *Lectures on Revival*. They constitute lessons that God's servant learned in days when tens of thousands came to a saving knowledge of the Lord Jesus. I have found nothing more heart-searching, more pungent and powerful and more satisfying than these messages by Finney" (Edman, from the Preface, *Finney Lives On*). "No other book on the subject has been so mightily used of God. It has been translated into many languages and circulated around the world . . ." (Preface, *Lectures on Revivals of Religion*).

Finney's life spanned two mighty periods of American and British Christian history, the First and Second Great Awakenings; wearing out two of his three wives, radical to the last, he passed away peacefully on Sunday in Oberlin, August 16, 1875. Written on his tombstone is the Scripture summary of his life as his memorial: "The Lord be with us as He was with our fathers; let us not fail nor forsake Him."

Chapter Seven

The Campmeetings and Revivals

The worst thing happened to America as a reaction to winning Independence in 1776 and establishing her Constitution in 1789: she forgot the spiritual roots of her freedom. Doctrinal division and party politics had hurt Great Awakening converts; then from France and Great Britain came a flood of rationalistic literature. Dr. Timothy Dwight described it as "the dregs of infidelity vomited on us . . . the whole mass of pollution emptied on this country. An enormous edition of the *Age of Reason* was published in pre-revolutionary France and sold in America for a few pence; and where it could not be sold, it was given away" (Fischer, *Reviving Revivals,* p. 162). The effect on U.S. colleges was disastrous. Students looking for an excuse to rebel against the society of the day embraced rationalism and even called themselves by the names of famous skeptics and infidels.

Bible Colleges like Harvard, Princeton and Yale became centers of skepticism, atheism, and anarchy. Christian students were snubbed, sneered at, and openly ridiculed. They became such a minority that on some campuses they had to meet secretly. In shades of the radical movements of the late 1960s, students of those days held mock communion services, forced the resignation of a Bible College President, and attempted to burn down a church!

Frontier Awakenings

But God had a surprise in store; young men and women banded together to pray. College preachers like Timothy Dwight, who took over Yale in 1795, began to see conviction spreading as they counter-attacked with powerful sermons filled with relentless logic and often real anointing. Over half the student body there confessed conversion before the year was out.

And even along the early frontier in Daniel Boone's day some powerful revivals broke out. Francis Asbury was sent from England to the frontiers with the mandate, "Offer them Christ." Peter Cartwright and other Methodist circuit-riding preachers on horseback took on the Wild West. In his book *The Awakening That Must Come* (Broadman Press, Nashville, Tenn. 1978), Lewis A. Drummond, the Billy Graham Chair of Evangelism professor at Southern Baptist Theological Seminary, describes these powerful frontier revivals in the days of Daniel Boone. This movement, in the late 1780s, was thus part of the Second Great Awakening:

"Caught up in the awakening were two North Carolina Presbyterian ministers, James McGready and his protégé, **Barton Stone**. . . . Trekking through the Cumberland Gap they took up their ministries in Kentucky" (Drummond, *The Awakening That Must Come*, p. 14).

McGready was an "impassioned preacher, diligent pastor and fervent man of prayer." In June of 1800, he called on the people of south-central Kentucky to gather for a four-day extended observance of the Lord's Supper. People came expecting blessing, and God met their faith. The Holy Spirit fell on them powerfully.

The First Campmeeting

Barton Stone, later a leader of the Disciples of Christ, said:

> There on the edge of the prairie. . . . multitudes came together . . . The scene was new and passing strange. It baffled description. Many, very many fell down as men slain in battle, and continued for hours together in an apparently breathless and motionless state, sometimes for a few moments reviving and exhibiting symptoms of life by a deep groan or piercing shriek, or a prayer for mercy fervently uttered." (Fischer, *Reviving Revivals*, p. 165-166)

Friday and Saturday saw floods of repentant tears and then times of exuberant rejoicing. The climax came on the final day when John McGee, a Methodist minister gave the closing exhortation. His own words:

"I . . . exhorted them to let the Lord omnipotent reign in their hearts and submit to Him and their souls should live. . . . I turned again and losing sight of the fear of man, I went through the house shouting and exhorting with all possible ecstasy and energy and the floor was soon covered by the slain" (Drummond, *The Awakening That Must Come*, p. 15).

People had come in unprecedented numbers from the hundred-mile radius of the Red River. Because there was insufficient accommodation, they brought bedrolls and tents for their housing; thus the first campmeeting was born. McGready said:

> No person seemed to wish to go home. Hunger and sleep seemed to affect nobody–eternal things were the vast concerns. . . . Sober professors who had been communicants for many years now were lying prostrate on the ground crying out in such language as this: "Oh! How I would have despised any person a few days ago who would have acted as I am doing now! But I cannot help it!" . . . persons of every description, white and black, were to be found in every part of the multitude crying out for mercy in the most extreme distress. (Drummond, *The Awakening That Must Come*, pp. 15-16)

The Cane Ridge Revival

Barton Stone, at the invitation of Daniel Boone, had preached and served at the Cane Ridge Meeting House in Bourbon County. Stone was so overwhelmed by the Red River revival that he went home and, in May 1801, called for a similar meeting in Cane Ridge, "which was attended with blessing." A second meeting in August was then called. To the utter astonishment of all, over twenty thousand people arrived for the six-day camp meeting! It was an incredible event, for this was the sparsely populated frontier. Among the thousands converted was James B. Finley, who later became a Methodist circuit rider. He wrote:

> The noise was like the roar of Niagara. The vast sea of human beings seemed to be agitated as if by a storm. I counted seven ministers, all preaching at one time, some on stumps, others in wagons and one standing on a tree which had, in falling, lodged against another. . . . Some of the people were singing, others praying, some crying for mercy in the most piteous accents, while others were shouting most vociferously. While witnessing these scenes, a peculiarly-strange sensation such as I had never felt before came over me. My heart beat tumultuously, my knees trembled, my lips quivered, and I felt as though I must fall to the ground. A strange supernatural power seemed to pervade the entire mass of mind there collected . . . I stepped up on a log where I could have a better view of the surging sea of humanity.
>
> The scene that then presented itself to my mind was indescribable. At one time I saw at least *five hundred* swept down in a moment as if a battery of a thousand guns had been opened upon them, and then immediately followed shrieks and shouts that rent the very heavens." (Mendell Taylor, *Exploring Evangelism*, p. 142)

The American frontier was set ablaze. The Presbyterians and Methodists caught fire, and then the flame broke out among the Baptists in Carroll County on the Ohio River.

Between 1820 and 1830 alone, Methodism doubled to become one of the most formidable forces for spiritual and social change on the frontier. Baptist revivalism had its birth in this movement; the camp meeting motif spread all over eastern America.

The frontier was radically transformed. Instead of gambling, cursing and vice, spirituality and genuine Christianity characterized the early Westward movement. It was God's great hour. It stopped skepticism in its tracks and returned the helm of the country to the godly.

The French historian Alexis de Tocqueville, who wrote the classic *Democracy in America*, once doubted it could survive. He saw that such freedom depends on a moral foundation of revealed truth mediated through religious institutions. But returning in 1831 he found the nation transformed. The churches were strong and people were helping each other build barns, singing like the Amish in the film *Witness*. He went home to write "*America is a Nation with the Soul of a Church.*" It took the Great Awakening to both ensure and preserve democracy.

The 1857 Revival

Which comes first, revival or judgment? In the 1857 Revival (from which issued the awakenings in Ireland, Scotland, Wales, and England a year or two later), a near socio-economic collapse jolted America away from her apathy into a national cry for spiritual reality. Though in 1860 more than five million out of her thirty million population were Protestant church members (and around three million of these evangelical Baptists or Methodists) these numbers (as in our time) seemed to have little effect on the nation. For ten earlier years (1845-1855), America's spiritual life steadily fell apart. Dr. J. Edwin Orr lists five contributing factors that led to a great economic collapse in the country, again uncannily like our day:

1. Gain, gambling, and greed. Speculation, spectacular wealth, and prosperity for an elite few widened the gap between the haves and have-nots, with a crumbling economy and a corresponding rapid increase in violent crime.

2. Occult domination. A nation hungry for the supernatural turned to Spiritualism, which gained a popular foothold over many minds.

3. Immorality. A Playboy philosophy of "free love" was advocated and accepted by many.

4. Commercial and political corruption. Bribes, graft, and illegal business practices were rife in the nation. The unity of the 1820s tore apart in the deepening hostility of the industrial North to the agricultural South, which threatened to secede. National laws still legalized the cruel system of slavery.

5. Atheism. Agnosticism, apathy and indifference to God, to the church and its message abounded on every hand. "The decline was four-fold; social, moral, political and spiritual" (Orr, The Fervent Prayer, p. 1).

And judgment came. Both secular and religious conditions combined to bring about a terrible economic and social crash; thousands of merchants were forced to the wall as banks failed and railroads went into bankruptcy. Factories shut down; vast numbers were thrown out of employment. New York City alone had thirty thousand idle men. By October 1857 people had despair and hunger staring them in the face.

A Revival of Holiness

In Hamilton, Ontario, Walter Palmer, a Holiness Methodist physician and his talented wife, Phoebe (herself a firebrand preacher), began a series of meetings soon reported in a New York journal as an "extraordinary revival" with three to four hundred converts. Walter and Phoebe, in common with many of Finney's converts of the era, were ablaze with a burning desire to implement the message of personal and social holiness and from such a practical sanctification to extend the Kingdom of God throughout the whole earth.

Phoebe began with the premise "God requires present holiness" and Finney's logic, "God would not require what we cannot do." She called for a complete consecration to God, spouse, children, possessions, reputation, and (for women)—the willingness to preach! From such an act of simple faith and corresponding testimony, she urged a present possession of holiness, rather than the life-long process of Wesley in his initial emphasis. Her preaching, teaching, half-a-dozen books, and editing of *The Guide To Holiness* left "an indelible impact on both Methodism and the wider Church" (Nancy Hardesty, *Great Women of Faith*, pp. 88-90).

Phoebe was already deeply involved in slum work, a prison ministry, a mission to the poor (The Five Points Mission), juvenile delinquent homes, orphanages (one for five hundred black children), a ministry to the deaf, and the precursor to the Y.W.C.A., the Ladies Christian Union. Now the foremost Methodist advocate of Christian sanctification, she spread benevolent responsibility everywhere through home groups, campmeetings, and the churches. Here the message of personal holiness and social righteousness found its greatest expression of power. Timothy Smith says in his *Revivalism and Social Reform*:

". . . a third and quite utilitarian impulse of the holiness revival, (was) the hunger for an experience which would "make Christianity work." Finney, the reformer, Mrs. Palmer, the pioneer of many benevolent and missionary enterprises, and William E. Boardman, organizer and executive head of the United States Christian Commission, did not seem like mystic dreamers to their generation. . . . they rang the changes on . . . the theme that the Spirit's baptism was the secret of pulpit power and the fountain of that energy which alone could accomplish the evangelization of the world" (Smith, *Evangelical Origins of Social Christianity*, p. 145).

Later, the Palmers helped spread the message and fire to Great Britain, preaching there over four years. Eventually some twenty-five hundred people were reported converted, especially under Phoebe's ministry, with many more making commitments to the "deeper life."

The First Fruit

Only twenty-one were saved when this Canadian revival began, but it grew steadily until anywhere from twenty to forty-five were converted each day, with all classes kneeling at the altar, from little children to the city mayor. "Laity" leadership here was a key, which became true of the whole later awakening; this initial notice was soon followed by increasing reports of local small awakenings in various states. In December of that year, a convention on revival was called by the Presbyterians. Two hundred ministers and many laymen attended, and much of the time was spent in prayer. Baptist and Methodist pastors in New York set aside a day a week for all-day intercession for an outpouring of the Spirit. By the New Year, messages were preached all over the East on revival.

Prayer in the Inner City— Embracing Our World

Prayer was such a key in this 1857 Fourth Great Awakening that it has been called "The Prayer-Meeting Revival." God laid a call on Jeremiah Lamphier, a forty-eight-year-old upper New York born businessman, who was converted in 1842 during a revival in the Broadway Tabernacle built by Finney a decade earlier. Seeing the terrible need in the city for God, he gave up his business in order to be a city street missionary. With social collapse staring the city in the face, Lamphier walked the streets, passing out ads for a noonday prayer meeting to be held Wednesdays at the Dutch Church at the corner of Fulton Street in downtown New York. For five, ten, fifteen, twenty, twenty-five minutes, he waited alone, his faith tried. But then, at 12:30, six men came in, one after another. By the next week, there were twenty. By the first week in October (just before the stock market crashed), they decided to meet daily instead of weekly.

Within six months over ten thousand businessmen were meeting every day in similar meetings, confessing sin, getting saved, praying for revival. Most of the organizers of the prayer meetings were businessmen; people had meetings in stores, company buildings and churches. With hardly an exception, churches worked together as one, with no time for jealousy. By common consent doctrinal controversies were left alone.

Great Ministries in a Time of Crisis

On the eve of the Civil War, America began to live again; in just two years, over a million converts were added to churches of all denominations. From February to June in 1858 alone, some fifty thousand persons a week were making commitments. The social and ethical effects continued for almost half a century. Human service agencies like the United Way, the

American Red Cross, and the YWCA began, staffed with community volunteers. YMCA converts ministered to both the North and South Armies during the Civil War; there were over one hundred fifty thousand converts among the Confederates alone. The blessing spread to Great Britain, covering every country, which had over twenty-seven million people, of whom a third attended State and Free Church services. It first touched Ireland, then Scotland, Wales, and finally England. There were one hundred thousand converts in Ulster, one hundred thousand additions in Wales, three hundred thousand in Scotland and more than half-a-million in Great Britain by 1865. Three hundred thousand joined Methodist, Baptist, and Congregational churches. Over a million converts were ultimately added to the churches in England.

Some of the great remembered ministries of history developed during this awakening. The revival saw the flowering of the ministry of D. L. Moody and Ira Sankey and the world-changing influence of William and Catherine Booth and the Salvation Army. Hudson Taylor's revival-based concept of interdenominational missions, the China Inland Mission, in time became the largest Protestant or Catholic missionary body.

A large number of philanthropic societies developed and prospered. Concerned about the hurt, lost and unwanted, they cared for children, reclaimed prostitutes and drunks, and rehabilitated criminals. City Missions expanded evangelism into theaters, open-air meetings, and slum visitations; the Open Air Mission, founded in 1853, flowered under evangelistic teams directed by Gawin Kirkham (J. Edwin Orr, *The Fervent Prayer*, pp. 120-127). The Awakening was primarily an urban rather than rural movement, the "English-speaking world fast becoming one of ever-enlarging cities with huge concentrations of population that had left forever the influence of rural churches behind" (J. Edwin Orr, *The Fervent Prayer*, p. 128).

Care for the Poor—Shaftesbury

One first effect of the revival was a new and intense sympathy for the poor. "God has not ordained," protested Anthony Ashley Cooper (Lord Shaftesbury), "that in a Christian country there should be an overwhelming mass of foul, helpless poverty" (Orr, *The Second Evangelical Awakening*, p. 99). As a boy of fourteen, he watched with horror as a drunk burial party, shouting a lewd song, dropped the coffin of the pauper they were carrying to burial. They fell in a heap in front of him, cursing and swearing. "Good heavens!" he muttered. "Can this be permitted because a man is poor and friendless?"

From that day on, this teenager (who would grow to become a tall young aristocrat, full of fun and life, and described by one woman as "the handsomest man I ever saw") purposed to give his life to the poor and oppressed. He wrote in his diary at twenty-six: "Time was when I could not sleep for ambition. I thought of nothing but fame and immortality. But I am much changed. I desire to be useful to my generation, and die in the knowledge of having advanced true happiness by having advanced true religion" (Garth Lean, *Brave Men Choose*, p. 46).

He faced terrible times and conditions, and fought for justice with tireless, passionate determination. Children "sometimes four or five, but generally between seven and thirteen were shipped by bargeload" to other cities to do the work of men. Bound by "apprenticeship" until they were twenty-one and completely at the factory owners mercy, children were employed at cotton mills for thirteen, fourteen, fifteen, or even sixteen hours a day. During rush periods they were sometimes working twenty-four hours a day, with only half an hour off for dinner." Their whip-wielding overseers were paid by each child's output (Garth Lean, *Brave Men Choose*, p. 45). Ashton attacked these terrible social evils and many others like them in public and in Parliament. To those "who said of London's thirty thousand naked, wandering, homeless children, 'What will you do with them when educated?' he replied, 'What will you do with them if left where they are?' (Lean, *Brave Men Choose*, p. 46).

Marxism—A Counterfeit Compassion

These industrial conditions he fought and suffered over were the same ones observed by another would-be world-changer: Karl Marx.

For thirty-four years Marx lived within a few miles of Cooper (or Shaftesbury); he was in London during the years of the great revival. Marx was certainly not ignorant of Christian things. His sister-in-law was active in the evangelical Lower Rhineland Revival that accomplished some tremendous social improvements while Marx was growing up in Germany. The sad thing was that Karl lost three of his own children through malnutrition during his early years in London. He blamed it on the failure of a "sneaking and hypocritical" Christianity to change the system. With Engels (whose family part owned one of the cotton mills) he set out to destroy it and everything around him.

Bitter, covered in boils and full of hate, he sat in the British Museum writing *Das Kapital* when Moody came to London to preach. He hated Christians, not because he failed to see any real Gospel power to transform society, but because of his own counterfeit conversion, and subsequent failure. He believed they had to be, like himself once, nothing but self-deceived hypocrites. Having already written off Christianity, he now had nothing but spite for their doing good, and in this way delay the day of violence which could usher in his own proud and perverse dream of a new world in his image.

False Assumptions

Christian meekness, humility, steadfastness, obedience, and kindness Marx put down as cowardice, self-contempt, abasement, and slavish subjection. It must have been hard to live with his rage when a godly revolutionary like Shaftesbury contradicted Marx's false assumptions every day. Later, Marx's disciples were to confront another awesomely holy radical in the person of Catherine Booth, whose own fiery spiritual and practical attacks on corrupt society disturbed them so much that, for a century, the Salvation Army was the only religion officially banned in the Soviet Union.

Shaftesbury believed "what is morally right cannot be politically wrong and what is morally wrong cannot be politically right." He originated more Royal Commissions of social investigation than any Parliamentarian in all British history, extending benefits to all classes of working people, pushed through more change than Marx ever did, and eventually earned the loved nickname "The People's Earl." The Hammonds, economic historians critical of his entire approach, nevertheless admitted of his social reforms, "He did more than any single man or any single government in English history . . ." (Lean, *Brave Men Choose*, p. 39).

Ministry to Orphans and the Young

Nor were they the only agents of social compassion. Tom Barnado was the youngest of a brilliant Dublin family. After attempting to explain away examples of conviction as "emotional hysteria," he finally became a Christian. He founded the famous Dr. Barnado Homes in London's tragic East End; later through the whole country. George Mueller's orphanages had of course been in operation many years, keeping up to ten thousand children alive and happy through his work of faith. But something more needed to be done for young working people.

George Williams, converted at sixteen one Sunday winter evening in 1837, launched the Teen Challenge of his generation, the Young Men's Christian Association on June 6th, 1844. He, with some of his new converts had "looked with deep concern and anxiety upon the almost totally neglected spiritual condition of the mass of young people engaged in the pursuit of business ... we regard it to be a sacred duty, binding upon every child of God to use all the means in his power and to direct all his energies in and out of season towards the promotion of the Saviours Kingdom and the salvation of souls . . ." (J. E. Hodder Williams, *The Life of Sir George Williams*, p. 114).

Two men's messages helped give him heart for this vision; *Finney* of America and *Binney* of England. Williams was deeply stirred to evangelism, revival, and prayer through Finney's *Lectures on Revivals* and *To Professing Christians*, which he gave out to his new converts. He was also influenced by the English preacher Thomas Binney, who preached stirring, contemporary sermons against cant and hypocrisy, calling on young men to rise up and do battle for character and honest work. "Probably no man of his time developed so pre-eminently in the pulpit the tendency of the thinking and reading of the age. (Binney) preached the reality of the battle that is life, and as he pictured it, the fight was glorious, the victory sure" (J. E. Hodder Williams, *The Life of Sir George Williams*, p. 38). The YMCA, helped by men like D. L. Moody, reached out both in the U.S. and Britain and mobilized thousands of young men for evangelism.

A Revival of World Missions and "Keswick"

Men like David Livingstone held out the challenge for Africa during the revival; Mary Slessor, converted in Dundee in 1860, joined the United Presbyterian mission in Nigeria and did extraordinary work among the tribes (p. 139). The seed of the Keswick Conventions of London, Oxford, and Brighton in 1873-5 was laid by Evan Hopkins, a newly converted young clergyman who had read William Edwin Boardmans' hugely successful treatise, *The Higher Christian Life*, published in 1860 at the height of the Awakening. He joined with Canon Harford Battersby (active in the Carlisle Awakening) to begin the conventions that gained a unique leadership position in the Christian world.

A majority of its leaders were either evangelists or converts of the Revival. Henry Varley ministered there. D. L. Moody, Reuben Torrey, A. J. Gordon, A. B. Simpson, J. Wilbur Chapman, and Handley C. G. Moule all supported it or spoke there; Andrew Murray and F. B. Meyer became its public voice. In Britain, Arminians and Calvinists got on well together over Boardman's writings, discussing differences "fraternally." But in the United States, "holiness" churches splintered in debate and "heated defence" over opposition from church officials, fanaticism, and attacks on Holiness doctrine—a situation that sadly persisted for one hundred years.

D. L. Moody 1837-1899

As Finney dominated American frontier evangelism in the middle third of the 19th century, the stout, simple and sincerely affectionate shoe-salesman, D. L. Moody, did for the final third. He was the evangelist of the urban frontier, more than forty years after the initial awakening. He ministered to the industrial city's work force until 1904 and the outbreak of World War I. Moody's mother was widowed when he was only four years old. She was left bankrupt, their creditors taking everything, even their firewood. She remained a widow for fifty-four years but kept all her nine children despite dire warnings that they would end up "in jail or with a rope around their necks." Her one motto was "My trust is in God." Moody (led to the Lord by his own Sunday School teacher, Edward Kimball) began his own, Sunday School with street kids neglected and rejected by the church. This school, started in 1858 in a vacant saloon, became the largest in Chicago, and eventually a church. In 1860 he gave up his shoe business (five thousand dollars a year) to "live by faith" (one hundred fifty dollars for the first year!).

Moody's "Second Blessing"

In 1864, with his own building on Illinois St., he was elected the Chicago President of the YMCA. There he met two little old ladies, Mrs. Sarah Cooke and Mrs. Hawxhurst, who joyfully interceded for his spiritual lack: "You are good, but you haven't got it. . . . We have been praying for you . . . You need power!" "I need power!" said Moody. "Why I thought I had power! . . . They poured out their hearts that I might receive the anointing of the Holy Ghost. There came a great hunger in my soul. I knew not what it was. I began to cry as never before. The hunger increased. I really felt that I did not want to live any longer if I could not have this power for service" (V. Raymond Edman, *They Found the Secret*, p. 83).

A Tale of Two Fires–Chicago and the Spirit

In 1871 (a night he did not finish with an invitation) a cow in a barn kicked over a lantern and a two hundred million dollar tragedy struck. The Great Fire of Chicago burned fifty churches to ashes, laid waste a third of the city, killed nearly two hundred people and left between seventeen thousand and eighteen thousand homeless. Fire also destroyed the new YMCA, Farwell Hall, built at the cost of two hundred thousand dollars three years before. Heart sick, Moody set out to try to raise funds for the homeless. While visiting New York in 1871 for this, and "crying all the time God would fill me with His Spirit" he had "such an experience of His love that I had to ask

Him to stay His hand" (Edman, *They Found The Secret*, p. 83).

This baptism of power moved Moody beyond his role as an untiring evangelist. He became a man who time and time again saw revival in his passion for souls. He began powerful evangelistic meetings with the musician Ira D. Sankey, whom he had met the year before. "The sermons were not different; I did not present any new truths; and yet hundreds were converted. I would not now be placed back where I was before that blessed experience if you should give me all the world!" (Edman, *Deeper Experiences of Famous Christians*, pp. 83-84).

From that time on, he asked God to help him win at least one soul a day. He never missed. Moody once witnessed to a woman. Her husband was annoyed. "Why didn't you tell him to mind his own business?" he snarled. "If you had seen the look on his face and the way he talked," she said, "you would have known it was his business." Moody's whole life was marked by soul-winning. "Are you a Christian?" he asked one man. "Mind your own business!" the man retorted. "It *is* my business." "Then," said the man, "you must be D. L. Moody."

Next year, the evangelist visited Britain again and was startled to hear the Australian Henry Varley say, "Moody, the world has yet to see what God will do with a man fully consecrated to him" (J. C. Pollock, *Moody*, p. 99). He returned home with a dream in his soul. He thought: "He didn't say a gifted man, a handsome man, a talented man, an educated man. He just said a man. And by the grace of God I will be that man!" Moody went back to Chicago for Sankey, and in June 1873, both families returned to Liverpool to "win ten thousand souls" by invitation of the Anglican clergyman William Pennefather. When they arrived Pennefather was dead. They began anyway. Crowds gradually increased until by Edinburgh they not only had the peoples' enthusiastic approval, but "after careful study, the ministers unreserved backing."

He introduced the noonday prayer meeting of the 1857 Revival again; evening meetings were jammed, crowding the largest auditoriums. They preached in Dundee, Glasgow (thousands were converted); Belfast in the fall of 1874 (again, several thousand converted); and then in Manchester, Sheffield, and Birmingham, each with growing success. Finally, they preached in London, climaxing with twenty thousand people nightly in the Agricultural Hall at Islington. William Taylor of California continued these meetings, while Moody moved on to preach to the poor in Bow by day and the rich in the Haymarket Opera House each evening. These meeting lasted twenty weeks and attracted two million five hundred thousand people.

C. T. Studd and the "Cambridge Seven"

Out of Moody's 1882 Cambridge University meetings came wonderful results from what initially seemed a disaster. Moody said, "There never was a place I approached with greater anxiety. . . . Never having had the privilege of a University education, I was nervous about meeting University men" (Pollock, *Moody*, pp. 228-229).

Seventeen hundred students noisily crowded into a hall that first evening to hear the "hick" American evangelist who could somehow say "Jerusalem" in only two syllables and, funnier still, didn't know any different. They "drowned out seventy brave undergraduates who tried to join in the hymns with vulgar songs." They yelled, "Hear, Hear" to Vicar John Barton's opening prayer, shouting derisive "Encores!" to Sankey's solo, and greeted Moody's' one-syllable pronunciation of "Daniel" by "bringing down the house with cheering, jeering, clapping, and stamping" (Orr, *Campus Aflame*, p. 90).

Yet Moody bravely hung in there. Only a hundred came the next night, but one was Gerald Lander of Trinity college, who (so embarrassed by the "civilized" behavior of his colleagues the previous night) apologized to Moody. God touched Lander; he later became Bishop of Hong Kong. Over half of the audience responded to Moody's appeal that night. The next night a hundred or more waited behind for counsel. The final meeting drew eighteen hundred and launched a worldwide interdenominational movement. Handley Moule, kneeling beside Moody on the platform, heard him say, "My God, this is enough to live for" (Pollock, *Moody*, p. 239).

C. T. Studd was the toast of England, captain of its champion cricket team, its top sportsman, and inheritor of a small fortune. His brothers wrote to him about Moody's challenge, and out of this eventually came the "Cambridge Seven," all Moody's helpers and some of his converts, who toured universities and challenged students for missions. Studd both gave up his cricket and gave away his fortune in the form of large sums to Booth, Moody, and George Mueller's orphanages. His wife, not to be outdone by her husband's devotion, sold all their wedding presents. She loved him so much that Studd had to write her a little poem to say every day: "Jesus thou art more to me/ than Charlie Studd will ever be." Together with other "holy madmen," they launched out to redeem another generation of spiritual warriors from the ranks of the "Chocolate Soldiers." Studd took as his motto, "If Jesus Christ be God and died for me, no sacrifice I make can be too great for Him" (McDonald, *True Discipleship,* p. 60).

Student Missionary Movements

At the same time, students from twenty other universities in the U.S. banded together to form the Student Volunteer Movement, the forerunner of Inter-Varsity Christian Fellowship, the Student Christian Movement and the Student Mission Association. This vision of world missions was a key factor in breaking America's protective isolationism. In their first International Conference of 1891 in Cleveland, they had 352 schools and colleges represented; within a generation, they involved forty thousand students in seven hundred campuses. The list of young leaders that came out of the revival spirit on these campuses reads like a "Who's Who" of world missions: John R. Mott, E. Stanley Jones, Robert Wilder, Samuel Zwemer and Robert Speer. Nobody laughed when they spoke their watchword: "*The evangelization of the world in this generation*" (McKenna: *The Awakening That Must Come,"* p. 38).

What do we learn from this third great awakening in the U.S. and Britain? Surely this: true revival always changes the "moral climate of a community"; when God finds someone with the courage to pray, preach, and live a life before Him of holiness and compassion, He can literally change the face of a nation. Moody spoke to more people about Christ than any other man in history up to his time. What was needed was neither the recognition nor ordination of man; what really counted was the touch and the hand of God on ordinary people who were "wholly consecrated to Him."

Chapter Eight

Contributions of the Awakenings

Two awesome centuries of manifested power: the First and Second great Awakenings, up to and including the 1858 Revival were all escalating demonstrations of the greatness and glory of God at work in His people. While building on the strengths of the Reformation, the revivalists that followed corrected some of its weaknesses. They held Reform convictions of the absolute authenticity and inspiration of Scripture. They did not forget the great truths of justification by faith, the Lordship of Christ, and the sovereignty of God. They had learned also from their Puritan spiritual forbears a call to discipline and holiness in the true child of God. But these next-generation believers went a step further than the Reformers were able to go. They restored neglected facets of the Gospel we sorely need again today.

The Obligation of Man—Responsibility

This [is] the generation of them that seek him, that seek thy face, O Jacob. Selah (Ps. 24:6).

Now also when I am old and greyheaded, O God, forsake me not; until I have shewed thy strength unto [this] generation, [and] thy power to every one [that] is to come (Ps. 71:18).

If my people, which are called by my name, shall humble themselves, and pray, and seek my face, and turn from their wicked ways; then will I hear from heaven, and will forgive their sin, and will heal their land (2 Chron. 7:14).

And if it seem evil unto you to serve the LORD, choose you this day whom ye will serve; . . . but as for me and my house, we will serve the LORD (Josh. 24:15).

Who shall ascend into the hill of the LORD? or who shall stand in his holy place? He that hath clean hands, and a pure heart; who hath not lifted up his soul unto vanity, nor sworn deceitfully. He shall receive the blessing from the LORD, and righteousness from the God of his salvation (Ps. 24:3-5).

And thou, Solomon my son, know thou the God of thy father, and serve him with a perfect heart and with a willing mind: for the LORD searcheth all hearts, and understandeth all the imaginations of the thoughts: if thou seek him, he will be found of thee; but if thou forsake him, he will cast thee off for ever (1 Chron. 28:9).

For the eyes of the LORD run to and fro throughout the whole earth, to shew himself strong in the behalf of [them] whose heart [is] perfect toward him (2 Chron. 16:9a).

Blessed [are] they that keep his testimonies, [and that] seek him with the whole heart (Ps. 119:2).

Seek ye the LORD while he may be found, call ye upon him while he is near (Isa. 55:6).

That they should seek the Lord, if haply they might feel after him, and find him, though he be not far from every one of us (Acts 17:27).

But without faith [it is] impossible to please [him]: for he that cometh to God must believe that he is, and [that] he is a rewarder of them that diligently seek him (Heb. 11:6).

If the Son therefore shall make you free, ye shall be free indeed (John 8:36).

But now being made free from sin, and become servants to God, ye have your fruit unto holiness, and the end everlasting life (Rom. 6:22).

For the law of the Spirit of life in Christ Jesus hath made me free from the law of sin and death (Rom. 8:2).

Stand fast therefore in the liberty wherewith Christ hath made us free, and be not entangled again with the yoke of bondage (Gal. 5:1).

Now the Lord is that Spirit: and where the Spirit of the Lord [is], there [is] liberty (2 Cor. 3:17).

Early Reform zeal to stress God's ultimate Lordship and absolute power sometimes failed to provide a sturdy base for our own mere human responsibility and obligation. Each generation inherits this creative tension between form and freedom, structure and flexibility, divine rulership and human response. It may err towards either legalism or antinomianism (a belief that the faith necessary for salvation does not involve obedience to moral law), a bullying moralism, or an easy-going carnality. To say "everything is God" may create just as big a problem as believing "everything is man." Somewhere along the way, the Gospel stress of the early Church and the Fathers of the first three centuries was forgotten; man's ability to respond freely to God's dealings got lost, at first theoretically and later practically. Forster and Marsden of Cambridge, in their definitive analysis of this problem, note:

> The doctrine of "free will" seems to have been universally accepted in the early Church. Not a single church figure in the first three hundred years rejected it, and most of them stated it clearly in works still extant. . . . We find it taught by the leaders of all the main theological schools. The only ones to reject it were heretics like the Gnostics, Marcion, Valentinus, Manes (and the Manichees), etc. In fact, the early fathers often state their belief on 'free-will' in works attacking heretics. They then go on to summarize the main points of this consensus:
>
> 1. Rejection of free will is the view of heretics.
>
> 2. Freewill is a gift given to man by God—for nothing can ultimately be independent of God, and;

3. Man has free will because he is made in God's image and God has free will. (Forster and Marsden, *God's Strategy in Human History*, p. 244)

It should be noted here that this stress on human freedom was not absolutely unbounded; man is only free so far. He was not free to save himself or to earn some kind of favor with God by good works outside of surrender to Christ. The early church did not believe that man without God's help could do God's work, nor that His grace was given as we deserved.

But neither did they believe that faith itself was an "irresistible gift," or that human beings were not really free or able to reject or respond to God's Spirit. Some of the best of the early Reformers, anxious to guard the Church from a Pelagian works-righteousness and humanism, began instead to adapt a picture of God and a view of His rulership perilously close to fatalism. We can trace the genesis of this error historically to the fourth century and some of the philosophical speculations of Augustine.

A Misguided View of God

Some of the best of the early Reformers began to believe not only that God allowed evil in the world but taught that He willed it, that all that happened was the result of God's express design and purpose, that all acts in the universe could be ultimately traced to God's decree.

Now, in the kindly light of a developing Church's understanding in history, we can thank God for the good they accomplished, without considering them or their teachings infallible. We must avoid one major consequence of this early extreme view: its practical stress on force rather than persuasion. Some came to believe that if the only will in the universe were God's will, no creature could resist that coercive will. If all men were the way they were by the decree of God, then the elect of God (themselves changed without choice), were perfectly justified in using force on a human level to accomplish God's will.

This explains, while it does not excuse, the violent, unjustifiable words and deeds of some of the early Reformers. They were, after all, only trying to be consistent with their theology.

But God is merciful. He raised up other generations that moved the Church towards a more Christ-like understanding.

Different Schools of Thought

All of the revivalists of the First and Second Awakenings, whether Calvinist or Arminian, believed and strongly practiced human responsibility. Some, like Whitefield, fearlessly preached Augustine's view of Divine election as selection, trusting that those that responded were the elect, and those that did not were not. But they did not let it hinder them from stressing "Ye must be born again!"

Others, like the careful and scholarly Wesley, were theologically opposite. Also in the highways and byways with the same Gospel, they were convinced instead that Christ died for all men and that "whosoever will may come." Neither side in revivals became locked into the kind of fatalism one church board of another time adopted, responding to a young shoemaker's offer to go overseas as a missionary with "Sit down, young man! When God wants to evangelize the heathen he will do it without your help."

William Carey did not "sit down." He went to India and became the father of modern missions. And if we learn anything from the first two Awakenings, it is this: the Church has a real and significant role in the purposes of God. As Francis Schaeffer put it, each choice significantly affects history. What you do in response to God can change your world forever. "If any man will do His will, he shall know . . ." said the Lord Jesus (John 7:17). And "to as many as believed on Him, to them gave He the power to become the sons of God, even to them that believe on His name" (John 1:12).

Holiness unto the Lord—Purity

Thou shalt be perfect with the LORD thy God (Deut. 18:13).

For the law made nothing perfect, but the bringing in of a better hope [did]; by the which we draw nigh unto God (Heb. 7:19).

And thou, Solomon my son, know thou the God of thy father, and serve him with a perfect heart and with a willing mind: for the LORD searcheth all hearts, and understandeth all the imaginations of the thoughts: if thou seek him, he will be found of thee; but if thou forsake him, he will cast thee off for ever (1 Chron. 28:9).

Thy people [shall be] willing in the day of thy power, in the beauties of holiness from the womb of the morning: thou hast the dew of thy youth (Ps. 110:3).

And an highway shall be there, and a way, and it shall be called The way of holiness; the unclean shall not pass over it; but it [shall be] for those: the wayfaring men, though fools, shall not err [therein] (Isa. 35:8).

But now being made free from sin, and become servants to God, ye have your fruit unto holiness, and the end everlasting life (Rom. 6:22).

Having therefore these promises, dearly beloved, let us cleanse ourselves from all filthiness of the flesh and spirit, perfecting holiness in the fear of God (2 Cor. 7:1).

To the end he may stablish your hearts unblameable in holiness before God, even our Father, at the coming of our Lord Jesus Christ with all his saints (1 Thess. 3:13).

Follow peace with all [men], and holiness, without which no man shall see the Lord (Heb. 12:14).

Be ye therefore perfect, even as your Father which is in heaven is perfect (Matt. 5:48).

But the God of all grace, who hath called us unto his eternal glory by Christ Jesus, after that ye have suffered a while, make you perfect, establish, strengthen, settle [you] (1 Pet. 5:10).

. . . make you perfect in every good work to do his will, working in you that which is wellpleasing in his sight, through Jesus Christ; to whom [be] glory for ever and ever. Amen (Heb. 13:21).

The second great lesson restored to the church in these awakenings was a more practical realization of the churches understanding of sanctification. It was the major thrust of both Wesley and Finney, their chief concern next only to the glory of God and the salvation of souls. The "strangely warmed" heart Wesley embraced in Aldersgate was translated into fire by the 1 January 1739, Fetter Lane meeting, where he and his original band of Methodists called on God for power to live lives of holiness and effective service.

The Key to Power

> Mr. Hall, Kinchin, Ingham, Whitefield, Hutchins, and my brother Charles were present . . . with about sixty of our brethren. About three in the morning, as we were continuing instant in prayer, *the power of God came mightily upon us, inasmuch that many cried out for exceeding joy and many fell to the ground.* As soon as we were recovered a little from that awe and amazement at the presence of His majesty, we broke out with one voice, "We praise Thee, Oh God, we acknowledge Thee to be the Lord" (*Journals of John Wesley*, Vol. II, p. 125). It was after this that Wesley began to see much fruit. For him the "three pillars of the church" were repentance, faith, and holiness.

Charles Finney not only met Christ, he had his "mighty baptism in the Holy Spirit" the same day, an experience he later related as the key to leading an effective and dynamic life of faith. Timothy Smith, in his excellent introduction to Finney's *Oberlin Papers,* comments:

"Like John Wesley, Finney drew deeply upon Moses and the prophets but re-inforced that source by appeal to the long tradition of Puritan or covenant theology. Moreover his starting point was not Moravian pietism, but . . . the law of disinterested benevolence–what Wesley called perfect love" (Smith, *The Promise of the Spirit*, p. 19). Early, in having to deal with what he saw as terrible apathy, fatalism, and irresponsibility in the Church, Finney laid such a stress on human responsibility and freedom "as to allow the charge that he ignored the role of God's grace" (Smith, *The Promise of the Spirit*, p. 19).

Later, however, in a way that was to profoundly affect both America and England, he began to preach that such grace, in the baptism of the Holy Spirit, was the key to the sanctification of both society and individuals. Christians could "partake of the divine nature–the moral attributes or perfections of God" by the Spirit through the promises of Scripture; an inward holiness wrought by the Spirit of God, "the substance and spirit of the law written in the heart by the Holy Ghost" (Smith, *The Promise of the Spirit*, pp. 18, 22).

The Work of the Kingdom—Compassion

And this gospel of the kingdom shall be preached in all the world for a witness unto all nations; and then shall the end come (Matt. 24:14).

But ye shall receive power, after that the Holy Ghost is come upon you: and ye shall be witnesses unto me both in Jerusalem, and in all Judea, and in Samaria, and unto the uttermost part of the earth (Acts 1:8).

The Spirit of the Lord [is] upon me, because he hath anointed me to preach the gospel to the poor; he hath sent me to heal the brokenhearted, to preach deliverance to the captives, and recovering of sight to the blind, to set at liberty them that are bruised (Luke 4:18, Isa. 61:1).

But whoso hath this world's good, and seeth his brother have need, and shutteth up his bowels [of compassion] from him, how dwelleth the love of God in him? (1 John 3:17).

But truly I am full of power by the spirit of the LORD, and of judgment, and of might, to declare unto Jacob his transgression, and to Israel his sin (Mic. 3:8).

Then he answered and spake unto me, saying, This [is] the word of the LORD unto Zerubbabel, saying, Not by might, nor by power, but by my spirit, saith the LORD of hosts (Zech. 4:6).

And he shall go before him in the spirit and power of Elias, to turn the hearts of the fathers to the children, and the disobedient to the wisdom of the just; to make ready a people prepared for the Lord (Luke 1:17).

Another important link that had major consequences for the nations was the link between a genuine Christian life and the reformation of the world. Not until Moody's day did revivalists begin to give up on society. (The *Scofield Reference Bible* popularized an interpretation of prophecy that gave birth to an unfortunate "save-all-you-can-but-you-can't-stop-a-sinking-ship" mentality.) On the contrary, all the early reformers and revivalists were united in their belief that the Lord held Divine right to the deeds of society and all its disciplines, and it was God's will to both bring back such fallen structures under His dominion and to re-establish Christ's Lordship in every area of life.

Spiritual Backbone

It is a simple fact that John Wesley's Methodists did more to save England from what could have been the same bloodbath as the French Revolution than any other single factor of that century. Even earlier, though sometimes upheld in a more legal, Old Covenant way, this was the consistent theme of the Puritans and the early Reformers, as well as those who followed them, exploring the promises of the New Covenant. This was no ostrich head-in-the-sand approach to problems. They never believed "living in a hole would make you holy." Again referring to Charles Finney's contribution, Timothy Smith says:

> Never a Pelagian, I think, Finney had found a way to reclaim the doctrine of God's sovereignty without becoming a Calvinist either. He had discovered, he believed in Scripture, a Pentecostal version of covenant theology that opened the way to an evangelical unity that Wesley and Whitefield sought but were never able to accomplish. Rooting the experience of the Baptism of the Holy Spirit in the Old Testament covenant of holiness also insulated it against the anti-intellectual and mystical corruptions of it that Wesley feared and that, alas, forgetting Finney, twentieth-century Pentecostals seem often to have embraced. (Smith, *The Promise of the Spirit*, pp. 22-23)

Concern for Social Justice

Until this last century, no Christian thought his task was to just "take care of your own life and run up your bills for the Anti-Christ." The revivalists of the "Benevolent Empire" linked conversion and spiritual growth directly to the alteration of society. They had a grand and glorious vision of a mighty revival, perhaps spreading throughout the world in their day to prepare mankind for the Second Coming of Christ, who would return and set up His millennial kingdom. Smith sums up this key contribution best seen in the social dynamic loosed on society in the 1858 Revival as follows:

> When Finney discovered, apparently out of his own study of the English Bible, the logical and historical

> links between covenant and promise in the Old Testament and Jesus' covenant promise in the New of His continuing presence through the sanctifying Comforter, the Holy Spirit, the circle was complete. He then proclaimed, as Wesley himself had only rarely declared, that the entire sanctification of the believers moral will was achieved through the baptism of the Holy Spirit. That proclamation did not reduce but in fact radicalized Christian concerns for social justice. For it offered to Calvinist, Pietist and Arminian alike a way of repossessing the doctrine of the sovereignty of God over individuals as well as over the structures of society. (Smith, *The Promise of the Spirit*, p. 19)

Finney and his friends and brothers of both Awakenings attempted to prepare the world for Jesus to live in again. They did not live to see it. But their vision of society had much better immediate and long-term consequences than the dominant ones of our past few decades. As Lovelace points out, from Moody's time on, prophesying our inability by divine decree to redeem society may have helped us lose it.

The last half of the nineteenth century was the last time Christians unified personal and social holiness. After that evangelicals avoided social reform, and liberals with social vision abandoned evangelism. The split between personal redemption and social gospel, between national and international evangelism, created a chasm that we still need to breach in the twentieth century.

Still More to Come

Again, we can find flaws in these men and women of God. Attempting to correct religious fatalism, some failed to stress God's grace enough; zealous for holiness, others overdefined devotion, and did not give young converts enough time to work out deep-seated battles with the old life. Though much more evangelistic, compassionate, and certainly more Christlike in practical character than some of the earlier saints, they did not live long enough to see a flowering of some of the things they had just begun to experience in their lives: power to be free, power to live clean, and power to affect the world. In turn they saw them all as the pillar of fire moved on. And God is not finished. In the accelerating events of this century, He has restored still further facets of His awesome nature, supernatural power allowing Him due worship in spirit and truth, and His demonstrated power to heal a physically as well as morally sick world. Thus, we come to the next great point in history, one that begins at the dawn of the twentieth century. It leads to the final groundwork of what some believe may be completed in your time, His last and greatest demonstration of His glory.

Charles Parham and the Topeka Connection

"Find out what are the Bible evidences of the Baptism of the Holy Ghost." This was the assignment Charles Fox Parham (1873-1929) set to the young students of his Bible College of Bethel late in 1899. Yet this innocent directive planted the roots of what has now become the most powerful movement in modern missions.

Completing this study, his students concluded the single common evidence of this power was the one miracle gift unique to the New Testament–the gift of "other tongues." And some sincerely set themselves to seek God for it. At precisely the dawn of the twentieth century–1 January 1901–in the early hours of the new century, the Holy Spirit fell on one of the praying young women of the Topeka Kansas Bible school, Agnes Ozman.

The next few years were chaotic for Parham and his followers, conducting "whirlwind revivals in the South and Middle West" with some success. Five hundred ministers were won to the new cause in Zion, Illinois, and an estimated twenty-five thousand followers by 1906 (Synan: *And the Spirit Said Grow,* p. 33). But "despite momentary enthusiasm and some lively press coverage," says Nelson, Parham "struggled with a seriously faltering ministry until by winter of 1904-1905 his health had broken and he left for Houston to rest and recover with friends. As his strength improved, he began preaching again on Easter Sunday and opened a short-term Bible school in December to train evangelists. Part of the curriculum was, of course, the spiritual gifts Parham believed God was restoring to the Church.

William J. Seymour—God's Forgotten Giant

To this school came the thirty-six-year-old William J. Seymour (1870-1922), a black, one-eyed preacher who was then an already widely traveled evangelist based in Houston. Parham liked him and allowed him to attend his segregated school, letting him sit outside the classroom door (purposely left ajar). The two men enjoyed a brief but friendly and productive association. In January 1906 Seymour left for Los Angeles to pastor a mission congregation, still without receiving the baptism he was seeking. Only a week after arriving, his ministry was rejected by congregational lay leaders and founders who disapproved of his enthusiastic Pentecostal emphasis.

Seymour was left without a mission, without acceptance, and without approval, a deformed, middle-aged black man cut off from both his culture and his calling, and (despite his desire for God) about as rejected as a man could be.

Undaunted, Seymour formed a (predominantly black) home prayer group. They met regularly until Easter of that year. And God, the God who never forgets injustice and delights in mercy, saw fit, in one divine moment, to single out for blessing one man who represented best the beaten end-product of three hundred years of cruel slavery. During three climactic days of Holy Week (April 9-12), amid a ten-day fast, Seymour and the others found what they were seeking: "more of God—glossolalia and other charismatic phenomenon burst forth with unusual intensity and evident sincerity."

Azusa Street—The "Blessed Miracle"

It had once been a church. It was so run-down and ramshackle it had been used as a livery stable. It had dirt floors and was in the middle of the black Ghetto of Los Angeles; but it could hold over nine hundred people, and it only cost eight dollars a month to rent They needed it for what happened. They called the street of this old barn-like building "Azusa." It became a legendary site of divine visitation. The name itself derived from one of those gracious "coincidences" that mark God's mercy. It derives from a lovely tale about a Native American girl, Coma Lee, who had a prayer healing ministry. When her prayers restored an ailing Shoshone chief, he renamed her "Azusa"–Shoshone for "Blessed Miracle."

It is highly significant that the outpouring of the Holy Spirit that was to carry the message of world evangelism and much of modern missions around the world in our time took place initially in cosmopolitan Los Angeles ("City of the Angels" or the "Messenger City"). Douglas J. Nelson has contributed deeply significant insight to the culture-transcending roots of much in modern missions. In his Ph.D. thesis, *The Black Face of Church Renewal: the Meaning of a Charismatic Explosion*, he shows Azusa Street's key role in the revival history of multitudes of varied racial and ethnic groups.

At one communion and foot-washing service lasting till dawn, twenty nationalities participated. Los Angeles citizens were a microcosm of the unreached world–African and Native Americans, Latins and Asians. Services continued morning afternoon and night (sometimes without a break until the next day), seven days a week, for three and a half years! All kinds of people came (some, at first, to scoff), and many stayed to pray. Within a week even a prominent Jewish Rabbi announced his full support. Astounding healings and dramatic conversions were announced.

Of course, when the news of this reached Parham, he came down to Azusa to see his spiritual disciple, Seymour. In his initial visit, Parham was horrified at what he saw. Seymour radically disagreed with his previous mentor on two issues, mixing the races and happily allowing the sometimes strange manifestations of the Azusa meeting.

Some fell on the ground in apparent trances. One report described Azusa as sometimes resembling "a forest of fallen trees." Parham (like many evangelicals of his time), still segregated his Houston congregation and (because of the controversy he had already endured in Topeka) was deeply sensitive to the charge of Pentecostals being considered "holy rollers." He urged Seymour to comply to popular evangelical cultural expectation.

But Seymour refused. He felt that the Baptism of the Holy Spirit was "an essential and crucial element not only of Azusa but of true Christianity itself"; there needed to be a "great coming together in the church as at Pentecost, beyond the barriers of race, color, gender, nation, class or status, to demonstrate that God is no respecter of persons and that all believers are truly one in Christ."

Nelson notes that Seymour found in the Pentecostal experience the following:

> New spirituality not only expressed in glossolalia but, of even more significance, the overcoming of color lines and other lesser barriers. Glossolalia was considered integral but not primarily as the mark of individual spiritual attainment. Rather it was seen as a kind of energy to be released and directed to break the barriers blocking full Christian fellowship in the new spiritual community, thereby providing the most tremendous power of all, that of Pentecostal togetherness. The "Third Race," or human race beyond Jew or Gentile that early Christians considered themselves to be, remains to be recovered by modern Christianity. "The explosive spread of Seymour's Azusa achievement may be understood as the power of a spirituality allowed to operate without restriction from non-Christian limitations derived from race, color, gender, nation, class or status. The breathtaking outreach from Azusa corresponded to the original Pentecostal event it was emulating.
>
> Glossolalia proved sensational, but the truly revolutionary thrust from Azusa depended on the *overcoming of the color line* which opened the possibility of turning a racist world upside down. Azusa is a key not only for church renewal but also for social transformation, simply by its own witness to the surrounding culture. *The deepest truth of Azusa lay not in the simple fact that diverse people came together but in how they came together. The whites came with love and true repentance for the way they felt about blacks and had treated them. The blacks came with love and genuine*

> *forgiveness. Orientals, Hispanics, Native Americans and others participated similarly.* It was a revival of brokenness and bridge-building. Arthur Osterberg, who loved Azusa from start to finish, said, "The Azusa Revival began where every revival should rightly begin, in repentant tears. It began in tears, it lived in tears and when the tears ended, the Azusa Revival ended." (Nelson: *PH.D. Thesis,* U. Birmingham, 1981, pp. 66-67 n.10)

At the height of the revival, Seymour said, "We are on the verge of the greatest miracle the world has ever seen." His newspaper appeared in September, with an initial printing of five thousand copies followed by later editions growing to fifty thousand copies. Papers passed from hand to hand until they fell apart. By 1908, only two years later, the surging movement had taken root in over fifty nations. Though activities there peaked in 1909, by 1912 it was publishing literature in thirty-five languages from Iceland to Tasmania and thought to have penetrated every U.S. town of more than three thousand. Visitors arrived daily from as far afield as China. The Azusa St. Mission became a pilgrimage likened by its admirers to the "humble stable of old in Bethlehem" (Paul Elbert, Ed.; *Faces of Renewal,* pp. 172-191).

Seymour did not live to see the completion of his dream, but he fully expected the renewal to accomplish it. News of the renewal spread rapidly across the U.S. and internationally. Within weeks an ever-growing stream of ardent missionaries began leaving for virtually all points of the compass at home and every major continent abroad. Some were seasoned missionaries others simply domestic servants or washer-women. The fact remains that the Pentecostal-Charismatic renewal movement began among black people under the leadership of a black man and at a time when racial tension between poor whites and poor blacks was the greatest in America's history. Furthermore, Seymour attracted, welcomed, inspired, managed, and sent forth all kinds and races of people successfully for over three years of decisive beginnings. Even today the effects of that miraculous outpouring go on.

David Barrett's 1985 statistics showed that "The Pentecostal-Charismatic renewal . . . after a historically brief eighty-five years of growth, totals well over 114 million adult persons worldwide, including fifty-nine million practising members of Pentecostal denominations, seventeen million active in older more traditional churches, and over thirty-eight million others non-affiliated" (*AD 2000 Global Monitor,* March 1991 #5, p. 3). A *Christianity Today* Gallup Poll showed 19 percent of all adults (twenty-nine million persons eighteen and older in the US alone) identified with this renewal in 1980.

But recent growth in many places of the world is still more startling, 157 percent world-wide between 1975 and 1985. Decadal growth in many nations is the highest of the churches in the country; in Canada, 60 percent, Ghana 100 percent, Japan 107 percent, Sri Lanka 138 percent, New Zealand 150 percent, United States 173 percent, Australia 385 percent, Singapore 635 percent and Korea 742 percent! Nineteen hundred ninty-two world growth is some 21 million a year.

A 1990 MARC survey of British churches showed that although nation-wide some three hundred young people drop out of church every week, third-wave works like those of *Icthus Fellowship* are growing eight times faster than the drop-out rate of other churches. It is real evangelism, not church transfer growth.

In 1990, twenty-five thousand such Christians and leaders of over fifty Pentecostal ministries and denominations met in the Indianapolis Hoosier Dome with the theme "Evangelize The World Now!" It was the largest such gathering in Christian history.

Numbers in 1992, according to the Lausanne Statistical Task Force, stood at over 410 million, 626 thousand worldwide. This included over 204,500,000 denominational Pentecostals; 57,500,000 mainline and independent Charismatics, 44,600,000 Protestant or Anglican Charismatics; 80,600,000 Catholic Charismatics; 37,500,000 mainline "third-wavers," and some 58 million Chinese Pentecostals, an astonishing 24.2 percent of the total Christian population of the world.

The fourth largest Protestant U.S. denomination in 1990 was the Church of God in Christ, a predominantly black Pentecostal church with almost 4 million members in eight thousand congregations. The Assemblies of God in 1990 listed some 20 million adherents worldwide. No wonder C. Peter

Wagner comments, "In all of history, no other non-political, non-militaristic, voluntary human movement has grown as rapidly as the Pentecostal-Charismatic movement in the last twenty-five years" (Synan, *And the Spirit Said Grow*, from the Foreword).

What happened in Azusa released the most significant international healing force of our century. And between the initial outpouring in Topeka and the visitation at Azusa came the other astonishing movement of the Holy Spirit in Europe that we now know as the 1904 Welsh Revival.

The New Century Awakening (1904-1912)

Without a doubt, one of the most awesome movements of the Holy Spirit was the international outpouring at the turn of this past century. Only in the past few decades have scholars been able to accurately assess just how widespread and powerful this was. Until recently it was the greatest worldwide manifestation of God in history. J. Edwin Orr, one of the first to research and realize the immense extent of this harvest, notes that "the first manifestation of phenomenal revival occurred simultaneously among Boer prisoners of war in places ten thousand miles apart as far away as Bermuda and Ceylon. Missionaries and national believers in obscure places in India, the Far East, Africa, and Latin America seemed moved at the same time to pray." Another significant fact for our day, as true today in the 1990s of the West as it was in the 1890s, is that most of them had "never seen or heard of it happening in missionfields, and few had witnessed it at home. Their experience was limited to reading of past revivals" (J. Edwin Orr, *Evangelical Awakenings* p. 41).

Revival in the Far East

This prisoner-of-war work was marked by "extraordinary praying, faithful preaching, conviction of sin, confession, and repentance, with lasting conversions and hundreds of enlistments for missions," and spread to an economically depressed South Africa. At nearly the same time, awakening began in Japan with "unusual prayer, intensive evangelism, and such an awakening of Japan's urban masses to the claims of Christ" that "Japanese churches almost doubled within the decade."

Four years later, when Japan was involved in momentous war with Russia, it would have been impossible.

Nor was it confined to Europe, Africa, and Asia. R. A. Torrey and Alexander saw the most fruitful meetings ever held in Australia and New Zealand. These South Pacific awakenings launched their worldwide evangelistic campaigns. A "Mission of Peace" by the Salvation Army convert evangelist, Gypsy Smith, to war-sick South Africa touched off an awakening in the population. Worldwide prayer meetings intensified (Orr, *Evangelical Awakenings,* p. 114).

The Welsh Revival

But the best-known and farthest-felt happening of the New Century decade was undoubtably the Welsh Revival.

> With less than a score of intercessors when it burst, the churches of Whales were crowded for more than two years; one hundred thousand outsiders were converted, drunkenness cut in half, and many taverns driven into bankruptcy. Crimes were so diminished that judges were presented with white gloves signifying there were no cases of murder, assault, rape, robbery, or the like to consider. The police became "unemployed" in many districts. (Orr, *Evangelical Awakenings,* p. 114) Coal mines stopped work with transport difficulties. The pit ponies didn't understand commands anymore. They couldn't recognize their owners' redeemed language!

Orr comments that the World War I killed a high proportion of men who had been converted or revived and left a dearth of men in the churches. Coal mines were then hit by unemployment, which continued into the Depression of the 1930s. But at least 80 percent of the converts were still true after five years, and those converts not killed in World War I lasted until well into the 1930s. But since the revival took Scripture knowledge for granted, the next generation was not ready for a later onslaught of anti-evangelicalism that captured a generation of otherwise disillusioned Welshmen for Marxism (Orr, *Evangelical Awakenings,* p. 115): "There arose another generation after them, that knew not the Lord" (Judg. 2:10).

New Converts

Yet this outcropping of glory affected all nations.

> Thirty English bishops declared for the revival after one of their number, deeply moved, told of confirming 950 new converts in a country parish church. Other Protestant churches, equal in membership there, gained around three hundred thousand converts, bringing renewed obedience to the four great social commandments: reducing crime, and promoting honesty, truthfulness, and chastity (Orr, *Evangelical Awakenings in Southern Asia*, p. 106).

The after-effects of the Welsh revival swept Ireland and Scotland; under Albert Lunde, a great revival in Norway affected Sweden, Finland, and Denmark. Lutherans there called it "the greatest movement of the Spirit since the Vikings were evangelized." It broke out in Germany, France, and other countries of Europe, marked by prayer and confession. And though not really much noticed until recently, it reached out (just as Evan Roberts had predicted) and affected the world.

International Awakenings

India in 1905-1906 saw awakening in every province, with meetings in many places five to ten hours long. And the Christian population jumped by 70 percent, sixteen times faster than the Hindu population. In twenty years pupils in Christian schools in India doubled to 595,725; 90 percent of all nurses were Christian, mostly trained in mission hospitals. Amy Carmichael recorded some of the effects among the rescued *devadasis*, the little temple prostitutes she was ministering to in Dohnavur. On October 22, to quote one of the little girls, "Jesus came to Dohnavur." At the close of a morning service, she was obliged to stop, overwhelmed with the sudden realization of the inner force of things. It was impossible even to pray.

> It was so startling and *dreadful*—I can use no other word—that details escape me. Soon the whole upper half of the church was on its face on the floor, crying to God,

> each boy and girl, man and woman, oblivious of all others. The sound was like the sound of waves or strong wind in the trees. . . . the hurricane of prayer continued for over four hours. "They passed like four minutes." For the next two weeks, they gave themselves to the Word and prayer; counselling around the clock. Almost the whole compound got saved; it deeply affected the village. (Orr, *Evangelical Awakenings in Southern Asia*, p. 133)

In Burma, Southeast Asia, the same year the A.B.M.U. (American Baptist Missionary Union) baptized two thousand of the Karens (tribe people), a single church baptized 1,340 of the Shans in December alone. Don Richardson's *Eternity in Their Hearts* (a significant study of God's dealings with hidden peoples untouched by missionary movements), makes for some mind-blowing reading. It gives us some keys to the spiritual roots of this area's awakening.

Tribal Visitations

During the previous century, Adoniram Judson, the American Baptist missionary of 1817, had only one Buddhist convert in seven years of hard labor. Not surprisingly, he did not feel too effective in his missionary calling, and he gave himself more to Bible translation. Yet in his city an untouched people called the Karens passed his door each day, sometimes singing to one they called "Y'wa- the true God." One day Ko Thah-byu, a Karen ex-robber and murderer, came to Judson's house looking for work.

During Christian instruction by George and Sarah Boardman, Judson's helpers, he at first seemed spiritually dense, until they began to teach him about the Bible. Astonishingly, the Karen recognized it as the legendary "lost book" telling about his own people's unknown God, Y'wa, which he believed had arrived in Burma. Full of excitement and destiny, the Karen became a prophetic evangelist, and eventually entire Karen villages would respond to his ministry. By 1858 there were tens of thousands of Karen Christians, all missionary-minded. They went in turn to their neighbors, the Kachin, and within the next century some 250,000 Kachin were converted.

In the 1890s William Young saw the same thing happen again among the Lahu people, with tens of thousands converted. Finally, some disciples of Pu Chan, a local witch doctor of the head-hunting Wa, another tribal people, were led supernaturally to follow a pony on a two hundred-mile journey to find the "lost book of God." It stopped finally in a missionary compound in the city of Kengtung, where this same William Young was digging a well. "Hello," he said in Shan to the awed Wa disciples, staring down at this white-faced stranger. "May I help you?" When he held up his Bible and answered "Yes" in response to their trembling "Have you brought a book of God?," they fell at his feet, overcome with emotion, and immediately urged him to leave.

Instead Young, already with thousands of Lahu to teach, made a place for them to stay and train. The Youngs and their Karen converts, in addition to baptizing some sixty thousand Lahu, soon found themselves with another ten thousand baptized Wa converts, who in turn spread the gospel still further in eastern Burma and southwestern China.

Finally, across the border the Englishman James Outram Frazier of the China Inland Mission, having discovered the Lisu tribe, learned their language and crossed the border into Burma to see what he could learn about cross-cultural communication from the American missionaries. Instead he found there a Baptist outpost occupied by Karen missionaries, and they sent him a Karen helper who learned to speak Lisu. Similar traditions of a "white-faced helper" who would restore a long-lost "book of God" ushered in another awesome movement, bringing tens of thousands of Lisu Chinese into the kingdom (Richardson, *Eternity in Their Hearts*, pp. 74-85, 89-100).

Revival Comes to the Far East

All this opened the door to what happened in India later in the 1900s and to the recent revival among the Nagas today. Few Christians know that two entire states of predominantly Hindu India–Nagaland and Mizoram–boast a higher per capita ratio of baptized Christians than any other area of equal size anywhere in the world. Churches in Nagaland (1 million people) embrace 76 percent of the population. Mizoram counts 95 percent of their population as members.

The revival hit Korea in three waves—1903, 1905 and 1907—quadrupling the membership of the churches in a decade, creating the national church from almost nothing, and rolling on into the 1980s. It has produced in Seoul today three of the largest churches in the world.

Jonathan Goforths' ministry in Manchuria has been recorded, but the extent of the China Awakening between the Boxer Uprising and the 1911 Revolution has not been comprehended. Yet the number of Protestants doubled in a decade to a quarter million, twice the figure for the entire evangelical community. Missionaries pioneered secondary and higher education and laid the foundations of medical service.

In Indonesia the one hundred thousand Evangelicals in 1903 tripled in a decade to three hundred thousand. In subsequent movements of phenomenal power, one little island alone (Nias) won more than that, converting two thirds the population. Later, in a small town on the island of Timor, in 1965, four nights before an attempted Communist coup, God sovereignly began to pour out His Spirit.

The coup was averted, and in the subsequent anti-communist reaction, evangelistic teams went all over the islands with miracle ministries, healing the sick and raising the dead. In this Indonesian revival, water was reportedly turned to wine, food was multiplied, and men ate poison without harm and walked across a river thirty feet deep. The thirty thousand members of the churches in central Java recorded in 1961 jumped to more than one hundred thousand, almost doubling annually, and the Indonesia Bible Society found it impossible to keep up with the statistics.

The Wave Spreads

Latin America saw real inroads of revival in Brazil and Chile, preparing the ground for what took place during the last few decades. In 1952, praying with Demos Shakarian and Oral Roberts in California, Tommy Hicks saw a vision of South America as a vast field of golden grain and set out for Argentina in 1954. Substituting for T. L. Osborn, who had been originally invited there for evangelistic meetings with

President Peron's permission, Hicks began services on the 14th of April. Soon, six thousand people were at the services. The healing of a boy with a leg brace on the first night led to widespread publicity, and soon the meetings had to be moved to the larger Huracan stadium (seating one hundred thousand people). Then, incredibly, it rose to a quarter of a million. Some claimed aggregate attendances exceeded two million.

The stock of available Gospel literature in Latin America was all but exhausted. Over twenty-two thousand Bibles and twenty-six thousand New Testament were sold, and at least half-a-million decision cards were taken by the multitudes pouring through the stadium gates. The effect "broke the back of evangelical resistance"; Assembly Of God churches alone multiplied tenfold in ten years. Others ministering there later also saw greatly increased attendance. In 1957 Oswald Smith had a crusade in Buenos Aires supported by three hundred churches, with attendances between ten to twenty thousand and reaching an aggregate of two hundred thousand, with more than a thousand conversions. Peter Wagner approximates the resultant growth in Latin American evangelical Christians as fifty thousand in 1900; more than 1 million in 1930; two million in the 1940s; five million in the 1950s; ten million in the 1960s; twenty million in the 1970s.

Amazing Growth in Christian Population

The Edinborough World Missionary Conference recognized more progress made in all Africa in the first decade of the twentieth century than ever before. From 1903 to 1910, believers jumped from three hundred to five hundred thousand. The beginnings of African educational and medical services were due to its missionary impulse. But the full impact was not felt until the war years when in the next half-century phenomenal revival created an increase double that of the general population. Now, according to David Barrett's monumental *World Christian Encyclopedia*, some four thousand Africans are converted every day, three times that number growing up in Christian homes, with some African leaders aiming to see a majority of their nation converted.

The turn of the century revival was international and ecumenical. It touched all major nations and "involved all major churches—Anglican, Baptist, Bretheren, Congregational, Disciple, Lutheran, Methodist, Presbyterian, and Reformed, leaving (as in the days of the Puritans, Wesley, Finney and Moody), only the Roman Catholic and Greek Orthodox communities relatively untouched" (Orr, *Evangelical Awakenings,* p. 105).

There were charismatic phenomena—uncanny discernment, visions, and trances (but no glossolalia in Wales). Only in the aftermath of the India awakening (as in the converts of the Los Angeles revival at Asuza) were there outbreaks of the phenomena of "tongues" from which Pentecostalism spread widely.

Another Wave Rolls In

When news of the coming revival reached America, huge conferences of ministers met in New York, Chicago, and other cities to discuss what to do when it began in the U.S. They met just in time. The Methodists in Philadelphia soon had over six thousand new converts in trial membership. The ministers in Atlantic City claimed there were only fifty adults left unconverted in a population of sixty thousand! Churches in New York City took in hundreds on a single Sunday, one recording 286 new converts, of which 217 were adults, 134 men, and 60 the heads of families.

Miraculous Phenomena

The 1905 Awakening "rolled like a tidal wave through the South, packing churches for prayer and confession, adding hundreds to membership rolls. First Baptist of Paducah added a thousand in two months, and the old pastor died of overwork. In the Midwest churches were suddenly flooded by great crowds of seekers. Every store and factory closed in Burlington, Iowa, to let employees go to services of dedication and intercession. The mayor of Denver declared a day of prayer, and by 10:00 A.M. churches were filled, by 11:30 almost all stores, every school, and the Colorado legislature closed. Twelve thousand attended prayer meetings in downtown theatres and halls.

In the West great demonstrations marched through Los Angeles streets. United meetings pulled crowds of 180,000; the Grand Opera House was filled at midnight with winos and hookers seeking salvation. For three hours a day, business practically stopped in Portland, Oregon, with bank presidents and bootblacks all at prayer meetings while two hundred department stores closed by agreement from 11:00 to 2:00.

Orr records that church membership in seven major denominations jumped by 870,389 in 1906 alone; in five years it was 2 million and growing. This did not even include the Holiness, or Pentecostal converts, or those of younger denominations whose rate of increase was even greater. The Methodists (then the largest U.S. denomination) said the revival had "sparked the public conscience, overthrown corrupt officials, crossed party lines, and elected governors, senators, assemblymen, mayors and district attorneys of recognized honesty" (Orr, *Evangelical Awakenings,* p. 103).

The people of Philadelphia "threw the rascals out" and put in a dedicated mayor. "A wave of morality went over the country, producing a revival of righteousness. Corruption in state and civic government encountered a setback for a dozen years, and the country was committed in degree to civic and national integrity until new forces of corruption came back in the 1920s" (Orr, *Evangelical Awakenings,* p. 103).

Now let's take an in-depth look at eyewitness reports of the focus of this early Twentieth-Century awakening–the Welsh Revival under Evan Roberts.

Evan Roberts and the Welsh Revival

The slender, brown-haired young man working in a Welsh coal mine was a Christian. His family were good, solid, religious folk, steeped in Calvinist theology, proud of their purity of home life, and jealous of their moral stand. Photos show him as nothing special to look at: a boy with a plain, pallid face. He was not a brilliant student and certainly no orator. Only one thing marked his life–he was serious about God and serious about revival.

That message one night at church had done it: "Thomas was not with them when Jesus came." Ever since then he had set his heart on not missing God. "Remember to be faithful," the church elder had said. "What if the Spirit descended and you were absent?"

He had determined not to be. He was in chapel prayer on Monday, Sunday-School prayer on Tuesday, the Wednesday night service, the Band of Hope on Thursday, and Bible class on Friday. Through all weather and difficulties he came. He was determined to be there when revival came and didn't care about the cost or discipline. "I could sit up all night," he said, "to read or talk about revival."

And often he did. For thirteen months he had prayed for revival. He preached or prayed aloud and alone in his room, so fervently that his landlady thought him probably mad or possessed and turned him out. But that intensity and discipline worked iron in his soul. A minister later commented on the set of his heart: "He is true to the backbone and above all faithful to God and his conscience. He cannot be bought or bribed. His strength is his character, sanctified by communion with the invisible."

Seth Joshua's Visit

It wasn't a good month for meetings, and the few people that did come seemed spiritually hard. Seth Joshua was a sensitive and godly evangelist who had been saved through the Salvation Army. Every inch a man of God, he preached what David Matthews called "a strange, strong new note" that deeply touched one young man who came to listen. Joshua's campaign for Christ finally closed in disappointment. The people rarely responded, and nothing apparently happened. Joshua moved towns to Cardigan Bay, and the silent boy in his audience followed. If anything Cardigan Bay was even tougher. Almost at the end of another difficult meeting, Joshua prayed intensely, "*Bend us–bend us–bend us, O Lord!*"

Some think this sentence gave birth to the revival. It certainly became famous, and the young man who later led it said it often. But right then no one noticed. Shortly after he prayed this, a young girl (Maggie Evans) sprang to her feet in a terrible agony of the soul. The twenty-six-year-old Bible college student who had followed Joshua's messages night after night silently, and seemingly semi-consciously, rolled off his seat into the aisle. Silent, covered in perspiration, he lay there, apparently unable to move. One lady watching thought he would die on the spot.

Apparently he did. When the services finally ended, Evan Roberts came back to his Bible school a new man. Studies now seemed utterly impossible. Day and night without ceasing, he prayed, wept, and sighed for a great spiritual awakening for his nation.

"Go home," said the Holy Spirit to his heart. "Tell the young people of your church what has happened to you."

A Home Church Youth Revival

It began among the young. Mary, one of Evan's sisters, was sixteen. Syd Evans and Evan's brother Dan were twenty. The "Singing Sisters," (Priscilla Watkins, Mary Davies, Livinia Hooker, Annie Rees and Anne Davis) who later travelled with Roberts to minister, were all between eighteen and twenty-two. Deliberately, solemnly, Evan shared what was on his heart. They were words he felt impressed by God to give: "Not by might, nor by power, but by My Spirit saith the Lord." The hours flew by unnoticed. Passers-by wondered why the church lights were on so late. Something was happening in that youth meeting unlike any awakening that had happened before in Wales, something that was to shake the world.

Other Revivalists

Wales already knew about revival; God's previous instruments for these in 1859 were powerful, stirring preaching ministries like that of David Morgan. Even now in the nation there were men like Rhys Bevan Jones and Peter Price (with the best youth group in Dowlais). Price had hundreds of conversions in his church. England had Douglas Brown, and Scotland had Jack Troup and Duncan Campbell. But this was utterly different. Time and time again, in prayer and choked confession, the young man said what he had been challenged to do himself: "Obey the Holy Spirit; be filled with the Holy Spirit; do not grieve the Holy Spirit by disobedience."

A week later the sober, sedate Calvinist Congregation that gathered at Bryn Seian Church in Trecynon Aberdare had no clue what was about to happen that shocking morning. Instead of their usual minister, there were this young man and some equally young girls with him. Instead of announcing the customary hymn, one of the girls burst out in song, tears streaming down her cheeks. The whole congregation gasped. Before this impromptu solo finished, her friend joined in also. But the young minister in the pulpit stood utterly silent; and as the congregation watched, his body shook and tears coursed down his pale cheeks. A stillness fell on the people like the quiet before a storm. It only broke when one of the proudest members of the church fell on her knees in agonized prayer, confessing her sin. The meeting went on all day without a break. By night every church in the city was trying to get into the building. And so the Welsh Revival began.

Revival Fills the Newspapers

What is it like in such a divine awakening? Again, a rare volume written during the time gives us on-the-spot reports of what was happening as God moved across the land. Here are actual British and American newspaper accounts of this awesome phenomena, excerpted from *The Great Revival in Wales,* collected and published by Rev. S. B. Shaw in Chicago, 1905:

The *Methodist Recorder Report:*

> Wales is in the throes and ecstasies of the most remarkable religious revival it has ever known. It is nothing less than a "moral revolution." . . . Already, in five or six weeks, the fire has spread to six or seven counties and bids fair find its way . . . into every parish in Wales. . . . What has largely contributed to the rapidity of the movement is the widespread publicity given to it in the press—both secular and religious. Every day, for weeks past, the *South Wales Daily News* and the *Western Mail,* the two leading dailies of South Wales, have devoted three or four columns to reports of it.
>
> The converts already number many thousands. Mr. Evan Roberts calculates that in the mining valleys of South Wales alone there have been at least ten thousand conversions. And if we add to this the harvest gleaned in various other places, North and South, the number cannot be far short of twenty thousand.

The report in the *Ram's Horn* on "Evan Roberts Call From God."

> A wonderful revival is sweeping over Wales. The whole country, from the city to the colliery underground, is aflame with Gospel glory. Police courts are hardly necessary; public houses are being deserted, old debts are being paid to satisfy awakened consciences, and definite and unmistakable answers to prayer are being recorded.
>
> The leader in this great religious movement is a young man, twenty-six years of age, Evan Roberts. . . . He is no orator, is not widely read. The only book he knows from cover to cover is the Bible. He has in his possession a Bible which he values above anything else he has belonging to him. When . . . working in the colliery, he used to take his Bible with him, and while at work would put it away in some convenient hole or nook near his working place, ready to hand when he could snatch a moment or two to scan its beloved pages. A serious explosion occurred one day. The future Welsh revivalist escaped practically unhurt, but the leaves of His Bible were scorched by the fiery blast. "Evan Roberts" scorched Bible is a familiar phrase among his friends. (The page that the blast struck was II Chronicles 6—where Solomon as a young man prays for revival.)

The report continues:

> Little more than a month ago, Evan Roberts was unknown, studying so as to prepare for the Calvinistic Methodist ministry. Then came the summons, and he obeyed. He insists that he has been called to his present work by the direct guidance of the Holy Ghost. At once, without question and without hesitation, he was accepted by the people. Wherever he went, hearts were set aflame with the love of God.

A Visiting Journalist's Report

"The scene is almost indescribable. Tier upon tier of men and women filled every inch of space. Those who could not gain admittance stood outside and listened at the doors. Others rushed to the windows where almost every word was audible. When at 7:00 the service began, . . . two thousand people must have been present. The enthusiasm was unbounded. Women sang and shouted till perspiration ran down their faces, and men jumped up one after another to testify. One told in quivering accents the story of a drunken life. A working collier spoke like a practised orator; one can imagine what a note the testimony of a converted Gypsy woman struck when, dressed in her best, she told of her reformation and repentance. At ten o'clock the meeting had lost none of its ardor. Prayer after prayer went up . . . time and again, the four ministers who stood in the pulpit attempted to start a hymn, but it was all in vain. The revival has taken hold of the people, and even Mr. Roberts cannot keep it in check. His latest convert is a policeman, who after complaining that the people had gone mad after religion so there was nothing to do, went to see for himself, and bursting into tears, confessed the error of his ways and repented."

Prayer and Praise

"The dominant note of the revival is *prayer and praise.* Another striking fact is the *joyousness and radiant happiness* of the evangelist. It has been remarked that the very essence of his campaign is mirth. To the rank and file of church ministers, this is his most incomprehensible phase. They have always regarded religion as something iron-bound, severe, even terrible. Evan Roberts smiles when he prays, laughs when he preaches.

"He is a leader who preaches victory and shows how it may be won–victory over the dull depression and gloomy doubt of our time. Is it surprising that followers flock in thousands to his banner? A generation had risen that had not seen the arm of God working as it had done in 1849 and 1859. Now to all appearances the revival has arrived, and it has all the marks of previous great awakenings. Strong men are held in its grip; the Spirit of God stirs to their very depths whole neighborhoods and districts. There is a tumult of emotion, an overpowering influence, and a conviction of sin that can only be attributed to divine agency. Personal eloquence, magnetism, fervor, or mental power do not account for it. The only explanation is the one which the evangelist gives–'It is all of God'. . . .

"The revival seems to work especially among young people. Its form, which is that of prayer, praise and personal testimony, and its absence of method make it the most methodical expression of the emotions of young hearts aflame with the love of God" (Shaw, *The Story of the Welsh Revival*, pp. 5-6).

These characteristics of brokenness and praise dominate the awakening; when a man asked Evan if the revival would come to London, he smiled and said, "Can you sing?"

The Hand of the Almighty

William T. Stead, the famous London editor of the *Pall Mall Gazette*, thought by some to be the most powerful man in Britain, visited the revival. Here are excerpts of his impressions in an interview conducted by the *London Methodist Times* on his return.

"Well, Mr. Stead, you've been to the revival. What do you think of it?"

"Sir," said Mr. Stead, "The question is not what I think of it, but what it thinks of me, of you, and all the rest of us. For it is a very real thing, this revival, a live thing which seems to have a power and a grip which may get hold of a good many of us who at present are mere spectators."

Later the interviewer asks Stead:

"You speak as if you dreaded the revival coming your way."

"No, that is not so. Dread is not the right word. Awe expresses my sentiment better. For you are in the presence of the unknown. . . . You have read ghost stories and can imagine what you would feel if you were alone at midnight in the haunted chamber of some old castle and you heard the slow and stealthy step stealing along the corridor where the visitor from another world was said to walk. If you go to South Wales and watch the revival, you will feel pretty much like that. *There is something there from the other world. You cannot say whence it came or whither it is going, but it moves and lives and reaches for you all the time. You see men and women go down in sobbing agony before your eyes as the invisible Hand clutches at their heart. And you shudder*. It's pretty grim I tell you. If you are afraid of strong emotions, you'd better give the revival a wide berth."

A Christian in Lancashire read about what was happening.

ing. He and his daughter caught the "Midnight Special" train and arrived at 6:00 A.M. in Chester Station. He asked the porter, "Where is the revival? How do we get to the place where the revival is?" "Take the 8:00 train to Wrexam," said the porter, "from there, the local train to Rhos." "How will we know?" "*You'll feel it on the train,*" he replied. "Go down that road and you'll feel it down there."

George T. B. Davis's Report in America

Thirty-four thousand conversions in Wales:

"I have just returned from a two-day visit to the storm center of the great Welsh revival which is sweeping over Wales like a cyclone, lifting people into an ecstasy of spiritual fervor. Already over thirty-four thousand converts have been made, and the great awakening shows no signs of waning. . . . It was my good fortune to take two meals with Mr. Roberts and to attend three meetings he conducted. . . .

"It was 9:45 when we reached the place, and even at that hour there were scores of people seeking admission. But the gates were closed and guarded by policeman, for the church was already packed to the doors.

"My first impression! How am I to describe it? . . . a room meant to seat about seven hundred people crowded to suffocation with about fifteen hundred. Up in the gallery a young lady—almost a girl—was standing, praying with such fervor as I had rarely if ever witnessed before. One hand was upraised, and her tones were full of agonized pleadings; and though it was in Welsh, so that I could not understand a word she uttered, yet it sent a strange thrill through me. Then a young man arose and with rapt, upraised face prayed as though he were in the presence of the Almighty. The entire atmosphere of the room was white-hot with spiritual emotion, and my chief thought was: "*This is a picture what must have occurred in the early church in the first century of the Christian era.*"

"A hymn was now started, and my attention was riveted on Evan Roberts, who stood in the pulpit and led the music with face irradiated with joy, smiles, and even laughter. What impressed me most was his utter **naturalness**, his **entire absence of solemnity**. He seemed just bubbling over with sheer happiness, just as jubilant as a young man at a baseball game. He did not preach; he simply talked between the prayers and songs and testimonies and then rarely more than just a few sentences at a time.

"In appearance the young evangelist is of medium height, slender, brown-haired. He is extremely nervous in temperament, and his pallor showed the strain of the meetings on him." (This physical and spiritual strain was to later tell terribly on Robert's health.) "In the afternoon meeting, while describing the agony of Christ in the Garden of Gethsemane, he broke down and sobbed from the pulpit; scores in the building wept with him. It had been announced to begin at 2:00, but before 12:00 the building was packed. . . . The air was stifling, but the people minded it not a whit. They had forgotten the things of earth and stood in the presence of God. The meeting began about noon and went on at white heat for two hours before Mr. Roberts arrived, ending at 4:30 P.M." (Shaw, *The Great Revival in Wales*, p. 62).

What was the revivalist like close-up in a meeting like that? David Matthews records: "There came a sudden calm. Hearing a movement behind me in the pulpit I looked up. Evan Roberts was on his feet. Our eyes met for a few seconds. *I solemnly avow that those eyes searched me through and through. They burned like coals of fire.* In a split second my innermost soul seemed to be laid bare. I feared and shook. . . . Had there been a cover nearby, I most assuredly would have sought it."

Essential Conditions

A young U.S. reporter asked Evan for a message for America. He grasped his hand and gave him the following, amplified from the Western Mail's printed record of the heart of the message he was sharing with the world:

"The prophecy of Joel is being fulfilled. There the Lord says, 'I will pour out My Spirit on all flesh.' If that is so, all flesh must be prepared to receive. (You desire an outpouring of the Holy Spirit in your city? You do well. But remember, four conditions must be observed. They are **essential**.)

"1. The past must be clear; *every sin confessed* to God, any wrong to man put right.

"2. Everything *doubtful* must be removed once for all out of our lives. (Is there anything in your life about which you cannot decide whether it is good or evil? Away with it. There must not be a trace of a cloud between you and God. Have you forgiven everybody? If not don't expect forgiveness for your sins. It is better to offend ten thousand friends than grieve the Spirit of God—or quench Him.)

"3. *Obedience prompt, implicit, unquestioning to the Spirit* of God. (At whatever cost, do what the Holy Spirit prompts without hesitation or fear.)

"4. *Public confession of Christ.* (Multitudes are guilty of long and loud *profession. Confession* of Christ as *Lord* is of recent date. We forget there is a Trinity in the Godhead and that the Three Persons enjoy absolute equality. . . . Is not he (the Holy Spirit) ignored entirely in hundreds of churches? Hear the Word of the Lord: 'Quench not the Spirit.' That is the one way to revival.

When the fire burns it purifies. And when purified, you are fit to be used in the work of God. Christ said, 'And I, if I be lifted up, will draw all men to me.' There it is. Christ is all in all."

Thus it was for glorious year after year, with some churches open twenty-four hours a day, producing incredible effects on the world. Before it began Evan Roberts was a young man consumed with compassion over a world with no one to weep for it. God gave him a vision of a revival that would go around the world.

Yet Evan himself may never have known that the promise to him had been literally fulfilled. Only recently have we realized just how wide, how powerful, and how far-reaching this revival was. Roberts himself could never have seen the results we now know. All he had for his life's ministry was what God showed him one night, as a young college student, kneeling beside his bed in agonized prayer. Perhaps he thought he might be the one to carry it afar. Perhaps he believed that, like Whitefield or Moody, he might travel from a revived British Isles to other continents, carrying the message that reached such astonishing focus in Wales. But it was not to be.

What Happened to Evan Roberts?

This is a question perhaps that will never be satisfactorily answered in this world. Long after the awakening had begun to spread through the British Isles, the nationally famous Welsh preacher Peter Price publicly criticized him in print after Evans' short and embarrassingly unfruitful visit to his large and growing Dowlais Congregational church. Some thought earlier that Price himself, with a mighty record of evangelism and outreach among the young, might be the natural choice of God to bring awakening to Wales before it came to Evan Roberts' town of Loughor. The young revivalist apparently faced "hardness" in his earlier meetings there; half-an-hour into Price's service, Roberts stood to deliver a scathing "word from the Lord" that someone "near him" was "blocking the way of revival" by criticism of both it and him, and that unless it was dealt with he would leave. He "would not take part in mock worship where the Holy Spirit was grieved." He left shortly after (David Matthews, *I Saw the Welsh Revival*, pp. 85-86).

Price later wrote a letter to the *Western Mail* to correct misconceptions or misconduct he perceived in young converts of the revival. Unfortunately, it resulted in his denouncing Roberts' work as spurious ("*a sham Revival, a mockery, a blasphemous travesty of the real thing*") and his own work in contrast as an example of the genuine:

> My honest conviction is for Evan Roberts and his girl-companions to withdraw into their respective homes and there examine themselves and learn a little more of the meaning of Christianity (if they have the capacity for this) instead of going about the country pretending to show the Way of Life to people, many of whom know a thousand times more about this than they do. Why, we have scores of young colliers in Dowlais with whom Evan Roberts is not to be compared either in intellectual capability or spiritual power. (31 January 1905)

Reaction in Print

Of course, many people reacted in anger. Replies to Price's letter ran the gamut of "Your letter will reinforce the Devil's

Army—the publicans are in ecstasy . . . may God forgive your blasphemy. *Shame. Shame.*" to "The truth is, you are overwhelmed with petty jealousy." One said, "Why don't you wait and see the results and then try to judge a little? If you disagree with Mr. Roberts, you should have written to him and not through the Press; the seventy thousand souls won for Christ speak volumes, when the great portion of these were Servants of the Devil."

Some commended Price's stand: "I glory, with thousands of other level-headed people, in your many outspoken sentiments as to the 'Sham Revival.' The whole thing is nothing more than ignorant excitement and will die out as rapidly as it flamed up . . ." Another said, "I have not gone to hear him, and I don't intend to, but if he comes here, he will probably find many of my sort in his meetings."

This criticism, physical strain, and a growing disunity that Evan attempted to correct in some divisive breakaway works among the Northern churches led to one of the strangest endings of a ministry in history. Offered an open-ended rest at the home of the godly Mr. and Mrs. Jesse Penn-Lewis, Roberts accepted and from then on never returned to ministry!

The revival, of course, went on. It spread internationally, later deepening and mutating into the teaching and instruction of the hundreds of thousands of converts it had generated. But Evan Roberts effectively dropped completely and utterly out. He rejected all callers, ignored all letters, even refusing to see his own concerned family, much to the embarrassment of his hosts. Later, he co-authored with Jesse Penn-Lewis the controversial book *War on The Saints*. He attempted in this to describe the work of deception in the spiritual world. Some think he may even have overreacted by disavowing some of the genuine among the ever-present spurious incidents in the awakening.

Roberts simply vanished from the scene, perhaps in his own thinking, for the best. What was God's work, as he had always emphasized, after all would continue without him. And it did. He only emerged rarely after this at some public religious events, usually unnoticed and unheralded, and to all but a few who remembered (and God), essentially forgotten.

But the work God raised up through him went on around the world, affecting millions.

> God to take me home to heaven. I don't want to live. I don't ever want to stand in the pulpit and preach without the power of the Holy Spirit. It's a dangerous thing. (Graham, *Revival in Our Time*, 1950, pp. 105, 108, 119)

Divine Healing

And it happened. That hunger for power broke out in the birth of a radically distinct stream from the more traditional evangelical responses. Their immediate ancestors of the early 1900s claimed George Fox and his Quakers, John Wesley's early Methodists, the Plymouth Brethren, William Booth's Salvation Army, Azusa Street, and the holiness movement at the end of the nineteenth century as their roots. Scorned, laughed, at or ignored by many of the mainstream evangelicals, denied validity by an orthodoxy suspicious of fanaticism, false doctrine, and deception, they were criticized and denounced by psychiatrists, journalists, and medical doctors alike.

Some were hated, spat on, even shot at. Religious leaders named them, in derision at first, "holy rollers" and "tongues-speakers." Eventually, seeing they were here to stay, they called them "Pentecostals." But the best of these first pioneers of "latter rain" fasted, prayed, and paid a price to see through the ushering in of a significant restoration of spiritual power to the church that has since been repeated in other countries around the world.

From 1947 to 1958, many of these second-generation Pentecostals were called "faith-healers" because they saw a revival of divine healing that launched the ministries of many independent evangelistic teams. David Harrell again comments:

> In some ways the charismatic evangelists looked much like other revivalists in American history. They studied the techniques of figures such as Billy Sunday and Dwight L. Moody. They admired the success of Billy Graham. But they were not part of the same revivalistic stream—they were a **signs-gifts-healing, a salvation-deliverance and Holy Ghost-miracle revival.** Salvation from sin was preached, but whatever the intention of the evangelists, it was never the central theme of their meetings. All the

gifts of the Holy Spirit, including speaking in tongues and prophesying and all expressions of joy so common in Pentecostal worship, were present in the early revivals, but they were not the central theme. The common heartbeat of every service was the miracle–the hypnotic moment when the Spirit moved to heal the sick and raise the dead. (Harrell, *All Things Are Possible*, pp. 5-6)

Pioneers of the Healing Revival

Those first-generation Pentecostals eventually organized. "Western North Carolina and Eastern Tennessee had A. J Tomlinson and the Church of God, and the Midwest had the Methodist Charles Parham. Azusa Street was in 1906. By the end of World War II, the three largest churches were the Assemblies of God, the Church of God, and the Pentecostal Holiness Church."

Manifestations of the Spirit

What set them apart from other fellowships was the central teaching of "the abiding possibility and importance of the supernatural element . . . particularly as contained in the manifestation of the Spirit" (Donald Gee, *Wind and Flame*, p. 3).

Some had millennium vision. Alexander Dowie, the father of healing revivalism in America, built Zion in 1900 on six thousand acres of land north of Chicago; by 1902 ten thousand people had moved there as the paradise for the righteous. "Out of Zion" came F. F. Bosworth, a band leader in Dowie's church who moved to Dallas in 1910, pastored a strong independent church for ten years, and launched out on crusades. By 1924 there were reports of "some twelve thousand that sought the Lord for salvation."

John G. Lake

Also from Zion was Dowie's protege, John G. Lake, whom W. T. Stead called "the embodiment of the spirit of primitive Christianity." Lake owed much to what he saw of Christ in the life of W. J. ("Daddy") Seymour. Seymour "had the funniest vocabulary," records John G. Lake, "but there were doctors, lawyers and professors listening to the marvellous things coming from his lips. It was not what he said in words; it was what he said from his spirit to my heart that showed me he had more of God in his life than any man I had ever met up to that time. It was God in him who was attracting people" (Lake, *Adventures in God*, pp. 18-19).

A year before leaving as a missionary to Africa, John Lake received a vision in prayer of the various places where he would be and the extent of the spiritual work in each place. "I had faith to believe," he said, "that the thing God showed me would come to pass, and I have lived to see it through." For five years his African ministry, accompanied by wonderful miracles, stirred many. Andrew Murray said of him, "The man reveals more of God than any other man in Africa." With a scientific background himself, he even offered himself to a research clinic for testing, (he wanted to see just how God healed) and often invited doctors to witness God's healing power directly during prayer (Lake, *Adventures in God*, pp. 18-31). He would curse live bacteria under a microscope and then show them dead on the slide. Lake returned to pastor in Spokane, Washington, where, according to Gordon Lindsay, "one hundred thousand healings were recorded in five years." His ministry resulted in the establishment of hundreds of churches.

Astonishing Healings

Smith Wigglesworth (1859-1947), along with Stephen and George Jefferies (later of Elim), was the best-known of the British Pentecostals. This "apostle of faith," once a plumber and volunteer worker in Salvation Army missions, was a "commanding figure with twinkling small eyes in a stout face; rugged and refined at the same time, always dressed immaculately in a dark suit" (Hacking, *Smith Wigglesworth Remembered*, p. 18). Always smiling, never without a Bible (the only book he ever read), he saw almost every kind of healing miracle in his ministry, including fourteen raised from the dead, one of which was his wife Polly. "God will not allow those who trust in Him to become failures in the straightened place," he said.

In common with other early healing revivalists, he was concerned for purity as well as power. "I want to move you," he said, "to a greater hunger for holiness and purity. The moment you look up when you are in a place of affection with Jesus, the heavens are opened" (Hacking, *Smith Wigglesworth Remembered*, p. 93). He believed the two essential ingredients of ministry were the Holy Spirit's operation and personal holiness ("Every believer should reach a place where he has no desire except the desire of God.") Glorifying Christ and utterly self-effacing, he was bold to a point of roughness. Anointing people from his custom-made, little celluloid bottle of oil, he made several powerful international evangelistic tours in the 1920s and 1930s. Stanley Frodsham said he "filled the biggest halls, ministered to record crowds, and prayed for thousands" (Frodsham, *Smith-Wigglesworth, Apostle of Faith*, p. 93). "Seek to be filled with the Holy Ghost, for the peoples sake," he cried. "Seek only for God and the rain will fall" (Roberts Liardon, *Cry of The Spirit*, p. 46).

A Vessel unto the Lord

Maria B. Woodworth-Etter (born in 1844) of the United Brethren began an influential healing ministry in 1876 and later associated with the Methodist Holiness church, remaining active in revivalism until the 1920s. Her early life was marked by tragedies: she lost her drunkard father to a sunstroke when she was eleven, leaving her mother with eight children to provide for. Around sixteen she married. Fighting a constant battle with sickness and ill health herself, she lost five of her six children. Tragedy cast her more on Christ. Broken and seeking only to know God's will, she received a call to ministry. She had to battle her own prejudices over woman ministries, afraid of bringing reproach on Christ and ridicule from her friends and family. Finally accepting what God was obviously doing in her life, Maria launched out on a militant mission against sin in what some called "the most powerful (mission) seen in the twentieth century."

> I felt impressed God was going to restore love and harmony in the church. I visited those dissenting families; the third day of the meeting the trouble was all settled. All present came to the altar, made a full consecration, and prayed for a baptism of the Holy Ghost

> and fire. That night it came. *Fifteen came to the altar screaming for mercy. Men and women fell and lay like dead. I felt it was the work of God, but did not know how to explain it or what to say. I was a little frightened* . . . after lying for two hours all, one after another sprang to their feet as quick as a flash with shining faces and shouted all over the house. I had never seen such bright conversions or such shouting. . . . The ministers and old saints wept and praised the Lord . . . they said it was the Pentecost power, that the Lord was visiting them in great mercy and power . . . (*Maria Woodworth-Etter*, p. 37)

Another powerful woman evangelist of those days was the colorful and controversial Aimee Semple McPherson. She married Robert Semple in 1908, an Irish Pentecostal evangelist whose supernatural ministry had first swept aside her youthful skepticism. She headed out with him, scared and expecting, to Macao, China. Shortly after he arrived, Robert caught a fatal disease, and all alone with her new-born little girl Roberta, Aimee returned to America. Remarrying Harold McPherson in 1912 with the stipulation that God's call to ministry was first in her life, she had one child (Rolf) by him.

A Special Call

Though at first content just to be wife and mother, she came to feel she was avoiding her ministry. Her health broke, and near death she surrendered to the divine call. Aimee began as a tent evangelist. After a disastrous fire in a Durant, Florida, wooden tabernacle where a kerosene lamp blew up, she moved to Los Angeles. There, fifteen years after Azusa street, the Pentecostal message was getting a good hearing. Her illustrated sermons, complete with Hollywood style special effects ("I want to speak on the last days of Pompeii next week," she told her crew, "and I need a volcano to erupt behind me.") were the talk of California.

But above all Aimee had a powerful attraction for the sick and the lost in her exceptional ministry of healing. To this day people in Angelus Temple (her home church) can show you a room full of wheelchairs, crutches, and braces that people in her meetings had abandoned, instantly healed by the power of God.

Her last authorized biography recounts her story of being kidnapped and the swirl of controversy it generated. Aimee was without doubt the most talked-about Christian woman of her time. She died on 26 September 1944 in Oakland, California. It was the same city where she had, twenty-six years earlier, received the vision of the "Foursquare Gospel." This denomination she founded has now grown to over 790 churches with two thousand foreign mission stations, thirty-two day and Bible schools, and 117 daily or weekly radio broadcasts in the U.S. Canada and twenty-seven other countries, and has produced pastors and teachers of the spiritual calibre of the Hayford brothers (Jack and Jim) and Jack Hamilton.

International Unity

Charles S. Price was probably the most influential of post-war evangelists. With a law degree from Oxford, he emigrated from England to Canada as a young man, became a Methodist minister, and received the Baptism of the spirit under Aimee Semple McPherson's ministry. In 1922 he launched out from an independent church in Lodi, California, to become a full-time evangelist. He died in 1947, shortly before the outbreak of the post-war revival, sensing in his spirit a growing co-operation among Christians.

By 1943 a number of Pentecostal churches were able to join the N.A.E. (National Association Of Evangelicals), the successor to the fundamentalist organization that had refused them in 1928.

In 1947 American Pentecostals participated in a world convention in Zurich, and in 1948, eight major churches formed the Pentecostal Fellowship of North America. David du Plessis recorded that "the general effects of these international and national conferences have been noticed in city-wide and county-wide union meetings held by Pentecostal evangelists . . . it is not uncommon to find from five thousand to ten thousand, and more. Such meetings were unheard of before the first World Conference of 1947" (*Voice of Healing*, July 1965, p. 13). Oral Roberts was the featured speaker at the constitutional convention.

The Healing Revival 1947-1958

Time marched on. Many of the early Pentecostal pioneers passed on. Evangelicals had become more tolerant of the healing revival; after all, not many of them had gone off into some fundamental doctrinal error, been caught in immorality, or absconded with the collection to South America. The financial situation for Pentecostals had also somewhat improved; no longer did they have to live a hand-to-mouth existence on the sawdust trail.

But there was now a void; "The need of the hour was for leaders. Smith Wigglesworth and Charles Price died within a few days of each other and "fired many pure young hearts with a holy desire to pick up the torch of their ministry and carry it forewords . . . ," wrote Donald Gee in 1956 (Gee, *Pentecost*, p. 17). The deaths of the pioneer evangelists, including Aimee Semple McPherson, left a void. Some troubled, older Pentecostals wondered if the days of revival were over.

The Latter Rain Begins

In fact, as David Harrell notes, "the great Pentecostal revival identified by some as part of the prophetic 'latter rain' was about to begin. The pioneers of divine healing revivalism were gone, but 'almost simultaneously with their passing, God raised up . . . many others to carry on a new wave of revival that has reached nearly every nation of the free world'" (Harrell, *All Things Are Possible*, p. 30).

It erupted in 1947 with "astonishing force." The practice of praying for the sick was "revived on a scale hitherto unknown," wrote the historian John T. Nichol. Du Plessis said, "The sudden move towards mass evangelism has been just as unexpected and equally as little prepared for as the phenomenal growth . . . fifty years ago. It cannot be attributed to anything else than the spontaneous move of the Holy Spirit upon all flesh" (*Voice of Healing*, July 1965, p. 13).

That outburst from 1947-1952 was, at least numerically, an astonishing success." Vast crowds have gathered in many places in the world," wrote Gee in 1956, that "far exceeded those of a former generation of evangelists" (Gee, *Pentecost*, p. 17). This set off another period of worldwide Pentecostal growth.

William Branham

Gordon Lindsay, the editor of the *Voice of Healing*, became a teaching advisor, historian, and promoter of the revival with nearly fifty evangelists. A key figure of those times was the awesome (and later terribly controversial) William Branham, "an uneducated, timid, and poorest-of-the-poor Baptist evangelist" who, in 1933 at the age of twenty-four, began to preach in Jefferson where over 3,000 people a night came to his meetings. In 1946 (after reportedly receiving an angelic visit and a commission for healing) he preached in the Jonesboro, Arkansas, Bible Hour Tabernacle pastored by Rex Humbard's father. People gathered to the little city from twenty-eight states and Mexico, with some twenty-five thousand people attending. Unheralded by anything except his amazing gifts, he began to travel from city to city, creating astonishment and wonder wherever he went.

A Shreveport pastor's daughter, seeing him arrive outside her house to begin meetings in her dad's church, said:

> All things we heard about him seemed quite incredible, but as he travelled southward he stopped with us. . . . Could I ever forget the first time I saw him that Sunday afternoon in 1947 when a little '38 Ford turned in our driveway, and a slight, tired man with the deep eyes of a mystic got out and looked around. *As I watched from the window, I began to weep for no apparent reason, except that my heart seemed to break.* (Anna Jean Price, *Voice of Healing*, November 1995, pp. 9-10)

Under Lindsay's direction Branham teamed with the colorful Canadian Ern Baxter in Vancouver, British Columbia, in a fourteen-day series of meetings in four cities with over seventy thousand people attending, where 90 percent of the audience had never seen a miracle. In January they held revivals in Miami and Pensacola, Florida, and in the spring they began a huge campaign in Kansas City where they were visited by a young Oral Roberts just launching out on his own ministry.

A Man Set Apart

Branham's simple authority over sickness and demons made

a life-long impression upon Oral Roberts and the discouraged young missionary T. L. Osborn. In 1950 Billy Branham went to Europe. Seven thousand people filled Finland's largest auditorium night after night, hundreds sometimes even thousands standing outside. He filled the largest stadiums and meeting halls in the world. In 1952 he went to Africa; in 1955 returned to Europe, and his healing power became a worldwide legend. The younger deliverance evangelists viewed him as a man set apart, like Moses (Harrell, *All Things Are Possible*, p. 37).

The two strange signs (some later believed them to be more spiritualistic than spiritual) he had of "vibrations" in his left hand and the amazing "word of knowledge" gift nevertheless amazed tens of thousands. Bosworth wrote in 1950:

> Brother Branham is the most sensitive person to the presence and working of the Holy Spirit and to spiritual realities of any person I have ever seen. . . . When the afflicting spirit comes into contact with the gift, it sets up such a physical commotion that it becomes visible . . . and so real it will stop his wrist watch instantly . . . like taking a live wire with too much current in it. When the oppressing spirit is cast out in Jesus' name, (Branham's) red and swollen hand returns to its normal condition. (Bosworth, *Voice of Healing*, March 1950, p. 10)

A Divine Gift

Bosworth also recounts:

> The Angel told him (Branham) that the anointing would cause him to see and enable him to tell the suffering many of the events of their lives from childhood down to the present time . . . the great audience hears all this over the P.A. system. Brother Branham actually sees it enacted, and, pushing the microphone away so the audience won't hear it, he tells the patient any unconfessed and unforsaken sins in his life which must be given up before the gift will operate for his deliverance. As soon as such persons acknowledge and promise to forsake their sin . . . their healing often comes in

a moment before Brother Branham has time to pray for them. (Harrell, *All Things Are Possible*, pp. 37-38)

The gift, which many insisted was "exactly 100 percent," made him more than a channel for the gift of healing. He was a "seer as the O.T. prophets." An interpreter for him in Switzerland and later a historian said, "I am not aware of any case in which he was mistaken in the often detailed statements he made." A contemporary evangelist recalled, "I've been with him when he would meet a person he had never seen and immediately call him by name" (Harrell, *All Things Are Possible*, p.38).

Leonard Ravenhill, the evangelical revivalist and friend of A. W. Tozer, was already a well-known speaker. Already in the area with a night off, he was able to fill in for a tired Branham during a campaign. Branham (arriving to speak after all, another hour-and-a-half after "Len's" own long message) called for "the first twenty people up here" that God would heal.

After publicly identifying the first in the prayer line (an attractive young woman) by giving her name and city through the microphone, he spoke quietly and privately to her; God would heal her if she gave up her adultery. Indignantly, the man behind her protested. He was her husband, he said, and Branham had no right to say that! Turning to him in terrible quietness, Branham replied, "And God will heal *you* when you stop running around with your secretary." Then, speaking again through the microphone, he gave a thirty-minute, gentle-but-searing rebuke to the audience, warning them that God's love would reveal every secret sin that stood in the way of their wholeness with him. Returning to the prayer line, he found that every person had left.

Of Humble Spirit

People came many times just out of curiosity; he preached and prayed for the sick from three to four hours to exhaustion until carried bodily off the platform. There were no "hard cases" for him. In one 1950 meeting, "nine deaf mutes came in the prayer line, and all nine were healed" (Bosworth, *Voice of Healing*, January, 1950, p. 5). Most impressive was his quiet mastery of audiences; he "seldom raised his voice or got excited or disturbed" (Harrell, *All Things Are Possible*, p. 38). His sermons were largely stories of personal experiences, and he had a trait that impressed his audiences and colleagues alike, an "outstandingly humble spirit."

"There is nothing boisterous or arrogant about him," wrote an observer. "He is a meek and humble man . . . loved by all. No one begrudges him success or is envious of his great popularity" (Harrell, *All Things Are Possible*, p. 39). This humility and a refusal to discuss controversial doctrinal matters won him wide Pentecostal support through the 1950s.

During this time Oral Roberts took up the torch and led the way for others like Jack Coe and A. A. Allen, who took to the big tents. T. L. Osborn began to take a healing and deliverance message to the missionfield with extensive results; Tommy Hicks went to Argentina in 1954 with reportedly as many as four hundred thousand persons attending a single service.

By 1955 William Branham's finances had faltered through his own carelessness, and by 1958 he was deeply re-assessing his ministry. In the new decade, his problems seemed to intensify; by 1960 he began to stray doctrinally. On December 18, 1965, driving to Arizona, he was hit head-on by a drunken driver, and he died on Christmas Eve.

If ever a movement was a costly, consuming blaze of glory, this one was. "It was an exhausting, draining way of life: Branham was a broken man after little more than a year; Jack Coe was physically exhausted at the time of his death; A. A. Allen, an incredibly tough campaigner, tottered constantly on the brink of psychological collapse; the resilience of Oral Roberts became a legend among his peers" (Harrell, *All Things Are Possible*, p. 6).

The Blossoming of the Charismatic Renewal

Ostracized even by the major Pentecostal churches, the independent evangelists came face to face with seemingly insurmountable obstacles. By 1957 nearly all recognized that what had begun in 1947 was over. But there were new opportunities in 1958. Thousands in traditional churches became interested in the charismatic message; hundreds of thousands of religious Americans were dissatisfied with their own lethargic denominations and were searching for a more dynamic experience.

As the charismatic renewal flowered, many of these second-wave healing evangelists turned their works into missionary ministries, consciously or unconsciously adapted to the traditional churches blossoming interest. Evangelists became teachers more than healers and recast their revival teams into teaching organizations. The time for the third wave had come.

CHAPTER TEN

The Third Wave

The 8 April 1966 *Time* magazine cover read, "Is God Dead?" The 1960s counter culture flowered out of the compost-heap of what some called the "post Christian era" with a deadly vengeance; 1966 and 1967 introduced Timothy Leary, Ken Kesey, Haight Ashbury, free love, and acid rock. By 1969 there was *Woodstock*, the peak of the flower child movement and the musical event of the decade.

Then it soured. In 1971 there was the tragedy of Kent State. In Oakland, California, Hell's Angels stage guards murdered one of the Altamont festival fans while Mick Jagger of the Rolling Stones cavorted about on stage, singing "Sympathy for the Devil." The time was ripe for a reaction to the age's utterly abandoned immorality.

Into this vacuum swept wide-spread awakenings affecting the streets, traditional evangelicals, and mainline denominations. They were respectively (but not always respectably), the Jesus and the Charismatic movements, and Church renewal.

The Jesus Movement (1967-1975)

Suddenly they were everywhere. Until the Jesus movement, everyone in America knew what a Christian looked like: a white, Anglo-Saxon, Protestant, Republican cheerleader, or a football player with crew-cut, white shirt, and tie. Then the oddest looking people began to speak in the strangest places about the ultimately-avoided subject–Jesus. Rejecting a caricature of Christianity that had estranged them from more orthodox avenues of faith, the new converts simply called themselves "Jesus People." Full of zeal, often with strange ideas and interpretations, not always of unquestionable purity or orthodoxy, they nevertheless exploded across the nation, forcing most of the traditional churches to either re-examine their approaches or react in horror. The Jesus movement could never, in the full sense, be termed a revival. But it laid the groundwork and contributed towards a wave of fresh life that, purified and trained, set the stage for much that has happened in our present generation.

Grass Roots

Some of those early radical pioneers are now considered among today's orthodox; blue jeans were exchanged for three-piece suits, and TV programs and fund-raising seminars replaced street preaching out of a van. Nevertheless, some of the best of the Jesus movement survived its traumatic years and now hold either key leadership positions of ministry or still vitally participate in mutated forms of their original callings.

Jesus Papers. There were several key publishers of the street papers of those days. The most prominent was Duane Pederson, the founder of the *Hollywood Free Paper*. It was competing with the *Los Angeles Free Press* (top circulation: ninety thousand). Ten thousand copies of the first issue of the *Free Paper* were printed and over 150,000 copies of an issue two years later. Over 200,000 copies of a special edition were distributed at the 1971 Rose Parade. The *Oracle*, a top San Francisco "hip" paper had an international circulation of nearly one hundred thousand; its editor-publisher, David Abraham, twenty-three, professed conversion in 1970 and re-issued it in 1971 as a Christian paper.

Carl Parks' *Truth* (Oct.1970) merged with Linda Meissner's *Agape* for a circulation of over one hundred thousand. Jack Sparks (Christian World Liberation Front/Campus Crusade 1969) published *Right On!* (later *Radix*), an attempt to deal with urgent social and moral issues in an intelligent way. It grew from 20,000 copies with its first issue in 1 July 1969, to 100,000 copies later on. Special issues averaged sixty-five thousand copies. Jack also published a hip translation of the Gospels and Epistles, and later a book on the cults.

Early Gatherings

There were the street ministries and coffee-houses. Arthur Blessit, of Sunset Strip, launched out in 1967 with seventeen other kids from five churches in his "Love-Inn" at Griffith Park, Los Angeles. Then, he began the coffee-bar *His Place* in 1968 on the Strip. In two years some ten thousand decisions were recorded (an average of a dozen decisions a night, but up to five hundred kids an evening). Arthur (a Baptist who later symbolically ran for president in the late seventies), despite recent family problems, continued to the hot spots of the world, carrying a custom cross as a testimony to the saving power of Christ.

Some worked with Third World young people in radical movements as well as with organized street gangs—men like Harold Brinkely and Ralph Garcia of *Youth for Truth* in Sacramento, California (1967), an outreach to groups like the Black Panthers. Gang converts like Tom Skinner (an ex-member of the Harlem Lords) and Nicky Cruz (converted under Dave Wilkerson's ministry in New York) went on to develop national evangelistic crusade ministries.

Outreach Groups

There were early attempts at Christian communes like Dick Keys' Clayton House in San Francisco, 1967; but when the ex-Four-Square pastor Chuck Smith and his first street-redeemed assistant Lonnie Frisbee joined together in the first (1966) Santa Ana Calvary Chapel, perhaps the best-known survivor of those days was born. Related outreaches like the House of Miracles under John Higgins were established after some rocky early attempts in 1968. Under the leadership of

Calvary Chapel in 1970 alone, four thousand prayed to "receive Christ," with over two thousand baptized in the Pacific Ocean. Smith's church received much media attention and has continued to clone other Calvary Chapels headed up by young ministries affected by the work.

Moishe Rosen and Jews for Jesus was founded in 1970 in New York and San Francisco. It continues to aggressively evangelize both Jews and Gentiles with street and literature evangelism.

David Wilkerson, the Assembly of God minister who received a call from God to the gangs and addicts of New York city, had perhaps more influence than any other single figure of this time in bridging the gap between orthodox Pentecostals, new charismatics, and the disenchanted street young. His book *The Cross and the Switchblade* was the single most influential book of both movements, *Teen Challenge*, the most powerful work of its decade. Wilkerson's ministry continues in a prophetic national call to revival and the streets in his Times Square church. His children also minister. His son Gary helped co-found effective street churches like the Broadway Revival Tabernacle in Highland Park, Detroit, a street church situated in a triple-X rated movie theatre. Spiritual callings can be passed on. Tim Dilena, the other co-founder of this powerful work, is the son of Paul Dilena, the police captain who first helped David in New York.

Calls to Conversion Among the Young

Then there was the visionary Baptist, Bill Bright, with his Campus Crusade. Called of God in 1951, in his last semester at Fuller Theological Seminary, Bright began the work at UCLA. He relocated his headquarters to Arrowhead Springs, California, in 1963, with a staff of 125. By 1972 he had a staff of over one thousand, with two-thirds out in the field. His vision then was of a staff of ten thousand by 1975 to influence a further 5 million Christians. They in turn, in one year, would influence 50 million.

After a number of popular media events like Explo '72 and "I Found It," Bright reached out to work with other groups like America for Jesus in an attempt to give direction and leadership to the new generation of young Christians. Co-workers like the internationally-known Josh McDowell have had wide influence in international university campuses and contributed some excellent apologetics works such as *Evidence That Demands a Verdict.*

Hal Lindsay's *Late Great Planet Earth* was the best-selling book of the decade. He thought the decade entering maturity at the time of the Second Coming was born in the few years after the creation of Israel in 1948. (That placed end-time events around 1990, give or take a few years.) In apocalyptic times such intense scenarios of the future fate of the earth influenced many to reconsider the Christian claim to truth.

By December 1969 the *Time* cover read "Is God Coming Back to Life?"

Moving On

There were of, course, some inevitable doctrinal and moral digressions of varied consequence along the way, along with some sad losses of those who had earlier been leaders in their areas. Tony and Sue Alamo, Victor Paul Wierville, Linda Meisner (the Jesus People Army with an early membership of five thousand), David Berg (whose 1967-1968 Teens for Christ became in 1970 the Children of God), David Hoyt (of Atlanta Jesus People)—all were deeply involved in attempts to minister to the counterculture. For some, practical problems like hurt, rejection, and bitterness were never resolved. Others fell victim to deception as a consequence of their confusing individual vision with an independent spirit. Some just got discouraged along the way and reacted tragically. Events like Sun Myung Moon's attempt to infiltrate government, media publicity over charges of brainwashing, kidnapping, and de-programming, prominent warnings in airports, and the Manson and Jonestown tragedies created strong public reaction against early successes in recruitment. But there was more to come.

The Charismatic Renewal (1958-1974)

Without a word of greeting, Smith Wigglesworth strode into the office of David du Plessis. He unloaded to that startled Assembly of God executive what was to prove a significant prophetic word: that du Plessis soon would go around the world, helping spread the good news of the restoration of spiritual gifts and power to Christians of all persuasions and backgrounds. Wigglesworth then left abruptly, apologetically returning moments later to offer belated greetings and introductions.

Events like this were common in the early days of that spiritual outpouring in the early 1960s that ultimately involved millions of people in a fresh attempt to see the prophecy of Joel fulfilled: "In the last days I will pour out of My Spirit upon all flesh" (Joel 2:28).

A New Awakening

In the 1960s it came as a "new wave"—the Charismatic movement, a neo-Pentecostal awakening "as remarkable as its predecessor." Charismatic clinics and Full Gospel Businessmen's conventions listed names like Derek Prince (PAOC), Kenneth Hagin (raised Baptist, became AOG in 1938), John Osteen, (Southern Baptist), Gerald Derstine (Mennonite), and Bob Mumford (Elim Bible Inst. Prof. of Bible and Missions). There was Michael Harper, the English Anglican, and Bob Frost, the California biologist. David Harrell says, "The force of the new revival astonished American religious leaders" (Harrell, *All Things Must Pass,* p. 156). It began to be called a "Third Force" in Christendom and was made the subject of a special article in the *Encyclopedia Britannica.* Rex Humbard and Kathryn Kuhlman (Evangelical Alliance), highly successful independents who never associated themselves with the earlier healing revival, were thrust into a position of leadership and honor. Humbard built a pioneering TV ministry around his Akron, Ohio, Cathedral of Tomorrow church. Kathryn packed them in each month in the Los Angeles Shrine and other huge auditoriums with astonishing demonstrations of God's healing power.

Many evangelicals, caught somewhat unprepared either experientially or theologically to either denounce or embrace the best of the movement, remained at a wary distance. Others, in various attempts to constructively (or otherwise) criticize what was perceived as either unscriptural or unnecessary, issued some form of standard public denial. Most of this is mild today. Early editions of books on the cults often associate the "Tongues Movement" with Jehovah's Witnesses and Mormons; at least one major denomination in a small nation purchased full-page ad space in a national newspaper warning about Pentecostal "demon-possession" and felt constrained to call a public meeting for their denomination. Their exhibit? A life-size photographic blow-up of a famous evangelical, arm-in-arm with a well-known Pentecostal, during the dedication of his new University with the solemn words, "See? He has joined the ranks of the Anti-Christ!"

Certainly, some early aspects of the charismatic movement earned and deserved valid criticism; there were much zeal, little knowledge, few scholarly defenders, some Penthouse amidst the Pentecost, and no shortage of power- or money-hungry charlatans to exploit what was going on. Some non-participating fundamentalists and evangelicals traded horror stories of reported moral and religious excess in the movement. Others reacted with disdain or suspicion if not downright hostility.

Usually, however, these disclaimers are made today in a somewhat guarded fashion. The cutting edge of many awakenings around the world involve exactly the same experiences, and simple people unspoiled by our own theological prejudices are happily repeating various aspects of the book of Acts. It is difficult to make any blanket denials lest one be found to "fight against God." Now that we have the opportunity to observe exactly similar occurrences during the work of revivals in other nations largely cut off from the West's particular idiosyncrasies, it takes a brave soul to categorically deny all that happened in this movement as a "work of the flesh," "deception," or worse. The verdict of history is that for millions God spoke to them during this outpouring and used it to bring genuine life, joy, and a heartfelt desire for godly experience and truth.

The Catholic Charismatics

One of the most controversial aspects of the Charismatic movement (at least to those Protestants who still jealously nurse what was obtained through great cost by the Reformation), was the Catholic Charismatic renewal. If Baptists' "speaking in tongues" is a hard enough pill to swallow, (and to admit that such things might be "of God" seem to strain all credulity to breaking-point) what shall a theologian in the Reform tradition make of a nun or priest who does the same thing?

To many Protestants this was the final evidence of the anti-Christ. If God was going to work miracles among Catholics, He would at least first make them Protestant. Old flames here have by no means died down, even after three decades. Most charismatic Protestants who are unable to deny the reality of a Catholic brother's or sister's walk with God simply content themselves in the wisdom and sovereignty of God; that "errors of doctrine" (as in Protestantism) are more easily corrected when one meets the Lord and has some living experience of the Truth other than that of a learned theological tradition.

Ralph Keifer was a key figure among the first Catholic Pentecostals. In Pittsburgh, Pennsylvania, in 1967, a retreat he conducted broke out in charismatic manifestations that later spread to Notre Dame. The first annual Catholic Conference held at South Bend, Indiana drew one hundred people; in 1970 nearly thirteen hundred; next summer approximately five thousand registrants and five hundred gate-crashers turned up, and the movement mushroomed to an estimated fifty thousand people.

In recent years, the proliferation of home study groups and the non-Catholic doctrinal or authority structure leanings of many of those involved has drawn some official disapproval and, in some cases, active suppression. Divisions into streams seen as more or less faithful to Rome are occurring. But the movement continues to expand and grow all around the world, especially in Latin American nations, where the bulk of the population is at least nominally Catholic.

David Harrell notes the shift in evangelical opinion:

> Once scorned by most of the nation's religious leaders and the press, by the 1970s Oral Roberts had become a man of prestige and stature. In 1974 David du Plessis was included in the list of the eleven most influential Christians in the world, based on an informal poll conducted by seven major church magazines. Kathryn

> Kuhlman's ministry was both successful and respectable. Full Gospel Businessmen's meetings took the Charismatic message into the banquet halls of the best hotels in the world and boasted as members some of the world's wealthiest, most glamorous and powerful. . . . (Harrell, *All Things Are Possible,* pp. 4-5)

Early Pentecostal Reaction

And how did the earlier Pentecostals view this new wave? Some, themselves just beginning to enjoy a new acceptance or at least a diminished criticism from other Evangelicals, found themselves in the odd position of not being able to really side with it. Many retained a respectful but reluctant new denominational distance. Others, who had earlier learned the hard way the value of continued flexibility in the things of God, adapted well.

Typical of these successful bridgers was Gordon Lindsay, who, Harrell says "more than any other man brought system and unity . . . contributing an orderly mind, keen business sense, boundless energy, badly needed literary skills, and an ecumenical spirit" (Harrell, *All Things Are Possible,* p. 53). He had an aristocrat's bloodline in the healing movement; born in Zion City in 1906, he was influenced by John G. Lake in Portland in 1920 and converted under Charles Parham's ministry. With Lake's help he travelled as an evangelist for eighteen years, first alone and later with his family, conducting over 150 campaigns. Work with the Assemblies of God, a short time in the Foursquare church, and many friends in other Pentecostal groups "prepared him as perhaps no other to establish communication with a variety of Pentecostals." When World War II began, he stopped travelling, took a church in Ashlan, Oregon, and later joined Branham.

Christ for the Nations

In April 1948 he began the *Voice of Healing* magazine; when Branham retired, leaving him to work with other young evangelists, he invested his savings to continue it. Reaching thirty thousand readers per month in the first year, it was a phenomenal success. In 1949 Lindsay arranged the first convention of healing revivalists in Dallas, Texas; the following year (except for Roberts and Branham) a *thousand of virtually every important healing evangelist in the nation* met in Kansas City. Through the fifties he held workshops and attempted to avert clashes between these and established Pentecostal churches. His overview of the movement was without equal.

Lindsay died on 1 April 1973 the historian and theologian of the movement, leaving his wife Freda, daughter Shira (Carol) and younger son Dennis to captain a native church ministry, one that funded by 1973 over three thousand overseas church building programs in over eighty-three nations, a literature work involving his older son Gil that distributed over 15 million books, including more than two hundred of Lindsay's own titles in forty-six languages and printed Christian materials in Russia, his vivacious daughters' Jewish mission in Israel, C.F.N., and a prayer/tape ministry that sent out some two thousand teaching cassettes a month.

F.G.B.M.F.I.

The Full Gospel Businessmen's Fellowship International was founded in 1952 by Demos Shakarian, a friend and disciple of Charles Price and an organizer of Oral Roberts' 1951 Los Angeles campaign. Its growth showed the great appeal of the charismatic message outside organized Pentecostal circles. By the mid-sixties, it had established three hundred chapters with approximately one hundred thousand members. By the early seventies their *Voice* magazine had a circulation of over 250,000. In 1972 Shakarian reported a membership of three hundred thousand and an annual operating budget of more than one million dollars. It was accepted by thousands of successful middle-class people and grew explosively to its present international influence.

Bridging the Gap

There was real need for wisdom. Talented teachers began to replace gifted preachers and healers. Some of the earlier revivalists adapted to meet the challenge. Oral Roberts joined the Methodists and founded Oral Roberts University. Gordon Lindsay started his Christ for the Nations International, the first international school drawing over one thousand students.

T. L. Osborn established a world missionary organization specializing in native evangelism. All appealed to both mainline Pentecostals and charismatics. Many new independent evangelistic ministries flourished. Some, like David Wilkerson, a third-generation Assembly Of God minister, had Pentecostal backgrounds. Many were "Spirit-filled" ministers from traditional churches, who brought teaching skills and theological training not always evident in the healing revival. Other Assembly of God ministers like Morris Cerullo, a Jewish Christian (who showed "unusual ability to blend healing revivalism and charismatic teaching"), and Jimmy Swaggart (the piano-playing, singing and preaching relative of the rock pioneer Jerry Lee Lewis) became ministry bridges from the healing revival of the 1960s to the 1970s. They helped create cooperation among old-line Pentecostals and (especially so for Cerullo) "succeeded in attracting support from the religiously dispossessed classic Pentecostals and neo-Pentecostals." Again, Harrell notes: "Once an object of derision, by the 1970s Pentecostal religion became almost fashionable. Many judged it the most vital force in American religion. By 1975 around 5 million or more Americans were taking part in the charismatic revival" (Harrell, *All Things Are Possible,* p. 137).

Much attention has already been paid to figures in the early charismatic movement in other works, like Harald Bredesen, John & Elizabeth Sherrill, and Michael Harper. Like the Jesus movement, the Charismatic movement had its glaring weaknesses and drew a sometimes just share of both criticism and detractors. But it did one thing: it broke down some barriers that had choked and stultified evangelicals and compelled an entire re-examination of the work and ministry of the Holy Spirit. Without question the movement recaptured the interest of hundreds of thousands in spiritual things and led to many conversions and miracles as people of traditional and orthodox evangelical backgrounds were forced to re-examine their faith in the light of these unusual experiences.

Church Renewal Movement

Since much of this was a parallel to the Charismatic movement, an attempt to integrate into, rather than come out of, the mainline churches, we will not spend much time here examining the differences. Names like Jack Hayford, pastor of the Church on the Way in Van Nuys, California, Larry Christenson of Minneapolis, and Dennis Bennet of Seattle, stood out as pastors who worked to bring renewal within their denominational structures. Others, like Derek Prince, Bob Mumford, and Charles Simpson, with international recognition as teachers and interpreters of the movement, attempted to see some sort of unity and leadership established across the charismatic renewal with some limited success, though not without misunderstanding, opposition, and excesses. Men like Ralph Wilkerson in Anaheim, Jerry Cook in Oregon, and Gerry Fry of San Jose in the U.S.A., and Michael Harper, Jean Darnell, and others in Great Britain pioneered renewal churches modelled on both lessons learned and teachings developed from the needs of the young adults saved during those decades. Another neglected side-benefit of these renewals was the renewed hunger for teaching. That more than any other factor of the seventies, led to the great proliferation of books, audio and video cassette taped lectures, and the "seminar" approach to Christian instruction.

On the Threshold

Its strength was its emphasis on a direct, immediate and personal experience with God and with the power of His Spirit; its weakness was at first a zeal without knowledge, and more recently, a knowledge without zeal. In fresh forms and as a third wave, it regenerated itself in the eighties in ministries to the church like John Wimber's and his "Power Healing" seminars. It can be recognized in the call to intercessory prayer, the simple life-style, and the prophetic sensitivity of the Kansas City Metro Vineyard Fellowships, with their desire to see a restoration of purity and power in the emerging ministries of men like Mike Bickle and Paul Cain, a survivor of the 1940s Healing Revival, and the evangelical revivalist Len Ravenhill. It has taken a social dimension in influential churches like those of John Perkins in Washington, Tommy Barnett in Arizona, and Roger Forster and Graham Kendrick of Ichthus Fellowship in England. It finds musical expression in worship tape ministries like Scripture in Song, the Make Way Praise Marches, and Integrity Music.

Restoration, Reconstruction, and Reformation

In recent years some third wave leaders have drawn ideas and structural help from other streams of teaching that developed in the late seventies. The "Faith," or "Word," churches drew from the teachings of men like Kenneth Copeland, who (despite criticism for what is perceived as sometimes shaky theology and materialistic or mystic leanings) has encouraged many people to trust God and His Word. Biblical authority, church structure, and ministry leadership have been the focus of works like those of Dick Iverson and Frank Damazio of *Church Life Library.* Rick Joyner's *Morningstar Journal* and the writings of men like Francis Frangipane have helped influence a new focus on Christian holiness and a fresh return to loving Christ. Bill Hybels of Willow Creek Community, Blaine Bartel with his *Fire N'Lite* videos, Francis Anfuso of *Twenty-First Century Ministries,* and the recent Carmen projects are examples of the creative use of multi-media in modern ministry. New street-level ministries like those of Phil Aguilar and his "Set Free" churches, Harold Warner's "Potters House" outreaches, Sonny Arguinzoni's Victory Outreach, Bill Wilson's children's church in New York, and more radical works like those annually encouraged by Scott Hinkle in his National Street Ministries conference prick the conscience of the complacent and stretch the boundaries of what the church is to look like in twenty first century ministry.

Another key force is the small but deeply influential Christian Reconstruction movement. Drawing originally from the detailed and scholarly thought of men like Cornelius Van Til and Rousas J. Rushdoony, it has since contributed much original, effective, and trenchant literature in the field of the application of Biblical and Covenant law to a culture anticipating revival. It is helmed by twentieth-century reformers like Gary North, Ken Gentry, Greg Bahnsen, James B. Jordan, and Gary Demar and implemented in various levels by many men effective in ministering in the areas of political influence, like the ex-Marxist radical Dennis Peacock.

North saw three great streams influencing the church in the West in this century; Presbyterian Theology, Baptist Schools, and Pentecostal High Technology. He and other Christian

Reconstructionalists spent most of the eighties developing a body of literature like the "Biblical Blueprint" series, attempting to relate Biblical law to every key area in society. As he succinctly puts it "When this revolutionary shift of faith comes, what will Christians recommend in place of today's collapsing humanist culture? . . . Christianity, in its orthodox form, challenges all forms of power religion. It offers comprehensive redemption–the healing of international civilization" (North, *Christian Reconstruction*, Institute for Christian Economics, p. 51). It is in allied wisdom and strength, from the gifts of the first Reformers revived in our time down to the experiences of today's inheritors of the work of the Spirit, that is needed in our day. Many see in this at last a real answer to the reviving of entire nations.

The third wave is still shaping in our time. It is by no means complete and by no means mature. It is a groundwork, an opening door, a preparatory step. Above all, it leaves us in the West with a challenge to see "much greater things than these" in what well may be the Last Great Awakening.

Ministries Today

What of the current possibilities in modern ministries? Groups and ministries born out of the preceding two decades had a hunger to transcend what they perceived as sub-standard levels of consecration and commitment in much of our evangelical witness. Today some still make significant impact.

Larry Lea (originally of Beverly Hills Baptist in Texas, then pastor of Church on the Rock) made a dynamic impact internationally in his crusade to take intercessory prayer to the churches of the cities. Along with the labors of men like David Bryant of IVF (Concerts of Prayer), Dick Eastman with his Change The World School Of Prayer, and Gary Bergel's Intercessors For America prayer conferences have sprung up all over the nation. There are also strong intercessory groups influenced by women of prayer like Joy Dawson and those in the leadership of works like Woman's Aglow and the "Lydia" networks.

Tony Salerno, like Wesley, was converted while in the ministry. Burdened for the young in both the church and the inner city, he took a small team of young converts to minister in Reedley, California, at the invitation of a godly ex-missionary pastor who for years had prayed for revival. A genuine outpouring of the Holy Spirit resulted in the small town's being deeply affected, with many converted (including Barry McGuire) and the establishment of what was called Agape Force. Modelled on the early Salvation Army structure and vision, the Agape Force, through travelling groups like Candle, Silverwind, Gingerbrook Fare and their international "Field Stations," profoundly influenced contemporary worship music, children's records, drama, and street ministry. Though now disbanded, many ex-Agape Force people continue to minister in creative ways in both street-sensitive ministry and media.

Bob Weiner founded Maranatha! Ministries, a confrontive and Charismatic outreach spanning two decades of ministry among university students. Founding campus churches by open-air preaching, prayer for the sick, a strong emphasis on Christ's Lordship, holy living, and intensive discipleship, Maranatha! Ministries' vision for the campuses of the world made them good contenders as the "Pentecostal Methodists" of the eighties. Weiner's missions ministry continues in outreaches to the Soviet Union, and outgrowths of Maranatha! Ministries like Campus Teams International and Greg Ball's Champions for Christ still affect thousands.

Jesus People U.S.A. is an example of the cream of the Jesus movement surviving and flourishing into the 1990s. Stressing community, practical involvement with the poor and disprivileged, and a simple, radiant life-style, this Chicago-based work has consistently upheld content in its communication. Glen Kaiser's Resurrection Band (a band to wake the dead) was one of the leading early "Jesus Rock" groups, and *Cornerstone*, their full-color, intelligent, contemporary magazine, is perhaps the best and most influential of all Jesus Papers.

Branching Out

Some ministries, like People of Destiny (originally in Washington, D.C.) under the leadership of influential young ministers like Larry Tomczak, Charles Mahaney, and Che Ahn, have established communities of practical care and help for their neighborhood areas. They also minister among other language groups and refugees in large cities.

Doug Coe, also in Washington, D.C., and others of the "brothers" on Capitol Hill work (low-profile and largely behind the scenes) to deeply affect and influence many high-level government leaders for Christ, like Chuck Colson. Working by friendship evangelism, they encourage events like the National Prayer Breakfast in the U.S. and other nations.

Mario Murillo is another key voice calling for change on the West Coast and other parts of the nation. Gifted with great communication skills, a prophet's burden, and street wisdom, he founded Resurrection City in Berkeley during the late 1960s. Murillo was a key instrument in bringing a Gospel of repentance, faith, and healing to a new generation. A Mexican-American with a touch for the disenfranchised young, he has consistently shown a creative, sometimes controversial, touch as an iconoclast of current issues of idolatry. In both 1982 and again in 1991, in the midst of great personal conflict and trial, Mario saw great outpourings of the Holy Spirit in the West Coast. His vision to see the whole Bay Area deeply affected by the Gospel has since spread to other states. In similar molds are his associate Mike Stevens, where burden for awakening has taken him around the world, and Jacob Aranza, another Mexican-American whose annual ministry to hundreds of thousands of high school students is both street smart and revival-based.

Keith Green, the zealous young founder of Last Days Ministries did more in eight years for God than many see done in a lifetime. His newsletters, pointedly convicting songs, and concerts deeply influenced both musicians and new Christians across the country and contributed towards a restoration of old principles set in new vocabulary, as well as a fearless attack on modern-day areas of sin and compromise in the world and the church. He was killed on July 28, 1982, in a small plane accident with some visiting friends, his pilot, and two of his children. Last Days, under the direction of his recently remarried wife and co-founder Melody Green Sievright, continues Green's work with a new emphasis on missions via their link with YWAM, the music schools of Jimmy and Carol Owens, and care for the unborn and the poor.

Missions Ministries

Perhaps one of the most significant forces for international missions among young people is the work of Youth with a Mission, founded by Loren Cunningham. It now annually mobilizes thousands of young people in a variety of capacities for short-term missionary service around the world. It is currently the largest evangelical, interdenominational youth missionary movement in the world, with some seventy thousand plus people involved annually and a dream to plant a base among every one of 3,000 two-million people segments. Among YWAM's top leaders and directors are men like Don Stevens of Mercy Ministries, with its international rescue and training ships like the *Anastasis*; Floyd McClung, who brings to YWAM his former experience among the counterculture and street people of Holland, and Denny Gundersson of the Northwest, who helms concerns for indigenous peoples like Native Americans. YWAM has prodigious influence around the world. Men like Danny Lehman encourage personal evangelism. John Dawson writes and preaches to spark interest in spiritual warfare and reconciliation in cities, working locally with street ministry groups. (Some, like Bobby Chance's Centrum and Judy and Ron Radachy of the Holy Ghost Repair Service in Hollywood, specialize in reaching the victims of child pornography and prostitution.) YWAM has literally hundreds of bases around the world, including the University of Nations in Kona, Hawaii, and it annually trains, mobilizes, or influences in missions hundreds of thousands of young people.

A second work of international significance in missions is Operation Mobilization, founded by the fiery George Verwer, a convert of an early Billy Graham crusade. Growing out of his missionary work in Mexico during his Bible-school student days, Verwer's low-profile O.M. has established a solid, interdenominational, and challenging work, specializing in a literature ministry through the medium of two large, internationally-travelling ships, the *Logos* and the *Doulos*. Verwer's burden is for the unreached peoples of the world, especially in India and among the Muslim peoples. Bringing the Gospel to between 250-300 million in India alone over the past thirty years, Operation Mobilization's work among these wholly unevangelized peoples may no doubt one day be recorded in history as significant a contribution in modern missions as that of William Carey.

Growing Concern for the Young

Some of the long-established groups like Campus Life, working with high school young, have had recent fresh infusions of zealous new leadership. Men like Doug Burleigh, Young Life's president, represent high quality attempts to vitalize the organizations well-established chapters in the nation. A growing front of dedicated young Gospel artists and musicians who look on their talents and gifts as ministries first have made a steady impact in Jesus Festivals and concerts across the nation since the late 1970s. See You at the Pole, a national prayer day for high school and junior high students that began in 1989, involves over a million students a year and is coordinated by groups like the National Network of Youth Ministries.

There is, too, the wide influence of Bill Gothard, whose Institutes of Basic Youth Conflicts mushroomed into crowds of twenty thousand or more for practical seminars on principles of Christian living. Although criticized for what some have perceived as a too-pietistic and rigid approach in controversial issues like contemporary Christian music, divorce, and education, Gothard has had a profound influence on the Evangelical consciousness. His missions excursions, first in New Zealand and then Russia have resulted in significant international influence. In 1992 over twenty-two thousand Russian high schools officially adopted his curriculum.

Media Influence

A molder (and often perverter) of public opinion, television touches the inner sanctum of the home. Some far-sighted Christians have successfully captured sections of this giant platform with a voice for God. Pat Robertson of CBN (the Christian Broadcasting Network), and Paul and Jan Crouch of TBN (the Trinity Broadcasting Network) are the best known among the charismatics with established networks.

In recent years other faces, both new and old, male and female, have appeared in regular slots in both cable and other network programs, offering a varied bill of fare aimed mostly at Christians, with some creative programming recently geared towards the housewife and children. Their alternate perspective in news events and their ability to inform and nationally mobilize Christians in key issues are a powerful influence. There is some question as to whether the two-dimensionality of television (with its intrinsic tendency, common to media, to make people "hearers" and not "doers" of the Word) can ever trigger revival. But if one ever happens, the channels to make such an event known are already in place, and millions can be affected in minutes.

Recent examples of this are the astonishing audience response to CBN's "block-booking" channels for the Gospel, first in Latin America in the late eighties (over 4 million conversions) and then again in the nineties. Conversion response in Russia and other Baltic states to programs like "Superbook," an animated children's series of Bible stories, brought a response of more than a million hand-written letters requesting ministry. More than 30 million responded to the 1991 to 1992 Soviet Youth TV special, "What Are You Living For?"

John Giminez, a former "Addicts For Christ" convert from New York and previous pastor of the Rock Church in Virginia Beach, deserves mention for his visionary effort to make public a consciousness of America's need for change and return to Christ. His attempts to bring closer together charismatic and evangelical leadership across the nation for public affirmation of faith and repentance birthed the rallies called "Washington for Jesus." Men like Sonny Arguinzoni and Victor Torres (other street-saved pastors) carry burdens for ex-street people needing spiritual homes. A street-concerned national ministry is the need of the hour in many Westernized countries struggling with poverty and gang violence.

The Jesus festivals are an ongoing series of regional gatherings under various names across the country. Initiated in 1972 in Pennsylvania, Jesus '76 drew an estimated sixty thousand during the bicentennial year, as also did Creation '93. Some, like Larry Andes' Fishnet, Harry Thomas's Creation, the original Ichthus, and various other Jesus regionals regularly drew an attendance of fifteen to fifty thousand from all denominations. Besides offering opportunity for artists, musicians, and singers, they have become a major platform for Christian challenge, teaching, and opportunity for both mass evangelism and missionary recruitment. This concept has spread internationally.

The international "Praise Marches" begun by Graham Kendrick and Roger Forster in England and now helmed by various young leaders in participating countries around the world are recent, creative, and healing demonstrations of the life of the church to the street. In 1993 they drew some 1.34 million participants in the streets of 758 cities in forty nations and will culminate in a satellite-coordinated World March involving millions in 1994, beginning in New Zealand (the "uttermost part of the earth from Jerusalem"), where the sun first rises in the world.

Hope, indeed, for the nations. It is yet too early to tell what God can and may do with those that remain faithful to their calling and to their convictions. One thing is sure: a new breed is in the ranks, "satisfied with a dissatisfied satisfaction," hungry to see something holy happen. And with them comes a glimmer of genuine light.

CHAPTER ELEVEN

Where Do We Stand?

Two-Thirds World Awakenings

"That they should seek the Lord, if haply they might feel after him, and find him, though he be not far from every one of us" (Acts 17:27).

We come to the latter half of the twentieth century and a brief overview of God's moving among major non-Western peoples. Significantly, much of the explosive growth and national awakenings among the Church worldwide are taking place here.

Africa has given us men of the calibre of Bishop Festevo Kivengere, as well as many new young prophets and evangelists. In the Africa of the turn of the century, only one out of thirteen thousand were Christians. Now one out of three are reported as Christians! Africa has experienced many powerful revivals typical of the Belgian Congo outpouring on C. T. Studd's 1914 mission-field. "The whole place was charged as if with an electric current. Men were falling, jumping, laughing, crying, singing, confessing, and some shaking terribly. It was a terrible sight. . . . This particular one can best be described as a spiritual tornado. People were literally flung to the floor or over the forms, yet no-one was hurt. . . . As I led in prayer, the Spirit came down in mighty power, sweeping the congregation. My whole body literally trembled with the power. We saw a marvellous sight, people literally filled and drunk with the Spirit" (*This Is That*, pp. 12-15).

Many of these African revivals are marked by supernatural manifestations–visions, prophecies and healings. and have deeply affected many parts of the continent. Men like Reinhard Bonnke hold a vision for all of Africa to be reached for Jesus: "This is not a day of the sickle, but of the combine harvester!" There are some twenty thousand new converts each day in Africa. Some estimates project at the present rate of growth that by the year 2000, 50 percent of Africa will be converted. (So what about the "heathen in Africa"?)

For thirty-five years there has been continuous revival in East Africa in countries like Kenya, Tanzania and even in Uganda, under a man like Idi Amin. With seven hundred new churches in Kenya in 1980 alone and more than two new churches a day, national leaders like President Moi were praying God would make them president of the first fully Christian nation. The African Indigenous Church movement recorded over a million converts in 1970.

Revival on a Nigerian University Campus

William Kumuyi, a Christian mathematics professor at the University of Nigeria in Lagos, began some years ago a Bible study centered around the subjects of revival and holy living after being challenged by reading some of the works of previous revivalists like Wesley and Finney. The study, which started with thirty-five people, soon overflowed into the university campus, with some two thousand attending. By 1992 Pastor Kumuyi's Deeper Christian Life Ministry was one of the five largest churches in the world, with some seventy thousand worshippers every Sunday, requiring five services a day, the first beginning at 7:00 A.M., with three Bible classes each Monday night involving some fifty thousand people. Kumuyi was ministering to 150,000 people a week.

African revivals are powerful examples of simple faith in a miracle-working God amidst sometimes terrifying persecution and political instability. They are a real testimony to the West of love under suffering.

The Numbers Multiply

Korea leads the world in large churches, especially the near-legendary David (Paul) Yonggi Cho and the Full Gospel Church in Seoul, with his "Fourth Dimension" vision, prayer, and bold trust in God. Over 20 percent of South Koreans are now estimated to be Christians; Seoul alone has two thousand churches. Full Gospel, by March 31, 1982, had 250,000 members, and seated thirty-two thousand. Prayer Mountain maintained a twenty-four-hour prayer meeting, and a new facility was built in December 1982 for seating ten thousand. Working with over 220 on its pastoral staff, Full Gospel then had seventeen senior pastors, forty-five elders, 282 senior deacons 3,468 regular deacons, five thousand home meetings, and seven services a Sunday, with afternoon worship with between fifty to sixty thousand in each service! By 1990, 180,000 were attending worship services, with more than eight hundred thousand in membership. His brother Yong Muk Cho, who started a sister church with five thousand members also in Seoul (Nambu Full Gospel) by 1992 had two hundred thousand members with some forty thousand in each Sunday worship service. Church growth in the Assemblies of God in Korea alone, over the years 1969 to 1982, was an astonishing 742 percent, in addition to that of the Baptists (240%), Presbyterians (135%), Methodists (130%) and the Salvation Army (86%). These numbers are even more impressive when you consider that at the turn of this century there were no Christian churches at all in Korea. Billy Graham ministered to a crowd of 1,150,000 in Yoido Plaza in 1973; the 1980 Here's Life Korea crusade drew 2,700,000, (the largest single preaching crowd in history) with a combined attendance in four days of over 16.5 million.

Obeying the Laws of Revival

China has had a number of gracious visitations from God. Jonathan Goforth, inspired by the Welsh Revival and reports from Korea, was deeply challenged by Finney's writings. He was determined to know the laws of revival and obey them. In the aftermath of strife, bitterness, and hatred that followed the massacres of the Boxer Rebellion, the young doctor challenged the divided missionaries to prayer and confession of sin. Missionaries and Chinese leaders from twenty-one stations were desperate for God. One woman leader said to Goforth, "We have prayed dry for revival here. If God doesn't send revival this time, I don't see how it will be possible for us to continue in prayer. We have exhausted every prayer promise in His book" (Rosalind Goforth, *Goforth of China*, p. 186).

Goforth had only four days. Beginning with an account of an earlier revival in Manchuria, he led the people in prayer where general brokenness and confession of sin commenced. "Mr. Goforth's message was 'Not by might, nor by power, but by My Spirit,'" said one missionary.

> The Cross burns like a living fire in the heart of every address. What oppresses the thought of the penitent is not any thought of future punishment but . . . of his unfaithfulness, of ingratitude to the Lord who has redeemed him, the heinous sin of trampling on His love . . . it has pricked them to the heart, moved them to the very depths of their moral being, and caused multitudes, no longer able to contain themselves, to break out into the cry "God be merciful to me a sinner!" (Rosalind Goforth, *Goforth of China*, pp. 186-187)

From leaders to Bible school students and then on to the general population in different provinces, the ensuing revival touched whole communities, deeply cleansed and strengthened the church, and reached thousands for Christ.

Hungry for the Word

Today, ministries like Paul Kauffman's World Outreach in Hong Kong have produced much literature and prayer for Communist China, laying a strong foundation for what God is now doing there. In 1930 missionaries felt "the doors to China are closing," and for thirty years they apparently did. Mao's revolution, however, did five things that only helped the future spread of the Gospel–he simplified language, constructed roads and communication systems, taught people to read and write in one dialect, and finally removed ancestor worship and every trace of religion!

Now into the spiritual vacuum left by his death, Christ is dealing again with this vast continent of the highest population group in humanity. Recent violent government reaction to attempted freedom among the young has only served to intensify prayer and increase the determination of the church to see this great nation receive the Gospel.

By the 1980s there were over fifty thousand house churches in China, with six to thirty people in each, most under thirty-five years of age. The Three Self Movement estimated anywhere between 10 and 20 million believers out of a population of 960 million in China. In January 1980, over 350,000 Bibles were mailed in, two hundred thousand more in inland regions; In the 1983s "Operation Pearl," nearly 80 percent of a million Bibles were successfully distributed after being brought in at night by sea. The secret supply boats were met by so many Chinese Christians (in numbers estimated between five and twenty thousand believers) that the alerted local army believed it was a revolution. By 1990, according to the estimates of the Lausanne Statistical Task Force, there were at least 50 million Chinese Pentecostals. There are some twenty-eight hundred new converts a day in China (*Current Thoughts/Trends,* March 1991, p. 12, Abstract. #7028).

In Japan also the Gospel began to make significant inroads into the nation in the early 1980s; from 1984 to 1988, churches reported significant growth rates of 20 percent (Baptist/Mennonite), 22 percent (Reformed/Presbyterian), and 35 percent (Interdenominational), with the Pentecostals experiencing a massive 107 percent increase.

Latin America continues to grow explosively. In 1900 there were only fifty thousand evangelicals in Latin America; in 1930, over a million; in 1940, 2 million; 1950, 5 million; 1960, 10 million, and in 1970, 20 million (Peter Wagner, *Look Out! The Pentecostals Are Coming*). David Barrett records that of Brazil's 99 million Catholics, 60 million are involved to some degree in Spiritism and 11.4 million are actually Protestants.

Americans like "Hermano Pablo" (Paul Finkenbinder), who labored to creatively evangelize through the media, and men like Juan Carlos Ortiz and Edward Miller, inheritors of the Argentinian awakening during the visit of Tommy Hicks, have done much to make known what God has done in this continent.

Christian Broadcasting Network's three-day media blitzes in Guatemala, El Salvador, and Nicaragua reaped impressive results; over 38 percent of 6,500 people interviewed in Guatemala City said they had received Christ during the broadcast, with another 9 percent responding during the survey interview. Local churches there registered a 41 percent growth rate in the first five months of 1990. In Nicaragua, of the more than 118,000 interviewed, 40 percent had become Christians, with a further seventeen hundred getting saved during the survey.

India, that spiritually-sensitive and troubled land, has had much spiritual investment from the days of the shoemaker William Carey through R. J. Ward (Britain), Praying John Hyde (U.S.) 1897, and Amy Carmichael (Ulster) 1906. Intelligent Western missionaries like E. Stanley Jones were given open doors to very high levels of government and leadership in the early 1940s; later healing evangelists like T. L. Osborn ministered to large crowds with simple demonstrations of God's present power to save and deliver. Today the practical Christian care and compassion shown by the Nobel-Prizewinning Albanian nun Mother Teresa and her late Assemblies of God missionary friend in Calcutta, Mark Buntain, were a constant testimony to the reality of Jesus' love. A number of young evangelists from the West have seen large responses in recent years in mass crusades for evangelism coupled with prayer for the sick. *Every Home Crusade* is on their third coverage of every home in India; TransWorld Radio has had remarkable success in beaming the Gospel to remote villages. Recent film showings like Campus Crusades' *Jesus* and the locally-produced biography of Christ, *Ocean Of Mercy*, have had phenomenal Gospel impact on villages. India sends out 4,500 missionaries, while another 120,000 serve at home as full-time Christian workers with thirty thousand mostly cross-cultural workers. A third of all these are charismatics (AD 2000, April 1991, #6, p. 2).

The Communist World

"We must engage in a most decisive battle against reactionary clergy and suppress their resistance with such cruelty that they will remember it for several decades to come." So said Lenin in 1922. "Religion," said Karl Marx, "is the opiate of the people."

Yet by the nineties the Communist world was one of the great contemporary harvestfields of our time. It was easier to preach the Gospel in many places of the Communist world than it was to preach in the streets of the United States of America. Here was one of the most explosive opportunity windows in the world, as millions of people who revelled in new-found governmental freedoms opened up to the promise of personal freedom implicit in the Gospel.

A Soviet unbeliever wrote:

> I have just turned over the last page of a great book, and am overcome by feelings of gratitude and happiness. But there are bitter questions which remain unanswered. Why only now? Why so late? Half my life is gone. . . . To think that such a treasure had been hidden from me. Who decided, and on what grounds, that this book was harmful for me? In our time of unrest and brokenness, when crystal palaces turned out to be cardboard shacks, when once-majestic kings are now covered with shame, when under the granite edifices are unstable foundations of clay, then I know there is a book to which I can always return and it will help comfort and support me in the darkest hour. (George Otis, Jr., *Charisma Magazine,* Special Missions Report, August 1990)

Here, where suffering and persecuted Evangelicals have carried out determined intercession for their nations, recent political changes have triggered incredible opportunities for evangelism, with the Baptists and Pentecostal's key to leadership and life. The previous 640 registered Pentecostal churches in the USSR, with many more unregistered and 250 new Pentecostal churches opening in the past five years, have now exploded with thousands of new converts. Though in 1980, 137 million Soviets once claimed to be irreligious, an impressive 97 million even then still claimed to be Christian. In the late 1970s, Poland reportedly had some thirty thousand young

Christians meet together to seek God for the power of the Holy Spirit.

Men like Brother Andrew and Richard Wurmbrand helped the West become aware of the "underground church"; books like *Underground Saints, Tortured for His Faith, God's Smuggler, Tomorrow You Die,* and *Vanya* helped convey the reality of the spiritual battle. Amidst the persecution and suffering, there was birthed a reality and hunger for God often missing in the West. Now the recent massive restructuring of the Soviet empire has birthed tremendous opportunities for harvest, although the key focus must now be on strengthening the existing church for its own outreach.

Despite cold weather more than 125,000 people attended eleven stadium meetings conducted in Romania by Luis Palau, with over 39,400 responding. The 31 percent response rate was the highest Palau and his team have ever seen in their ministry. Nearly 80 percent of the ten thousand strong crowd at the final meeting indicated conversion (*Christianity Today,* July 22, 1991). A 1990 *Youth with a Mission Crusade* in Pakov, in the former USSR, resulted in nine thousand Soviets responding to Christ in a town of two hundred thousand (*Charisma,* Nov. 1990, p. 22). John Guest saw 2,700 of the five thousand attending his crusade in the USSR respond, with nearly eight thousand Soviets becoming Christians in Moscow's Gorky Park (*Charisma Magazine,* Oct. 1990). Daily reports of immense harvests come in from all over this awesome missionfield. The 1991 to 1992 CBN TV specials that aired all over the former Soviet Union have had phenomenal response, with over 30 million (primarily young people) requesting salvation literature in 1992 alone and over 4 million requesting follow-up booklets. Rallies to help plant new churches have had record attendances with thousands not having room to come, and one new church in Kiev began with a potential membership of over 2,500 new Christian families.

All around the world there are impressive signs of God's work, especially in the Third World and most Communist nations, but there remains much to be done, especially among the unreached lands, the "forbidden countries" (where to become a Christian carries an automatic death sentence) and the Muslim peoples of the world.

Yet with the recent Gulf War, more prayer was centered on the Middle East than at any other time in this century and many nominal Muslims have begun to radically reconsider their religious commitment in the wake of military defeat. In the aftermath of the massive Western military infusion where hundreds of soldiers were converted, hundreds of thousands of Bibles and Christian books are now in place in areas where they have been historically outlawed.

One entire African Muslim delegation to Mecca had a vision of Jesus and became Christians. The church is now established in both Iran and Iraq, and in some regions, like Algeria, awesome visitations of God have resulted in the supernatural conversion of almost an entire town's leadership overnight.

Asia still represents the great final continent of origins. In the justice of God, the "chain of Christianity" moving from there Westward over the centuries ought to find its completion. The task is by no means done; yet it has been frequently stated that more people will give their lives to Christ during this century than all previous centuries put together, and much of that will take place during this decade.

Now for the first time in Christian history, the "unfinished task" has a discernible shape and outline in the so-called "10-40 Window" of the world. Here nearly 95 percent of the unreached people-groups, nations, and world-class cities of the world can be seen to fit into a shrinking boundary roughly the shape of two outstretched hands over the center of the world. The "thumbs" cross over the area where it all began—Iran and Iraq, the Biblical Persia and Babylon. And this is the site where many Bible scholars believe it all began, the probable location of the original Garden of Eden. For the first time in contemporary missions history, we think we know what God is up to. He is going back to where it all began. He is taking back the ground in reverse. He is reclaiming what was lost in the Fall, and He is accomplishing this final task in our time.

As we leave this brief overview of the so-called Two-Thirds World peoples, we ought to be haunted by an embarrassing statistic: seven thousand, six hundred people in the West give up professing faith in Christ every day.

Allowing that many are nominal Christians, allowing that some never understood the Gospel in the first place, allowing any and all other factors we can assign to justify this tragic fact, this truth remains: with all our heritage, opportunity, Scripture, and teaching, we in the West must be held deeply responsible for our hard-heartedness and apathy. True, we are seeing the fruit of God's continuous renewing and purging work, but oh, we still need a great revival. In the light of all God's work in history, our final call is to one last awakening, one that sparks our massive volume of lapsed or professed Christians into complete consecration to the living Christ and a rebirth of genuine care and compassion for others. Shall we pray and believe then for—the last wave?

Sin in the Nation

The Current Darkness

From John Price's challenging study of the economic and political situation of the United States in *America at the Crossroads* and Patterson and Kim's 1991 survey, *The Day America Told the Truth,* come some shocking statistics. The question "Do we need a revival?" in the light of these kinds of facts is pointless. Much more to the point is this question: "Do we really want a revival?" Sometimes God has to let really bad things happen before we realize just how much we have left His loving laws. It has been so in many of the major revivals of the past, this "darkness before the dawn." It takes no scholar to realize that in the Western world it is dark enough now.

Crime. "America is the most crime-ridden society in the world; no other country is even close" (James Kilpatrick, *Nations Business*, April 1975). Even with the U.S. Bureau of Crime Statistics' records of 20 million personal crimes in 1988 alone (one hundred for every one thousand Americans), recent studies show official crime statistics are underestimated by about 600 percent! "Thirty-nine percent of people in America have already committed some kind of criminal offense, and more than half of all Americans (60%) have been victims of crime at least once in their life, with more than half victimized twice or more" (*TDATTT*, p. 173). One out of every four Americans will be a victim of a "Type One Crime," a serious offence against property, or a personal or potential injury like assault, robbery, rape, burglary, or murder. If there are four members of your family, statistics say one of them will be the victim of a crime of violence. One in six Americans was seriously abused as a child.

Homicide among young men is twenty times that of Western Europe and forty times the Japanese rate. Young men in Harlem are less likely to survive to the age of forty than those in Bangladesh. There is a murder every twenty-seven minutes. That means fifty-four lives are taken each day, and twenty thousand a year.

Overwhelming Statistics

Every seven seconds a larceny is committed. Every ten seconds a burglar plys his trade. Every seventy-eight seconds someone is robbed. A rape takes place every eight minutes. (The U.S. has twenty times the number of rapes reported in Japan, England, and Spain.)

Our role models are morally bankrupt: "Today's movie heroes are cynical loners, misanthropes, capable of expressing themselves with weapons only. . . . Children's programming now averages twenty-five violent acts an hour, up 50% from the eighties; 95% of all children's cartoons have violent themes" (*TDATTT*, pp. 122-123).

Americans had 4.6 billion dollars of property stolen in 1977 alone. There is only one arrest in every five reported crimes. A crook has a better than 80 percent chance of escaping arrest. If he does get caught, he stands a good chance of not serving time. A Gallup Poll says 45 percent of all Americans are afraid to walk in their neighborhoods at night, up from 31 percent in 1968. Almost 20 percent say they are fearful in their homes at night. Americans are the most heavily armed people on earth; 26 million carry a handgun or a knife with them when they go out.

Prior to 1775 religion and morals made up 90 percent of the educational content of school readers. By 1926 religious and moral teaching made up only 6 percent and has since dropped to an almost immeasurable amount. In the nineties just about everyone lies. There are more serious liars now than at any time in America's past as a nation. Ninety-one percent of Americans say they lie regularly; 36 percent are lies that hurt others, violate trust and have criminal or legal consequences. One in five Americans says he can't make it through a single day without conscious, premeditated lying. Lying has become a cultural trait in America; it is imbedded in our national character. Americans lie about everything—and usually for no good reason. The majority of Americans today (two out of three) believe there is nothing wrong with telling a lie (*TDATTT,* pp. 45, 49). And today's Americans no longer take counsel or advice from any kind of authority, religious or not; over 93 percent said they and nobody else determine what is right and wrong in their lives. Eighty-four percent confessed they had or would violate the rules of their religion if they personally thought it was wrong. When asked what beliefs people would die for, almost half (48%) said "None" (*TDATTT* pp. 27,28).

Sexual Sin. "In terms of the idealized couple of the past: virgins joined in holy matrimony faithful till death do them part; we found nothing but a shadow on the wall." Although more Americans believe that adultery and fornication head the list of what they personally consider shameful and immoral (above lying, drug use, and stealing), it has not stopped immorality. Ninety-two percent of sexually active people report having had ten or more lovers with a lifetime average of seventeen. Four in ten . . . had more than one lover in the past year. Single people have averaged a four-above-par twenty-one lovers, and four in the last year. Living together has now gained acceptance with a majority of Americans (over 50%). Only one in three Americans gave love as his primary reason for marrying. Forty-five percent agree that most marriages will end in divorce, with communication problems the number one reason in the nineties, and both infidelity and constant fighting a close tie for second. Almost one third of all married Americans (31%) have had or are now having an affair; and the majority (62%) somehow still think there is nothing morally wrong with the ones they're currently having. And how does this affect the children? Almost two thirds of the present eighteen-to twenty-four-year-old "baby-busters" (61%) lost their virginity by the age of sixteen; one in five kids in the nineties loses his virginity before the age of thirteen.

And the consequences are terrifying. Besides the more than fifteen other sexually transmitted diseases that are rampant in the Western world, some 2.2 million Americans feel reasonably certain they have AIDS, and another 7 million believe themselves at high risk for it. Almost half those who are gay and high-risk (42%) admit they still take no precautions; one in four already believes he has had sex with someone already infected (*TDATTT*, pp. 73,87,89,100-101,137-138). With 230 million of the killer virus able to fit on the period of this sentence and no presently known cure, AIDS is the first fatal, disease-causing organism that has circled the globe in less than one third of a generation. As Everett Koop said, it is "the first with the capacity to destroy an entire generation."

A Horrible Sin

Abortion. In Los Angeles during February of 1982, a twenty by eight by eight metal trash container was discovered, filled with the horrifying spectacle of five hundred dead and decaying little bodies, each four pounds or more, pickled in formaldehyde and stacked in leaking tubs like ice-cream containers. A week later authorities removed another four hundred more, many with perfectly formed faces and limbs, from the home of the man who once owned the now defunct medical lab that had dumped its grisly stock. County officials would not permit news and TV photographers near the scene. It shocked many as badly as the news of the Nazi holocaust. But we are in a holocaust. Satan must be afraid of what is coming in our generation–as he had done twice in Biblical history, in the days of Moses and Jesus, he has a contract on the children of our time. The nation that was horrified by the cyanide deaths of Jonestown and by poisoned Tylenol hardly seems bothered that more little people are killed in the U.S. annually by abortion than the total combined populations of Miami, Kansas City, and Minneapolis.

To get around constitutional protection, the Supreme Court defines babies as "non-persons" even though the Constitution does not define persons. It invented a new right, "the right of privacy," based on the convenience of the mother. It said, "Maternity or additional offspring may force on a mother a distressful life and future. Psychological harm may be imminent, and mental and physical wealth may be taxed by child care. There is also the distress for all concerned, associated with the unwanted child." William F. Buckley, Jr., has stated that, based on this reasoning, the whole of the adolescent class should be eliminated.

War on the Unborn

Once before in history, the Supreme Court tried to usurp God's authority over human lives. In 1857, just before the Great Revival, the Court determined that the free descendents of slaves could not be citizens and that slaves were not persons (the *Dred Scott* case).

We must remember that Hitler didn't start by killing Jews; he began with the mentally retarded. On 1 September 1939, in a private letter to two German doctors, he authorized them to give to incurable patients a "mercy death." Next, he killed those in retarded children's hospitals and homes, criminals in Nazi prisons, and finally old people's homes. Over forty thousand people were killed by Hitler before he began his anti-Semitic campaign. If the state can arbitrarily kill any of us who do not deserve to die, it can kill all of us. Here is a list of America's war dead:

Revolutionary War–25,324
Civil War–498,332
World War I–116,710
World War II–407,316
Korean War–54,546
Viet Nam War–58,095

War on the Unborn–9,500,000, January 1972 to January 1983 (Barbara Syska, Research Analyst, National Right to Life Committee, 419 Seventh St. N.W., Suite 102, Washington, D.C. 20004).

Christians and the Courtroom

Legalized Wrong. The late Francis Schaeffer, John Whitehead, and more recently Jay Sekulow and other Christian lawyers like those of the Rutherford Institute have all attempted to alert the nation to its critical situation in the lawcourts of the land, particularly in regard to recent cases pending Supreme Court decision. Cases mentioned include the following: ministers being held liable for counseling malpractice; Christian teachers forbidden to pray in public schools; HEW requiring Bible colleges to admit drug addicts and drunks as "handicapped people"; churches forbidden to build a religious school or day-care center in areas zoned as residential; parents prosecuted for sending children to religious schools not approved by a state board of education; and pastors arrested for operating a church school not approved by the state.

Secular humanism, as typified by the actions of groups like the American Civil Liberties Union, has deeply influenced the decisions of the Supreme Court and brought the country to a place Whitehead felt may trigger a "Second American Revolution." (See Schaeffer's *A Christian Manifesto* and Whitehead's *The Second American Revolution.*)

Financial Crisis

Economics. In 1929, just before the crash, personal debt had risen to eighty-eight percent of personal income. In 1950 personal debt was 50 percent. In 1974 it was 75 percent and has risen steadily ever since. An average of two hundred thousand businesses file bankruptcy every year. Of the ten largest business bankruptcies, excluding banks, in the two hundred-year history of the U.S., five have occurred since 1975. If banks collapse now, they do not close as in the past but are taken over by the government (Emergency Banking Act of 1961). "The U.S. government debt is now over 3.8 trillion dollars. The total yearly taxes of an average family in this nation only pay for three fourths of a second of government expenses" (Larry Burkett, Speech at CBA, 1991).

Inflation. "Exceeding 10% a year is called 'ruinflation' because it ruins an economy and ultimately destroys a people. That kind of inflation after WWI led to the election of Hitler. In 1919, right after the war, prices rose by 50%. By 1920 they were up 500%, and by 1922-1923, the last year of inflation, prices increased by 14,000%! By then an egg in Germany cost 80 billion marks and a loaf of bread 200 billion marks. Reischmark notes were issued in 100 and 200 million denominations; one lady taking a wash basket of money to a bakery to buy a loaf of bread found a thief had stolen the basket and dumped the money on the ground" (John Price, *America at the Crossroads*).

Suicide. Many more Americans kill themselves each year than the official statistics (thirty thousand a year) indicate, though most think it immoral and more than half believe it is a sin punishable by God in the next life.

There is no human solution in sight. As the Second Law of Thermodynamics points out, you can't get order in a system without a prior ordering energy and intelligence of a greater magnitude than the system needing help. As David said long ago, "It is time for Thee, O Lord, to work; for they have made void Thy law" (Ps. 119:126).

The Marks of a Revivalist

John Gillies, in his 1795 classic *Accounts of Revivals*, noted what he perceived as the marks of a revivalist. Here is a summary of these characteristics.

1. They were earnest about the great work of the ministry on which they had entered. They felt that as ministers of the Gospel they dared not act otherwise. They dared not throw less than their whole soul into the conflict. They dared not take their ease. They dared not be indifferent to the issue when professing to lead the hosts of the living God against the armies of the prince of darkness.

2. They were "bent upon success"; to be indifferent to their office would "prove themselves nothing short of traitors to Him and to His cause. As warriors they set their hearts on victory and fought in faith, anticipating triumph under the guidance of such a Captain.

3. They were men of faith. They ploughed and sought in hope. They knew in due season they would reap if they did not faint. They had confidence in God, in their Savior's commission, in the promises of Scripture, in and the Holy Spirit's almighty power and grace.

4. They were men of labor. They bore the burden and the heat of the day as freely offered to the Lord, keeping back nothing, grudging nothing, joyfully, thankfully, surrendering all to Him who loved them. They labored for eternity as men

who knew the time was short and the day of recompense was at hand.

5. They were men of patience. They were not discouraged though they had to labor long without seeing all the fruit they desired. They were not soon weary in well-doing.

6. They were men of boldness and determination. Enemies might oppose, timid friends might hesitate, but they pressed forward, in nothing terrified by difficulty or opposition. There is needed not merely natural courage in order to face natural danger and difficulty; there is, in our own day, a still greater need of moral boldness in order to neutralize the fear of man, the dread of public opinion, that god of our idolatry in this last age. Our age boasts of superior enlightenment, but it would bring everything to the test of reason or decide it by the votes of the majority.

7. They were men of prayer. It is true they labored much, visited much, and studied much, but they also prayed much. In this they abounded. They were much alone with God replenishing their own souls. "It was said of Wales in 1904 that you knew revival was on the way when you heard the '*Oh*' of desperation and urgency in the prayers."

8. They were men of most decided doctrine both in law and Gospel. There is a breadth and a power in their preaching—a glow and an energy about their thoughts and words that makes us feel they were "men of might." Their trumpet gave no feeble, uncertain sound either to saint or sinner, the Church or the world.

9. They were men of solemn deportment and deep spirituality. Their daily work furnished the best illustration of what they preached. No frivolity, flippancy, worldly conviviality, or companionships neutralized their public preaching or marred the work they were seeking to accomplish. They lived what they preached. (Gillies, *Historical Collections of Accounts of Revivals*, pp. vi-xi).

Chapter Twelve

Revival Features and Impacts

The Social Impact of Revivals

If one of the definitive marks of revival is its ability to change the "moral climate of a community," in what areas of society will we notice most change? Historically, we will notice it in the extremes, the upper and lower strata of a country's educational system, economic structure, moral stance, health care facilities, and the attitudes toward age and the media. There are the main areas that undergo significant amounts of change. God's work touches and transforms the outer limits of that society.

Revival Affects

The educational system includes teachers and students, educators and pupils. In our day the conflicts are over Christian vs. public schools, voluntary prayer, creationism, textbook censorship, and the teaching of the religion of secular humanism.

The economic structure involves wealthy and poor, business and slums. Today the call is for sweeping relief in the inner city, reassessment of presently adopted assumptions of both socialism and capitalism, waste, and the increase of major industries that are built around addictions, affluence, and joblessness.

The moral arena takes in the realm of both the Church and criminal, seminary and prisons. Today it deals, on the one hand, with both liberalism and Evangelical humanism, and on the other with rising crime, prison reform, and rehabilitation.

Health care facilities include doctors and the sick, psychiatrists and the insane; excessive cost and carelessness; Easternized holistic care; abusive drugs, childbirth, vaccination, and surgery procedures; abortion clinics, organ transplants and sperm bank misuse.

The media are those who define culture and help it proliferate. Today's media problems for the Church include challenged direct mail privilege, TV access by cable and satellite; and anti-Christian and occultic propaganda in the arts, including film, television, theatre, and the recording industry.

Age conflicts affect children and infants, the elderly or retired, and involve the areas of abortion and genetic manipulation, euthanasia, retirement homes, mandatory retirement, and inadequacy in pensions and health insurance plans.

The Church's Responsibility

Bill Gothard points out that where the Church fails in her commission, government must assume the burden, and thus it acquires that corresponding power of influence. Instead of the early nation's strong family-based and church-based education, we have amoral and humanistic public schools. Instead of her ministry of care and healing, we have the clinical and costly public hospital; instead of Christian charity, we have government welfare.

Having steadily conceded responsibility to the government in most other areas, we only seem to notice with alarm this loss when the same government begins to directly intrude on the Church herself, with taxation, zoning, and other abusive ordinances. Dorothy Sayers (the Anglican theologian and friend of C. S. Lewis and J. R. R. Tolkein) noted in her *Christian Letters to a Post-Christian World* that the poor always have to be cared for and the burden borne by the more well-off, whether church or government does it.

The difference is, with the true Church, support is a Gospel concern with gifts of compassion and care; with government it is a legal issue, and the money is exacted from the rich in taxes. The sad consequence is that love is thereby eliminated and replaced by law and civic duty.

Yet in each era of revival, an awakened Church returns to shoulder its abandoned responsibility to a hurting world. Indeed, much of that which is publicly charitable and socially compassionate in society has Christian roots, like many orphanages, hospitals, and rehabilitation and social centers. In 1842, Albert Barnes, a friend of the revivalists in his day, an author of a classic book on the atonement, and a pastor for forty years at the First Presbyterian Church in Philadelphia, said:

"One sin is interlocked with others and sustained by others . . . the only power in the Universe which can meet and overcome such combined evil is the power of the Spirit of God. There are evils of alliance and confederation in every city which can never be met but by a general revival of religion" (Barnes, *Revivals in Towns and Small Cities,* The American National Preacher, XV, 1841, pp. 12-13,15).

Civic Duty

William Arthur's book *Tongue of Fire*, released in half-a-dozen editions in England and America after 1854, laid out to the Methodists their duty to the inner city if they believed in deliverance from all sin and entire consecration. He warned that the two most dangerous perversions of the Gospel were to look on it as a "salvation for the soul *after* it leaves the body, but no salvation from sin while there" and as "a means of forming a holy community in the world to come, but never in *this* one." He said:

> Nothing short of the *general renewal of society* ought to satisfy any soldier of Christ . . . much as Satan glories in his power over an individual, how much greater must be his glorying over a nation embodying in its laws and usages disobedience to God, wrong to man and con-

> tamination to morals? To destroy all national holds of evil; to root sin out of institutions; to hold up to view the gospel idea of a righteous nation . . . is one of the first duties of those whose position or mode of thought gives them any influence . . .

In doing so they were "at once glorifying the Redeemer" by showing how lovely His influence over society was and taking out hindrances to individual conversions, some that directly incite vice, others that uphold a state of things that shuts God out. "Satan might be content to let Christianity turn over the subsoil" if he can continue to forever sow the surface with thorns and briars, "but the Gospel is come to renew the face of the earth" (Arthur, *Tongue of Fire,* pp. 145-146).

In the 1857 Awakening, Christian concern with poverty, the rights of women and children, working people, the evils of the liquor traffic, slum housing, and racial bitterness blossomed in a thousand movements and ministries to see the nation change. In England, Christians who disagreed on other areas stood together against the sin of the streets. Perhaps divided in method and mind-set like Shaftesbury and Booth, they were yet one in motive. Unable to let the nation alone, they fought both in government halls and on filthy streets the abuse of working people, their children, and the poor.

Briefly, here is a synopsis of some of the most recognized reform movements, many of which are still in active existence today in one form or another.

William and Catherine Booth's Salvation Army

By all accounts the one most obvious example of Christian social compassion and practical concern by any group in contemporary history is the Salvation Army. The works of the holy Army launched by the young Methodist William Booth (1829-1912) and his astonishing wife Catherine Mumford (1820-1890) are legendary. Almost every type of outreach and care for the poor and downtrodden imaginable were both attempted and usually successfully implemented by this radical band.

William's *In Darkest England and the Way Out* outlined a scheme for the rehabilitation of an entire nation, a grand social reconstruction plan a century ahead of its time.

Catherine's brilliant preaching and writing affected hundreds of thousands. Her temperance tracts, written under an assumed name, were widely distributed throughout Europe; though suffering from curvature of the spine, never to know a pain-free day in her life, and often lonely and confined, she read the entire Bible right through eight times by the time she was twelve years old. Shortly after, at fourteen, she mastered Finney's systematic theology, along with other volumes by Butler, Fletcher, Wesley, and other holiness writers. These influential works led to her strong messages on Christian perfection that were to characterize the Army's motivation for service to the world.

When Catherine died more people attended her funeral than had attended the Queen of England's (ten thousand). William was universally honored by statesmen and kings for his work with the poor and underprivileged; thirty-five thousand people attended his funeral. But one of the most radical challenges to sin in society the Booths made came from one of their sons, Bramwell, in a controversial media exposure that rocked a nation.

"Maiden Tribute"

Bramwell Booth's young and pretty wife, Florence, blue-eyed and normally serene, flinched as the full horror of the truth she had uncovered struck her sensitive spirit. Managing the "Refuge," a temporary haven for runaway girls, streetwalkers, and hookers, she was prepared for evidence of London's widespread prostitution, but not for what she discovered: a terrible network entrapping young girls—innocent children often younger than thirteen or fourteen. The network used false employment agencies, condoned hideous initiations, and then shipped the young girls as human sexual slave traffic to rich debauchers throughout England and sometimes (drugged and nailed alive into coffins) to the Continent.

The age of consent in "moral" Britain was then only thirteen in contrast to the Continent's twenty-one. Yet three times legal efforts to raise this age in England were met with defeat. One Member of Parliament wanted it lowered to ten!

London was steeped in prostitution: one in every fifty English women were hookers, with eighty thousand prostitutes in the city and two thousand pimps working Charing Cross alone. Their clients were "men in high places; not only members of Parliament, but Queen Victoria's cousin, the King of the Belgians, who spent 'eighteen hundred pounds a year debauching English girls'" (Richard Collier, *The General Next to God,* p. 111). Another lecher proudly boasted he had "ruined 2,000 women." One home near Farnham for "fallen children" housed forty girls under twelve; one at Newport another fifty girls under ten. "In only four instances had any of the perpetrators been punished. Two London men had outraged respectively sixteen and a dozen children; only one (of the men) was convicted. The plea? The children over thirteen had consented; and those under thirteen 'could not know the nature of the oath!' In eight weeks no fewer than thirty cases involving injury to forty-three girls between three and thirteen years old were brought before the courts" (Madge Unsworth, *Maiden Tribute,* pp. 17-18).

A Rescue Attempt

With her own baby daughter beside her, thinking of the anguish of other little girls and their degradation, Florence cried herself to sleep night after night. Bramwell, her tenderhearted husband, was shocked but secretly doubted it could be so bad. Determined to check it out, he shortly after met a seventeen-year old girl, Annie Swan, who had escaped during the entrapment process. Further questioning of other rescued street girls confirmed the horrible truth–a slave-traffic that "could not be matched by any trade in human beings known to history had been set in motion."

The twenty-six-year-old Salvation Army Chief of Staff then wrote, "I resolved–*and recorded the resolve on paper*–that no matter what the consequences might be, I would do all I could to stop these abominations, to rouse public opinion, to agitate for the improvement of the law, to bring to justice the adulterers and murders of innocence, and to make a way of escape for the victims!" (Bramwell Booth, *Echoes and Memories,* p. 120).

The Great Exposure

Working with a new convert, Rebecca Jarrett, a thirty-six-year-old ex-drunkard and twenty-year brothel-keeper, and the famous London editor William T. Stead, the Salvation Army launched a fantastic plot to confirm and expose the children's slave traffic—one that was eventually to embroil the Army in bitter controversy and result not in the arrest and conviction of the child traders, but of Jarrett and Stead. Jarrett posed as a procurer and Stead as "one of the wealthy debauchers to whom so many hundreds of the children of the poor were annually sacrificed." Obtaining a pretty child called Eliza Armstrong for two pounds from her own mother, they played out and documented the entire process, releasing it in the July 6, 1885, issue of the *Pall Mall Gazette*.

It "took the British public by storm, in a way that can be hardly paralleled in newspaper history" (Unsworth, *Maiden Tribute*, p. 25). Where it was opposed, young Bernard Shaw himself offered to go out and sell the paper; where it was in demand, enterprising newsboys sold the last copies at exorbitant prices.

The "dead" Criminal Law Amendment Bill was suddenly resurrected before a packed and excited House of Parliament. Within seventeen days over three hundred and forty three thousand signatures filled the Salvation Army's "monster petition" to the House of Commons. Two miles in length, the petition was carried by eight Salvationists onto the floor of the House. In a month the bill was law, and the age of consent was raised to sixteen. But the underworld, outraged at their exposure, counter-attacked. They took Stead and Jarrett to court, indicting them under an 1861 abduction act. This "most sensational trial of the nineteenth century" ended in Bramwell's acquittal, but Stead and Jarrett respectively received three-and six-month sentences. But they had succeeded. It cost them all dearly, but they broke the back of one of the most vile and vicious practices in England's history.

American Reform

And what of America? Her great national abomination was slavery; Africa was raped for America's prosperity, and a total of 10 million men and women were carried away. One hundred million died. The defenders of slavery claimed it was "a Christian institution," a "positive good" because "among other things, it brought the heathen from Africa and gave them the elements of a Christian civilization!" The 1857 revival was to so deeply affect the destiny of the United States that revival-created sentiments over this issue helped elect Abraham Lincoln to the presidency and ultimately led to the Civil War, the most costly attempt evangelicals ever made to see righteousness applied to a nation.

The Anti-Slavery Impulse

Gilbert Hobbes Barne's revolutionary study on the real roots of anti-slavery stands as one of the great historical discoveries of the movement. His book flew in the face of the five major interpretations of the causes of the Civil War. The lost papers and letters he found showed the true cause of anti-slavery. He "held up the religious faith of individuals, the moral ideals of heroes, the dedicated efforts of a handful of determined men, a Holy Band, who pitted themselves against the political might, the economic power, and the social folkways of a whole nation in order to stand up for what their hearts told them were eternal, universal, 'higher' spiritual laws" (Barnes, *The Anti-Slavery Impulse*, p. xix).

Can a revival message change a nation? Preaching in a day when some fifty thousand conversions were taking place each week, Charles Finney and other reformers of that time really believed that Christ, in the lives of His holy people, was going to change the world. They had a concern for personal and social perfection, a pure zeal fired by revival, and above all they had a message radical enough to overthrow the entrenched religious selfishness of their times.

> What made Finney an epochal figure was not his eloquence or his "new measures"; it was the new doctrine he preached. . . . The emotional impulse which Calvinism had concentrated on a painful quest for a safe escape from life, Finney thus turned towards benevolent activity. Converts, he declared, did not escape life; they began a new life "in the interests of God's kingdom." In this new life they have "no separate interests" . . . They should set out with a determination to aim at being useful in the highest degree possible. Among

> Finney's converts this gospel released a mighty impulse towards social reform. (Barnes, *The Anti-Slavery Impulse*, pp. 11-13)

In Finney's "Holy Band" there were self-effacing co-workers like Theodore and Angela Grimke Weld, and converts to holiness like the wealthy New York Tappan brothers. The crusade against slavery was a direct result of revival convictions and conversions "which led . . . to the formation of countless abolition societies, (and) the arousing of a religious crusade against slavery which was more significant and important in the election of Lincoln and the outbreak of the Civil war" than the egocentric bombastic rhetoric of William Lloyd Garrison, the "evil genius" in the East (McLouglin, Introduction, *The Anti-Slavery Impulse*, pp. viii).

"Abolition is essentially a revival," an anti-slavery paper explained, "a revival of the principles of liberty and social religion . . . the reformation was a revival of the entire system of Christianity which in the lapse of centuries has been transformed into a sort of idolatry." They looked on the American Revolution as a "political revival—a new and striking exemplification of the great doctrine of human rights" and Abolitionism as a "two-fold revival," of the "law of love in relation to man" and then "of the principles of liberty, as proclaimed by our forefathers. Its necessity has arisen from the national violation of this law, a national departure from these principles" (Benjamin P. Thomas, from the Forward, *Theodore Weld*, p. vii).

Oberlin and Lane Seminaries, set up to train evangelists and revivalists, were the first colleges to welcome black and white students and to allow men *and* women to enter the ministry. They likewise took a terribly unpopular stand against slavery because they believed it a sin against God.

God's Holy Agent

The roots of this revolution were first laid a century earlier by the Quaker radical, George Fox. In 1657 he warned against the practice of slavery based on the equality of all men in the eyes of God. Fox was no mere meditating mystic. Rufus Jones calls him:

> A brave and heroic character, a rugged, unpolished man battling with immense difficulties and oppositions, but revealing often a fine humor, and always a large patience and a mighty faith. . . . He learned to stand in a hostile world. He managed to endure a long series of prison confinements that would have broken any constitution not well supplied with iron sinew. His journeys, when he was out of prison . . . were usually difficult and dangerous and full of exposure to the elements of nature. (Jones, *Journal of George Fox*, p. x)

Fox's journal reads like the diary of some holy secret agent, a sacred revolutionary. Next only to his absolute certainty that he had a "direct and immediate correspondence with God" was his love for people resulting in a declaration of spiritual war on all that hurt them. He had, perhaps better than any other of his time and nation, a "clear, sure insight into the moral and social issues of his time."

Because Fox loved God, he really loved man. Jones says again,

> From his own first-hand experience, there emerged a profound conviction which lasted all his life that God and man are essentially related because their spiritual frontiers are continuous and undivided. There is something in man that is not of dust or earth or flesh or time, but of God. . . . Fox has many ways of saying this in his seventeenth-century phrases . . . faith gave him an exalted sense of the infinite worth and preciousness of man, of every man, of every type and degree. (Jones, from the Preface, *Journal of George Fox*, p. x-xi).
>
> Fox "put his finger with almost infallible certainty upon the sore spots and evil tendencies around him. He was as tender as a mother over all who were victims . . . of man's brutality, injustice, stupidity, greed, or carelessness. He hated every artificial fashion which contracted the full human life of any man or woman. He went about his task of liberating men and transforming society with an absolute confidence in God's guidance and in the power of His Spirit, with an unlimited faith in

human possibilities and in the effectiveness of the spirit of sincere love and kindness when put full into practice. . . . In any case, nothing has ever worked any better than this method of love and friendship, this transmission of the spirit of Christ." (Jones, *Journal of George Fox,* p. xii)

Ahead of Their Time

Dumond, a major authority on the Anti-slavery movement, asserts that the early Quakers were no ignorant "obnoxious group of meddlers" any more than the later anti-slavery leaders of the nineteenth century, as was charged and commonly believed. The Quakers, too, were originally rich, powerful slaveholders, who came to their decision through a "century of soul-searching and consultation." Then they "opposed slavery from the first to the last on moral and religious grounds—as a *sin*. They made tremendous financial sacrifices to rid themselves of the contamination. They never asked anything for themselves by way of profit—political, social or economic—from their friendship for the oppressed." "Nevertheless they were violently denounced, charged with inciting rebellion, suppressed, and finally driven out of Barbados because they sought to evangelize and educate their slaves. They were denied the poor privilege of freeing their slaves in the southern states and, in the early Congress of the United States, accused of treason and incendiarism because they petitioned for the suppression of the African slave trade" (Dwight Lowell Dumond, *Anti-Slavery–The Crusade for Freedom in America*, pp. 16-17).

Leading the early pre-Revolutionary abolitionists was the gentle New Jersey tailor John Woolman, "the greatest quaker of the eighteenth century and perhaps the most Christ-like individual Quakerism has ever produced." He was helped by the Philadelphia schoolmaster-organizer Anthony Benezet, whose friendship and correspondence with John Wesley led to that Methodist's tract *Thoughts on Slavery,* copied almost verbatim from Benezet.

Woolman, Dumond says, was a "humanitarian in the finest sense of the word; he knew the truth, spoke the truth, and men believed because they had no other choice. Wealth, war, and slavery were to him the three greatest enemies of the souls of men" (Dumond, *Anti-Slavery–The Crusade for Freedom in America,* p. 17). When they began thirty thousand slaves died every year, brought, sold, worked, and killed like cattle. When their spiritual descendents finished, a nation had suffered the judgment of God, and they had broken the legal back of the greatest abomination of the land.

The Need of the Hour

Anti-slavery in the United States, like abortion, prison reform, and other parallel civic controversies of our day, had to be tackled head-on as a moral issue. Our times call for another restoration of that godly imperative: a message that expects and demands practical holiness for both individual and community is the need of the hour.

We have simply ignored the teeth of true conversion; the society-affecting principles of prayer and fasting, confession and restitution, genuine forgiveness, reproof and rebuke, care for the poor, the old, the widows and orphans, and the necessity of every-believer evangelism.

Biblical repentance is three-fold: repentance from idolatry (false gods) personal iniquity (individual sin), and social injustice (corporate evil). Our modern version of "repentance" is counted as heroic if we pass stage one; counterfeit conversion is the order of the day. As Allein pointed out so long ago, we are supposed to repent not only from the world, the flesh, and allegiance to the Devil, but from our own righteousness—or in modern terms, our own rights or good things. Today we "suggest" an abandonment of the first three (as options for a "growing" Christian) and urge professed converts to "consecrate" their "good things." Only recently has the concern for genuine heart-purity become a watchword again in the young Church, not as an option, but as a mandate for the truly converted. Only in the last two decades has there been a serious interest again in dealing with entrenched evil in the structures of law, medicine, government, media, and education.

The Last Wave

Ezekiel hangs over a valley. Is it a dream, a vision, or a reality? At this point he may not know and hardly cares; far below him is an open graveyard. For all he knows, it may be the graveyard of a prophet who failed some ultimate test. And the question comes to Him on the wind, "Son of man, can these bones live?"

Ezekiel's Chapter 37 vision is a fascinating parallel to what happened in the preceding generation. First, the lonely, individual prophet preaching to a hopelessly decayed situation; then the Word creating a miracle of reconstruction; and last, with the Wind, a military resurrection.

The Radical Sixties

If we had any word to put on the turbulent sixties, it would have to be *radical*–radical politics, radical movements, radical "free" speech, radical everything. It was surely so in the Church. Shockwaves from the Jesus, Charismatic, and Church Renewal movements interlaced and interfaced with the craziness of the streets and general culture. Yet with death all around, the bones began to come together.

First Came the Darkness. Out of a first-generation ancestry based on mere legal memory of old morality and a second-generation parental license of new immorality, another generation arose, rejecting the values and traditions of both adult cultures. That generation was the counterculture of the sixties. Three of their characteristics were, as Charles Reich pointed out in his *Greening of America*:

1. Individualism. Of the counterculture's three commandments, the first undoubtedly was "Be true to yourself." "Doing your own thing" was "in," and conformity to anything was out. Independence became the virtue of the hour, borrowed (minus morals) from their pioneer-consciousness grandparents; technology was their servant, borrowed (minus status-serving trappings) from their jet-set organizational parents.

2. Existentialism. How do you react to a materialistic, rationalistic, and mechanistic view of the universe given by the "facts" of a Neo-Darwinian world-view? Some hung up "facts" altogether. They saw it like this: "If the facts don't match what

I know to be true by life and experience, then maybe there is something wrong with thinking." Like the smoker who read that cigarette smoking causes cancer, he determined to do something about it; he gave up reading. Experience-centeredness and the idea of "nowness"—that the past or future is unimportant—gave us a generation whose theme was "Let's live for today."

And just like the street, it was a decade of experience in the Church. Mainline churches asked if you had experienced renewal. Charismatics asked if you had experienced the baptism of the Holy Spirit. The Jesus People asked you if you had had an "experience with Jesus."

3. Independence. The most hurtful of all factors in the sixties, affecting both the Church and the streets, was a terrible spirit of selfish independence. Some church renewers told other families how to stick together when their own families were falling apart. Some Charismatics believed in miracles but got into trouble with money and immorality. Jesus People talked about "turning on to Jesus," but some still turned on with substances Jesus definitely did not approve of.

The image of the sixties was the Lone Ranger Prophet, independent from anyone, preaching to a congregation of the dead.

The Therapeutic Seventies

If the sixties were for radicalism, the seventies were for recovery. During the seventies people tried to get over the hurt they got by being radical in the sixties. As Tom Skinner said, "Yesterday's radical is today's conservative—he's so busy trying to conserve the things he got by being radical he can't afford to be radical anymore." In contrast to the violent sixties, the seventies were "mellow and laid-back"; the mood was conservative, apathetic, and non-violent. The East had come to the Western culture with a vengeance, and the "peace bomb" had exploded.

Terrible things were still happening in the world, and neither national nor international conditions markedly improved, but no one wanted to get involved. The sixties hurt too much. In reaction to the bitterness of that decade, the culture went about patching up her wounds in materialism and pleasure. Rock went out and disco came in.

By this time people had begun to realize that we were living (in William Buckminster Fuller's words) on "Spaceship Earth." The limits of resources, the dangers of pollution, and nuclear escalation all urged disagreement as an unaffordable luxury. The culture moved from radical to conformist, from individualistic to group-think, and from independent to communal. Kids switched from drugs to drink, and Travolta and Winkler took fans back to the innocent fifties with "Happy Days" and *Grease*. It was time again to forget the gutsy honesty and ragged emotions of the sixties and return to fantasy.

Getting Back to Scripture

The awful question came to Ezekiel. Was this the test of presumption or unbelief? Was this the thing God had asked of the disconnected former citizens far below him? "And He said to me–'Son of man, can these bones live?' And I answered, 'Oh Lord God, Thou knowest.' Again He said to me, 'Prophesy to these bones and say to them: Oh ye dry bones, hear the word of the Lord. . . . so I prophesied as I was commanded; and as I prophesied, there was a noise, and behold a shaking and the bones came together, bone to his bone" (Ezek. 37:3-7).

What did God do in the seventies in His church? Like the world around them, the church moved to community concern. Teaching seminars and Bible studies and tapes (both video and audio) became the new emphasis. And from the emphasis on experience (which had revived the mystical tradition), she moved back to scripture and content, reviving the contribution of the Reformation stream.

"Is this renewal scriptural?" the Church was asked. "Do these baptisms and miracles match the Word of God?" the Charismatic movement was queried. "Is the Jesus you experienced the Jesus of the Bible?" was the question put to the survivors of the Jesus movement. Churches with regular consistent Bible exposition grew by leaps and bounds; the thrust of the Church Renewal movement mellowed, the Charismatic movement passed on to discipling, and the Jesus movement became the new young orthodoxy.

In the seventies the Church set about patching up her wounds and getting her act cleaned up. The home, the family, marriage, and child-raising all came under examination. Issues like divorce, discipleship, and demons were debated. Stress was laid on the necessity of unity for revival; cults proliferated, and government reacted with broad suspicion; the Church felt the chill, and its members drew a little closer to one another.

The Sins of the Seventies

And so the body came together as Ezekiel watched, bone to his bone, flesh on flesh, still dead, but at least together. There was a great lifeless army in the valley, together, covered, looking definitely more promising, but without breath.

What were the sins of the seventies? Apathy, materialism, sloth, pride. As Ezekiel put it, "pride, fullness of bread, and abundance of idleness was in her and her daughters; neither did she strengthen the hand of the poor and needy" (16:49). The church became introspective, then self-serving. The blessing of God in financial prosperity was misinterpreted as a personal benefit, and on the eve of financial disaster and terrible social need in the culture, the Church built imposing structures as monuments to her vanity.

The Militant, Apocalyptic Eighties

With the invasion of Afghanistan, war in the Persian Gulf, and Ronald Reagan as president of the United States, the eighties came. What were the marks of this decade?

"Then He said to me—'Prophesy to the wind, prophesy son of man, and say to the wind: Thus saith the Lord God: come from the four winds, O breath, and breathe upon these slain that they may live.' So I prophesied as He commanded me, and the breath came into them, and they lived, and stood up on their feet an exceeding great army" (Ezek. 37:9-10).

God wrote across the eighties the word *militancy*. What goes on in the world is often a shadow, a reflection of what He does with His Church. In the eighties we heard martial music in the Church of the living God. We remembered the church as an "army terrible with banners," not an army that was just plain terrible. We once paid much attention to the building and almost none to the battle. The note of war was absent for a long time. But these things changed. God had ways of getting our attention.

One thing certain about apathy is that if you do not forsake it, it will forsake you. Things get so bad that something must be done. At the end of the seventies, the cultural mood suddenly changed, leaving political strategies based on the liberal seventies high and dry. New levels of stress, discontent, fear, and apparent helplessness and impotence all combined to give new light on old values; the country, much to the dismay of the liberals, swung for a moment towards conservatism. Still dead, but with a national hunger to somehow put it together and live again, they forged ahead.

The Revival to Come

And so here we are, left on the brink of the cliff like Ezekiel, listening for the sound of the wind. Do not think God has yet done all He intends to do. Revival is an act of mercy, and if ever the West needs mercy she needs it now. He has too much of an investment in the West to easily hand her over to the Destroyer. He has yet a destiny for her to fulfill. "I sought for a man," He speaks again to our times, "to stand in the gap." Can He find such a people in our generation?

As the world mobilizes for war, so His Church must see again. A battle for world dominion is joined, and the Devil does not believe in SALT Treaties with the sons of light.

As Gary North said so well:

> Christians are praying for worldwide revival. If such a revival comes, the last humanist truth will be abandoned. People will believe that the God of the Bible is not only possible (but that) He has, in fact, personally entered their lives. Christians today have a golden opportunity, an opportunity that doesn't come even as often as once in a lifetime. It comes about once in every two hundred fifty years. The last time it came for Christians was during the American Revolution era (1776-1789) . . .
>
> A showdwn is coming, in time and on earth. Christ vs. Satan, Christianity vs. Humanism, the dominion reli-

> gion vs. the power religion. You are being called by God to take up a position of judicial responsibility on the side of Christ. It is time to prepare ourselves for an unprecedented revival. It is time to prepare ourselves for the changing of the guard in every area of life, all over the world. Our preparation must help us answer the question: *I'm saved; what now?*" (North, *Christian Reconstruction–What It Is, What It Isn't*, p. 51)

In this book we have travelled through a past full of treasure. We have visited scenes of His visitation, seen a condensed, century-by-century sweep of Gods' work with mankind. The Reformation signalled a new freedom from guilt and gave a man the courage to face the world. The First Awakening told us how we could be clean as well as forgiven, and challenged us to take that cleansing to the world. The Second Awakening put the church back into the soul of the nation to win the thought battles for our minds and our hearts. The Third Awakening gave us back the keys and motivation to redeem a fallen society, to have an impact on the extended structures of sin in societies and cities.

In the New Century awakening, we began to learn again of the walls of separation that had long held us back from reconciliation. We learned to trust the Holy Spirit and to expect His intervention when we do not grieve Him. In the Healing and Charismatic movements we found God still supernaturally concerned with our physical bodies, that He could touch us to make us well and healthy, as well as sensitive and compassionate. We are learning again in the Last Wave not only spiritual warfare and worship but that marriages and families, towns and cities, and perhaps even nations can experience the grace of God in reconciliation.

And now God is speaking about prophecy to a world connected and networked together unlike any other time in history. God is speaking in visions and dreams to the first generation since the invention of print in Reformation times whose primary learning mode is visual and participative; people today see in pictures and find out what is true by doing it. In a planet without obvious solutions to the accelerating crisis of nature's own declining ability to respond to its fallen Caretaker, God is giving us words and mandates to heal the sins that affect the very planet on which we live. "All creation is yearning, longing to see the manifestation of the sons of God" (Rom. 8:19, Weymouth version).

The world can be witnessed to in a single generation. We can welcome Jesus back with our present of the finished task set by Him so long ago when He said, "This Gospel of the Kingdom must be preached for a witness to all nations; then shall the end come."

Watch the signs of the times, the spiritual analogies and metaphors of significant changes in nations and cultures around the globe; God is speaking to our world, and the earth shall yet be filled with His glory.

Can I venture a prophecy? He will "finish the work and cut it short in righteousness; some thirtyfold, some sixtyfold, some a hundred." The last shall be first and the first shall be last. He will sum up all He has ever done in history again. He will both raise up new works and revive old works to illustrate His glory. He will give to a generation without a vision or a record of His mighty works one last chance to arise and join them.

The Last Wave. *And you and I, living on the edge of eternity, have the fearful privilege of being a part of it. My brother, my sister–shall we go?*

Suggested Reading List

Works on Revival

1. *All Things Are Possible,* by David Edwin Harrell, Jr., Indiana University Press.

2. *Another Wave of Revival,* by Frank Bartleman,Whitaker House.

3. *The Awakening That Must Come,* by Lewis A. Drummond, Broadman Press.

4. *Dynamics Of The Spiritual Life,* by Richard Lovelace, I.V.F. Press.

5. *Evangelical Awakenings,* by J. Edwin Orr, Bethany. This is a set of five volumes, all in paperback and excellent reading. See Bibliography.

6. *The Flaming Tongue,* by J. Edwin Orr, Moody Press.

7. *The General Next to God,* by Richard Collier, Collins.

8. *The Great Awakening,* by Joseph Tracy. Out of print, but try the library.

9. *Historical Accounts of Revivals*, by John Gillies, Banner of Truth.

10. *Lectures on Revivals of Religion*, by Charles G. Finney, Bethany.

11. *Personal Declension and Revival*, by Octavius Winslow, Banner of Truth.

12. *Power From on High*, by John Greenfield. Out of print.

13. *Power Through Prayer,* by E. M. Bounds, Baker, Whitaker House, and Zondervan.

14. *Rain From Heaven*, by Arthur Wallis (formerly *In the Day of Thy Power*), Bethany.

15. *Reality,* by Arthur Katz, Logos.

16. *Reflections On Revival*, by Charles G. Finney, Bethany.

17. *Revival*, by Richard Owens Roberts, Tyndale.

18. *Revival Praying*, by Leonard Ravenhill, Bethany.

19. *Revivalism and Social Reform*, by Timothy Smith, Abingdon Press.

20. *Revival–Their Laws and Leaders*, by James Burns. Out of print.

21. *Why Revival Tarries,* by Leonard Ravenhill, Bethany.

REVIVAL BIOGRAPHIES

Revival Biographies

1. *Aimee–Life Story*, by Aimee Semple McPherson, Foursquare Publishing.

2. *All Things Are Possible*, by David Edwin Harrell, Indiana University Press.

3. *Aspects Of Pentecostal/Charismatic Origins*, by Vincent Synan, Logos.

4. *Autobiography of Charles Finney*, by Charles G. Finney, Bethany.

5. *Billy Graham*, by J. C. Pollock. Out of print.

6. *Christian Leaders of the 18th Century*, by J. C. Ryle, Banner of Truth.

7. *The General Next to God*, by Richard Collier, Collins.

8. *George Whitefield*, by Arnold Dallimore, Banner of Truth.

9. *Goforth of China*, by Rosalind Goforth, Bethany.

10. *Holy Company*, by Elliot Wright, MacMillan.

11. *The Jesus Movement In America*, by Ed Ploughman, David C. Cook.

12. *Journal of David Brainerd*, by Jonathan Edwards. Out of print.

13. *The Journal of George Fox*, by Rev. Norman Penney, Everyman's Library.

14. *Lord Shaftesbury*, by Florence M. G. Higham. Out of print.

15. *Moody*, by J. C. Pollock, MacMillan.

16. *Shout It from the Housetops*, by Pat Robertson, Logos.

17. *Signs and Wonders*, by Maria Woodworth-Etter, Harrison House.

18. *Smith Wigglesworth Remembered*, by William Hacking, Harrison House.

19. *Strangely Warmed*, by Garth Lean, Tyndale.

20. *Twenty Centuries of Great Preaching*, by a collection of authors, Word.

For Future Study

1. *A Christian Manifesto,* by Francis Schaeffer, Crossway Books.

2. *America at the Crossroads*, by John Price, Tyndale.

3. *America Is Too Young to Die,* by Leonard Ravenhill, Bethany.

4. *A Time for Anger,* by Franky Schaeffer, Crossway Books.

5. *Destined for the Throne,* by Paul E. Billheimer, Christian Literature Crusade.

6. *God's Strategy in Human History,* by Forster and Marsden, Send the Light Press.

7. *Is a New Wave of Revival Coming?* by Ralph Mahoney, World MAP.

8. *Lectures on Revivals of Religion*, by Charles G. Finney, Bethany.

9. *Operation World,* by P. J. Johnstone, Send the Light Press.

10. *The Promise of the Spirit*, by Charles G. Finney, Bethany.

11. *Rain from Heaven,* by Arthur Wallis, formerly *In the Day of Thy Power*, Bethany.

12. *Reflections on Revival,* by Charles G. Finney, Bethany.

13. *Revivalism and Social Reform,* by Timothy Smith, Abingdon Press.

14. *Revival Praying,* by Leonard Ravenhill, Bethany.

15. *The Revival We Need,* by Oswald J. Smith. Out of print.

16. *The Search for America's Faith,* by George Gallup, Jr., Abingdon Press.

17. *Today's Gospel–Authentic or Synthetic?* by Walter Chantry, Banner of Truth.

18. *The Truth Shall Make You Free,* by Gordon Olsen, Bible Research Fellowship.

19. *The World Christian Encyclopedia,* by David Barrett, Oxford.

20. *Youth Aflame!* by Winkie Pratney, Bethany.

Select Bibliography

Andrews, J.R., *The Life of George Whitefield,* Morgan and Scott, 1879.

Barnes, Gilbert Hobbes, *The Anti-Slavery Impulse*, Harbinger/Hacu Press, 1933.

Barrett, David B. and Johnson, Todd M., *AD 2000 Global Monitor,* Global Evangelization Movement, Rockville, VA, 1991.

Bartleman, Frank, *Another Wave Rolls In,* Whitaker House, 1982.

Best, Mary Agnes, *Rebel Saints,* Harcourt Brace, 1925.

Booth, Bramwell, *Echoes and Memories,* Hodder and Stoughton, 1925.

Bready, J. Wesley, *This Freedom Whence*, Light And Life Publishers, 1950.

Campbell, Duncan, *God's Standard,* Christian Literature Crusade 1967.

Collier. Richard, *The General Next to God,* Fontana/Collins, 1976.
Christian World Almanac, Tyndale, 1990.

Dallimore, Arnold, *George Whitefield*, Cornerstone Books, 1970.

Dowley, Timothy, *History Handbook of Christianity*, Eerdmans, 1977.

Drummond, Lewis A, *The Awakening That Must Come*, Boardman Press, 1978.

Dummond, Dwight Lowell, *Anti-Slavery Crusade for Freedom*, University of Michigan Press, 1961.

Durant, Will, *The Reformation*, Simon and Schuster, 1957.

Edman, V. Raymond, *Finney Lives On*, Bethany, 1951.

Edman, V. Raymond, *They Found the Secret*, Zondervan, 1961.

Edwards, Brian H., *Revival–A People Saturated with God*, Evangelical Press, Durham, England 1990.

Edwards, Jonathan, *Works of Jonathan Edwards*, Yale University Press, 1959.

Elbert, Paul (Ed.), *Faces of Renewal*, Hendrickson, 1988.

Finney, C. G., *Autobiography of Charles Finney*, Bethany, 1976.

Finney, C. G., *Heart of Truth*, Bethany, 1976.

Finney, C. G., *Lectures on Revival*, Bethany, 1979.

Finney, C. G., *The Promise of the Spirit*, Bethany, 1980.

Finney, C. G., *Systematic Theology*, Bethany, 1976.

Fischer, Harold A., *Reviving Revivals*, Gospel Publishing House, 1950.

Forster and Marsden, *God's Strategy in Human History*, Tyndale, 1973.

Fox, George, *Journal of George Fox*, Everyman's Library, 1940.

Frodesham, Stanley, *Smith Wigglesworth, Apostle of Faith*, Assembly of God Publishers, 1965.

Frodesham, Stanley, *With Signs Following*, Gospel Publishing House, 1946.

Gallup, George Jr., *Search for America's Faith*, Abingdon Press, 1980.

Gee, Donald, *Wind and Flame*, Heath Press, 1967.

Geikie, Cunningham, *The English Reformation*, Strahan and Co., 1879.

Gilles, John, *Accounts of Revival*, Banner of Truth, 1981.

Goforth, Rosalind, *Goforth of China*, Bethany, 1937.

Graham, Billy, *America's Hour of Decision*, Van Kampen Press, 1951.

Graham, Billy, *Revival in Our Time*, Van Kampen Press, 1950.

Greenfield, John, *Power from on High*, Christian Literature Crusade, 1950.

Hacking, W., *Smith, Wigglesworth Remembered*, Harrison House, 1981.

Hardesty, Nancy, *Great Women of Faith*, Baker/Abingdon Press, 1980.

Hardman, Keith J., *Charles Grandison Finney, Revivalist and Reformer*, Syracuse University Press, 1987.

Harrell, David Edwin Jr., *All Things Are Possible*, Indiana University Press, 1975.

Harris, R. Laird, *Theological Wordbook of the Old Testament*, Moody Press, 1980.

Highman, Florence, *Lord Shaftesbury*, MacMillan, 1945.

Hodder, Edwin, *The Life and Work of Shaftesbury*, Cassell and Co., 1870.

Hurlbut, Jesse Lyman, *The History of the Christian Church*, Zondervan, 1970.

Lake, John G., *Adventures in God*, Harrison House, 1981.

Lean, Garth, *Brave Men Choose*, Blandford Press, 1961.

Lean, Garth, *Strangely Warmed*, Tyndale, 1964.

Liardon, Roberts, *Cry of the Spirit*, Harrison House, 1989.

Lindsay, Gordon, *The Gordon Lindsay Story*, Voice of Healing, 1958., *Men Who Changed the World*, Christ for the Nations, 1959.

Lovelace, Richard F., *The Dynamics of Spiritual Life*, I.V.F. Press, 1980.

Lloyd, Jones, Martyn, *Revival,* Crossway Books, 1987.

MacDonald, Williams, *True Discipleship*, Walterick, 1962.

Marsh, Josiah, *The Popular Life of George Fox,* Charles Gilpin, 1847.

Matthews, David, *I Saw the Welsh Revival!* Moody Press, 1978.

MacNeil, *History and Character of Calvinism*, Oxford, 1954.

McKenna, David L., *The Coming Great Awakening*, Intervarsity Press, 1990.

MacPherson, Aimee Semple, *Aimee,* Foursquare Publishers, 1967.

MacPherson, Anna Talbot, *They Dared to Be Different*, Moody Press, 1967.

Miller, Basil, *John Wesley*, Bethany, 1966.

Miller, R. Edward, *The Flaming Flame,* Argentine Bible, 1973.

Nixon, Leroy, *John Calvin, Expository Preacher,* Eerdmans, 1950.

North, Gary and Demar, Gary, *Christian Reconstruction; What It Is, What It Isn't,* Institute for Christian Economics, 1990.

Olford, Stephen F., *Lord Open the Heavens,* Harold Shaw, 1980.

Orr, J. Edwin, *Campus Aflame,* Regal, 1971.

Orr, J. Edwin, *Eager Feet,* Moody Press, 1975.

Orr, J. Edwin, *Evangelical Awakenings in Africa,* Bethany, 1975.

Orr, J. Edwin, *Evangelical Awakenings in Eastern Asia*, Bethany, 1975.

Orr, J. Edwin, *Evangelical Awakenings in Southern Asia,* Bethany, 1975.

Orr, J. Edwin, *Evangelical Awakenings in the South Seas,* Bethany, 1976.

Orr, J. Edwin, *The Fervent Prayer,* Moody Press, 1974 .

Orr, J. Edwin, *The Flaming Tongue,* Moody Press, 1968.

Orr, J. Edwin, *The Second Evangelical Awakening*, Marshall Morgan, 1949.

Overton, J. H., *John Wesley*, Methuen and Co., 1891.

Patterson, James, and Kim, Peter, *The Day America Told the Truth*, Prentice-Hall, 1991.

Penn-Lewis, Jesse, *War on the Saints*, Christian Literature Crusade, 1978.

Pierson, A. T., *George Mueller of Bristol*, James Nisbet and Co., 1899.

Pollock, J. C., *The Cambridge Seven*, I.V.F. Press, 1955.

Pollock, J. C., *Moody*, MacMillan, 1963.

Pollock, J. C., *John Wesley Servant of God*, Victor Books, 1989.

Price, John, *America at the Crossroads*, Living Books/Tyndale, 1971.

Quiller-Couch, A. T., *Hetty Wesley*, Morgan and Scott, 1903.

Ravenhill, Leonard, *Why Revival Tarries*, Bethany, 1978.

Ravenhill, Leonard, *Revival Praying*, Bethany, 1979.

Reich, Charles, *The Greening of America*, Random House, 1970.

Richardson, Don, *Eternity in Their Hearts*, Regal, 1981.

Rifkin, Jeremy, *The Emerging Order*, G.P. Putnams, 1979.

Ryle, J. C.,*Christian Leaders of the 18th Century*, Banner Of Truth, 1978.

Schaeffer, Francis A., *A Christian Manifesto*, Crossway Books, 1981.

Singer, C. Gregg, *Theological Interpretation of American History*, Craig Press, 1964.

Smith, Timothy, *Revivalism and Social Reform*, Abingdon, 1957.

Snyder, Howard A., *The Radical Wesley*, I.V.F Press, 1980.

Synan, Vincent, *Aspects of Pentecostal/Charismatic Origins*, Logos, 1975.

Synan, Vincent, *And the Spirit Said Grow*, MARC, World Vision 1992.

Tari, Mel, *Like a Mighty Wind*, New Leaf Press, 1971.

Taylor, Mendell, *Exploring Evangelism*, Beacon Hill, 1964.

Thomas, Benjamin P., *Theodore Weld*, Rutgers University Press, 1950.

Tuttle, Mark (Ed.), *Christian History Magazine*: Various Issues, Christian History Institute, Worcester, PA.

Unsworth, Madge, *Maiden Tribute*, Salvationist Publishing, 1949.

Various Authors, *Champions Of The Truth*, Religious Tract, 1898.

Various Contributors, *The Story of the Welsh Revival*, Fleming H. Revell, 1905.

Walker, Williston, *A History of the Christian Church*, T. & T. Clark, 1930.

Wallis, Arthur, *In the Day of Thy Power*, Christian Literature Crusade, 1956.

Waugh, Alexander, *Biographical Sketches of Eminent Christians*, Religious Tract, 1850.

Wesley, John, *Journals of John Wesley*, Epworth Press, 1938.

Wesley, John, *Primitive Remedies*, Woodbridge Press, 1973.

Williams, J. E. Hodder, *The Life of Sir George Williams*, Hodder and Stoughton, 1958.

Woodworth-Etter, Maria, *Signs and Wonders*, Harrison House, 1916.

Woolsey, Andrew, *Duncan Campbell*, Hodder and Stoughton, 1974.

Word, *Twenty Centuries of Great Preaching*, Word Publishers, 1978.

Wright, Elliot, *Holy Company*, MacMillan, 1980.

W. E. C., *This Is That*, Christian Literature Crusade, 1954.

Notes

Notes

Notes